Reviews of National Policies for Education

Education in Thailand

AN OECD-UNESCO PERSPECTIVE

This work is published under the responsibility of the Secretary-General of the OECD and UNESCO. The opinions expressed and arguments employed herein do not necessarily reflect the official views of the OECD member countries, or of the UNESCO.

This document and any map included herein are without prejudice to the status of or sovereignty over any territory, to the delimitation of international frontiers and boundaries and to the name of any territory, city or area.

Please cite this publication as:
OECD/UNESCO (2016), *Education in Thailand: An OECD-UNESCO Perspective*, Reviews of National Policies for Education, OECD Publishing, Paris.
http://dx.doi.org/10.1787/9789264259119-en

ISBN 978-92-64-25909-6 (print)
ISBN 978-92-64-25911-9 (PDF)

Series: Reviews of National Policies for Education
ISSN 1563-4914 (print)
ISSN 1990-0198 (online)

The statistical data for Israel are supplied by and under the responsibility of the relevant Israeli authorities. The use of such data by the OECD is without prejudice to the status of the Golan Heights, East Jerusalem and Israeli settlements in the West Bank under the terms of international law.

Photo credits: Cover © eabff/Shutterstock.com

Corrigenda to OECD publications may be found on line at: *www.oecd.org/about/publishing/corrigenda.htm*.
© OECD/UNESCO 2016

This work is available under the Creative Commons Atribution-ShareAlike 3.0 IGO licence (CC BY-SA 3.0 IGO); additional terms may apply.

Foreword

Thailand's education system stands at a crossroads. As the country aims to move beyond the "middle-income trap", it needs to build a highly skilled workforce, able to compete in the ASEAN economic community. Significant investment has widened access to education and Thailand performs relatively well in international assessments compared to its peers. However, the benefits have not been universally distributed and Thailand has not received the return on its investment in education that it might have expected. Too many poor children do not attend school altogether, and too many fail to reach the minimum standards needed for full participation in society. Thailand risks developing a two-tier education system – leaving children in poorer rural households behind.

Thailand has embarked on an ambitious series of reforms which go some way towards addressing these challenges. It has modernised its curriculum from a content-based one with an emphasis on rote learning, to a standards-based one describing what students should be able to know and do in each subject. Schools and teachers, however, have not always been given the support and skills they need to implement this new approach. The country has a comprehensive system of standardised national assessments but lacks the capacity to ensure that its national tests reinforce the aims of the curriculum and support reform efforts rather than undermine them. It has raised the qualification levels of its teachers and school leaders, yet questions on the quality of their training and ongoing development remain. It has also invested heavily in rolling out digital devices into schools but seen little improvement in computer literacy as a result.

This OECD-UNESCO report offers insights on how Thailand can overcome these policy and implementation gaps. It identifies the strengths and weaknesses of Thailand's basic education system and makes a number of recommendations for further reform, drawing on international experience and best practices from high-performing systems around the world. The report encourages Thailand to focus on four priority areas to prepare students from all backgrounds for a fast-changing world:

- Conduct a thorough and consultative review of the curriculum, documenting clearly the common standards students should meet, which can be used to drive reform in the rest of the system.

- Build the capacity – at all levels of the education system – to reliably assess students for the full range of competencies identified in the revised curriculum, ensuring that a range of tests are used to generate the information needed to support individual student progress.

- Develop a holistic strategy to prepare teachers and school leaders to deliver education reform, including implementing the revised curriculum, and to tackle teaching shortages in the most deprived areas.

- Create a comprehensive information and communications technology strategy to equip all of Thailand's students for the 21st century, with an emphasis on improving teachers' skills to make the best use of technology in the classroom and improving rural Internet access.

Andreas SCHLEICHER
Director for Education and Skills and
Special Advisor on Education Policy to
the Secretary-General
OECD

Qian TANG
Assistant Director-General
for Education
UNESCO

Acknowledgements

This report is the result of a review of the Kingdom of Thailand's policies and practices in the field of education, informed by international experience and best practices. The review process draws from various sources, including a background report prepared by the Office of the Education Council of Thailand, a pre-review visit to Thailand to help define the actors and main policy issues, and a main review visit by a team of OECD, UNESCO and international experts in February 2015.

The OECD-UNESCO review team is indebted to the government of the Kingdom of Thailand which has graciously supported this review. Special words of appreciation are due to the Secretaries-General of the Office of the Education Council who have co-ordinated Thailand's involvement in the review process. We are especially thankful to Panthep Larpkesorn for his constant support and to the authors of the Country Background Report, which was helpful for our work. The review team would also like to convey our sincere appreciation to the many participants in the review visits who gave time from their busy schedules to share their views, experience and knowledge. A range of actors at all levels of government and from non-governmental and international organisations provided insights in the course of site visits to Bangkok, Chang Mai and Kanchanaburi. Notwithstanding such support, the OECD-UNESCO team encountered difficulties in accessing some information; these limitations affect the comprehensiveness of this report.

The members of the OECD-UNESCO review team were Francesc Pedró (UNESCO), Joint Team Leader; Elizabeth Fordham (OECD), Joint Team Leader; Eduardo Cascallar (external expert, United States); Kirsteen Henderson (external expert, Canada); Jan Hylén (external expert, Sweden); Francesc Masdeu (UNESCO); Sara bin Mahfooz (UNESCO); Andrew McQueen (OECD), Nyi Nyi Thaung (UNESCO) and Phil Stabback (external expert, Australia). The OECD took primary responsibility for Chapters 1, 4 and 5; UNESCO took primary responsibility for Chapters 2, 3 and 6.

The review team acknowledges the support from Andreas Schleicher, Director of the Directorate for Education and Skills (OECD); Richard Yelland, Head of the Policy Advice and Implementation Division (OECD); Qian Tang, Assistant Director-General for Education (UNESCO); and David Atchoarena,

Director of the Division for Policies and Lifelong Learning Systems (UNESCO). The review team is especially grateful to Gwang-Jo Kim, Director of the UNESCO Asia and Pacific Regional Bureau for Education, and staff in the UNESCO Bangkok Office – Ramya Vivekanandan, Jonghi Park, Maria Melizza Tan, Miron Khumar Bhowmik, Satoko Yano, Katherine Centore, Ratchakorn Kulsawet, Pirawaz Sahawiboonsuk, and Aliénor Salmon – who made such an important contribution to the organisation of the review visits and drafting of the report. Many people provided support, input and advice at different stages of the review process. We are grateful to Nicholas Adams-Cohen, Adrien Alain Boucher, Aurora Cheung, Jianhong Dong, Gerald Fry, Caitlyn Guthrie, Maki Hayashikawa, Daria Jarczewska, Thanomporn Laohajaratsang, Vivian Leung, Fengchun Miao, Sakshi Mishra, Anna Pons, Paulo Santiago, Désirée Wittenberg, Worapoj Wongkijrungrueang, and Felix Zimmerman. Sally Hinchcliffe edited the report, and Rebekah Cameron and Célia Braga-Schich organised the publication process.

Table of contents

Acknowledgements 5

Acronyms and abbreviations 13

Executive summary 15

Assessment and recommendations 19

    Introduction 19
    Thailand's education curriculum 20
    Student assessment in Thailand 23
    Thailand's teachers and school leaders 25
    Thailand's information and communication technology in education 29
    Moving forward 32
    Bibliography 36

***Chapter 1* Thailand's education system** 37

    Country overview 38
    The education system in Thailand 45
    Recent education reforms 53
    Conclusions 57
    Notes 57
    Bibliography 58

***Chapter 2* The basic education system in Thailand: A comparative policy perspective** 63

    Introduction 64
    Inputs 64
    Access and participation 71
    Educational processes 78
    Student outcomes 80
    Efficiency 86
    Conclusions 86
    Bibliography 88

Chapter 3 Thailand's education curriculum 93

Introduction 94
Policy Issue 1: Thailand's intended curriculum lacks clarity, consistency and relevance 99
Policy Issue 2: Education staff need more training and support to implement the standards-based curriculum 113
Policy Issue 3: Thailand has limited capacity to assess how well the curriculum has delivered its intended outcomes 118
Policy Issue 4: Thailand's curriculum review processes need to be put into practice 121
Conclusion 127
Notes 128
Bibliography 129
Annex 3.A1 Summary of the structure and contents of the Basic Education Core Curriculum (2008) 131

Chapter 4 Student assessment in Thailand 133

Introduction 134
The Thai context 136
Policy Issue 1: Thailand needs to build assessment capacity right across its education system 145
Policy Issue 2: National assessments need to offer greater validity and comparability of results 153
Policy Issue 3: Thailand does not have the right mix of assessment instruments to measure the full range of skills students need 165
Conclusion 175
Notes 176
Bibliography 177
Annex 4.A1 The information request made by the OECD/UNESCO team to the National Institute of Educational Testing Service 185

Chapter 5 Thailand's teachers and school leaders 189

Introduction 190
Policy Issue 1: Teacher preparation is inadequate to support the country's education reforms 196
Policy Issue 2: Thailand lacks a holistic strategy for professional development 204
Policy Issue 3: Administrative burdens, particularly in rural schools, keep teachers away from the classroom 214

Policy Issue 4: Thailand is not making effective use of the school leaders' role to improve teaching and learning in an increasingly decentralised system. 220
Policy Issue 5: Thailand's procedures for teacher deployment fail to meet local and national school workforce needs 227
Conclusions 240
Notes 241
Bibliography 242

Chapter 6 Thailand's information and communication technology in education 249

Introduction 250
Policy Issue 1: Thailand lacks the infrastructure to support effective ICT use in schools 254
Policy Issue 2: Digital learning materials are not yet fully incorporated into the basic education system 264
Policy Issue 3: Teachers need more confidence and capacity to use ICT effectively in the classroom 268
Policy Issue 4: Thailand lacks adequate capacity to monitor and assess ICT use in schools 276
Policy Issue 5: Thailand lacks a coherent framework for its significant investments in ICT 282
Conclusions 285
Notes 286
Bibliography 287

Annex A Contribution of stakeholders in Thailand 294

Figures

Figure 1.1.	Map of Thailand	38
Figure 1.2.	Fertility rates (total births per woman) and life expectancy, 1980-2012	40
Figure 1.3.	Annual GDP growth in Thailand, 1980-2014 and proportion of population living below the national poverty line, 2000-14 (percentage)	42
Figure 1.4.	Trends in global competitiveness in selected ASEAN countries, 2005-14/15	43
Figure 1.5.	The Thai formal education system	47
Figure 1.6.	Governance structure of the education system in Thailand	53
Figure 2.1.	Public expenditure on education as a percentage of GDP and of total government expenditure in Thailand, 1999-2012	65

Figure 2.2.	Public expenditure on education as a percentage of GDP and of total government expenditure, selected countries, 2012	66
Figure 2.3.	Public expenditure on pre-primary education as a percentage of GDP, selected countries, 2012	67
Figure 2.4.	Public expenditure on education per student as percentage of GDP per capita, by level of education, selected countries, 2012	68
Figure 2.5.	Expenditure by level of education as a percentage of total government expenditure on education, 2008-12	68
Figure 2.6.	Expenditure on education and teachers' salaries, selected countries, 2012	69
Figure 2.7.	Equity in resource allocation, selected countries, 2012	70
Figure 2.8.	Net enrolment rates, primary and secondary education, selected countries, 2012	71
Figure 2.9.	Change in net enrolment rate in pre-primary education, selected countries, 2006 and 2012	72
Figure 2.10.	Change in net enrolment rate in primary education, selected countries, 2006 and 2012	73
Figure 2.11.	Change in net enrolment rate in secondary education, selected countries, 2006 and 2012	73
Figure 2.12.	Trends in the share of children and youth not studying in Thailand, by age and income level, 1990 and 2012	75
Figure 2.13.	Gross graduation rate from lower secondary education, selected countries, 2012	75
Figure 2.14.	Rate of out-of-school children, by level of education and gender, selected countries, 2012	76
Figure 2.15.	Trends in gross enrolment rate in tertiary education, selected countries, 1999-2012 (percentage)	77
Figure 2.16.	Trends in tertiary enrolment rates for 19-25 year-olds in Thailand, by income quartile, 1986-2008	78
Figure 2.17.	Student learning time in school, selected countries, 2012	79
Figure 2.18.	Trends in mathematics, reading and science performance, PISA 2000-12	81
Figure 2.19.	Mean mathematics scores, and shares of low and high performers, selected countries, PISA 2012	82
Figure 2.20.	Share of resilient students, PISA 2012	83
Figure 2.21.	Mathematics score by region and locality type, PISA 2012	84
Figure 2.22.	Relationship between mathematics performance and pre-primary attendance, selected countries, 2003 and 2012	85
Figure 3.1.	The curriculum review	95
Figure 3.2.	Key components of the 2008 Curriculum document	100
Figure 3.3.	Roadmap for curriculum development	122
Figure 4.1.	O-NET results in %, Grade 12, 2008-14	140
Figure 4.2.	O-NET results in %, Grade 6, 2008-14	140

Figure 4.3. O-NET results in %, Grade 9, 2008-14 140
Figure 5.1. Teacher-related institutions in Thailand 195
Figure 6.1. Availability of computers at school, selected countries, 2012............. 256

Tables

Table 1.1. Real GDP growth of Southeast Asia, The People's Republic of China and India, annual percentage change 41
Table 1.2. Number of institutions and students in Thai formal education by responsible agency, school type and programme, 2013 48
Table 1.3. Education planning instruments in Thailand 56
Table 2.1. Development measures, selected countries.. 64
Table 3.1. Stakeholders in the curriculum development process........................... 123
Table 4.1. National student assessments in Thailand 138
Table 4.2. Subjects tested in the O-NET, 2015.. 139
Table 5.1. Teachers' employers, 2013/14 school year... 191
Table 5.2. Number of institutions offering accredited pre-service programmes, 2009/10 196
Table 5.3. Number of teachers needed by subject in schools experiencing a shortage, 2013/14 school year 228
Table 5.4. Schools hindered by a lack of qualified teachers, 2002 and 2013 229
Table 5.5. Employment exam results and jobs for shortage subjects, 2014 237
Table 6.1. Recommended download speeds 258
Table 6.2. Type and speed of Internet connections in schools, 2012.................... 259
Table 6.3. Internet connections for schools, 2012 259
Table 6.4. Use of ICT for teaching practices in classrooms (National percentages of teachers often using ICT for learning activities in classrooms), 2013 270

Boxes

Box 3.1. Learning theories and Bloom's taxonomy... 101
Box 3.2. Student performance standards.. 103
Box 3.3. An example of pedagogical guidance provided in the 2008 curriculum... 104
Box 3.4. Curricula and key competencies for the 21st century............................ 106
Box 3.5. ASEAN Curriculum Sourcebook... 111
Box 3.6. Professional development in Hong Kong, China................................... 117
Box 3.7. Student performance standards and supports for assessment in New Zealand.. 120
Box 3.8. International examples of curriculum development bodies 125
Box 4.1. External quality assurance of schools.. 144

Box 4.2.	Hong Kong, China: Developing in-service teacher training to facilitate assessment for learning	147
Box 4.3.	Item response theory	148
Box 4.4.	Building national capacity for assessment: the example of Cito in the Netherlands	152
Box 4.5.	Dimensionality: Technical considerations	160
Box 4.6.	Technical note on equating	162
Box 4.7.	School-based assessment: Lessons from New Zealand	170
Box 5.1.	Teacher preparation in Singapore	200
Box 5.2.	Pre-service programme accreditation in Korea	202
Box 5.3.	Moving towards a framework for good teaching: The example of Chile	207
Box 5.4.	Performance appraisal in Ontario, Canada	210
Box 5.5.	Pathways to teacher promotion	212
Box 5.6.	Improving the school working and learning environment: The example of England	216
Box 5.7.	Attracting, supporting and retaining teachers and school leaders in disadvantaged schools	218
Box 5.8.	Standards for school leadership	221
Box 5.9.	Succession planning in Singapore	222
Box 5.10.	Measures to improve school leadership in Hong Kong, China	226
Box 5.11.	Models for forecasting teacher supply and demand	230
Box 5.12.	Increasing the attractiveness of the teaching profession	233
Box 5.13.	Attracting teachers to poor and remote areas	235
Box 5.14.	Teacher recruitment policies in OECD countries	238
Box 6.1.	Assessing the computing and information literacy skills of young people	254
Box 6.2.	The European Commission's rural broadband proposal	260
Box 6.3.	International one laptop per child policies	261
Box 6.4.	The Paris OER Declaration	265
Box 6.5.	The Norwegian Digital Learning Arena	266
Box 6.6.	Norwegians SMILE	269
Box 6.7.	Professional development to foster ICT competency	275
Box 6.8.	Promising cases: Systematic monitoring systems	279

Acronyms and abbreviations

ASEAN	Association of Southeast Asian Nations
B-NET	Buddhism National Educational Test
BYOD	Bring your own device
CDC	Constitutional Drafting Committee
CEFR	Common European Framework of Reference for Languages
ESA	Educational Service Area
ETS	Educational Testing Service (United States)
GAT	General Aptitude Test
GDP	Gross domestic product
GERD	Gross expenditure on research and development
HR	Human resources
I-NET	Islamic National Educational Test
IBE	International Bureau of Education
ICILS	International Computer and Information Literacy Study
ICT	Information and communication technology
IPST	Institute for the Promotion of Teaching Science and Technology
IRT	Item response theory
ISCED	International Standard Classification of Education
KIDS-D	Knowledge, Imagination, Discover and Sharing - Digital project
LAO	Local administration organisation
LCR	Learner-to-computer ratio
MOE	Ministry of Education
MOI	Ministry of the Interior
N-NET	Non-Formal National Educational Test
NCPO	National Council of Peace and Order
NEA	1999 National Education Act
NESDB	National Economic and Social Development Board
NGO	Non-governmental organisation
NIDTEP	National Institute for Development of Teachers, Faculty Staff and Educational Personnel
NIETS	National Institute of Educational Testing Service
NQF	National qualifications framework
NRC	National Reform Council
NRSA	National Reform Steering Assembly

O-NET	Ordinary National Educational Test
OBEC	Office of the Basic Education Commission
OEC	Office of the Education Council
OER	Open educational resources
OHEC	Office of the Higher Education Commission
OLPC	One Laptop Per Child
ONESQA	Office for National Education Standards and Quality Assessment
ONIE	Office of Non-Formal and Informal Education
OPEC	Office of the Private Education Commission
OPS	Office of the Permanent Secretary
OTEPC	Office of the Teacher Civil Service and Educational Personnel Commission
OVEC	Office of the Vocational Education Commission
OTJ	Overall teacher judgement
OTPC	One Tablet Per Child
PAT	Professional and Academic Aptitude Test
PD	Professional development
PISA	OECD Programme for International Student Assessment
SAR	Self-assessment report
SBA	School-based assessment
SEAMEO INNOTECH	Southeast Asian Ministers of Education Organization Regional Center for Educational Innovation and Technology
SITES	Second Information Technology in Education Study
STEM	Science, technology, engineering and mathematics
TCT	Teachers' Council of Thailand
THB	Thai baht
TIMSS	Trends in International Mathematics and Science Study
TVET	Technical and vocational education and training
UNDP	United Nations Development Programme
UNESCO	United Nations Educational, Scientific and Cultural Organisation
VET	Vocational education and training
V-NET	Vocational National Educational Test

Executive summary

Thailand finds itself at a crossroads. In less than a generation, it has moved from a largely agrarian low-income society to an upper middle-income country and a key contributor to the economic growth of the Southeast Asian region. At the same time, Thailand has enacted major education reforms and invested a significant proportion of its national wealth into educating its youngest citizens. Overall participation rates in the school system are now high, particularly at the pre-primary and primary levels, and a large number of youth continue on to higher and professional education. However, not all sections of society have benefited equally from this expansion. Access and performance are particularly poor among children from disadvantaged backgrounds and those who live in rural areas. Moreover, half of Thai students in school are not acquiring the basic skills required for their own success and the country's continued development. Thailand will need to significantly enhance the effectiveness, equity and efficiency of its education system in order for students to achieve positive outcomes that match the country's investment in education and socio-economic aspirations. This review addresses four policy areas where reforms can have a transformative impact on learning: curriculum, student assessment, teachers and school leaders, and the use of information and communication technology (ICT) in education.

Curriculum

A clear, coherent and relevant curriculum is at the heart of any good education system. With reforms in 2001 and 2008, Thailand shifted its content-based curriculum to a modern standards-based approach describing what students should know and be able to do in each subject. The new curriculum is intended to support more learner-centred teaching strategies rather than focus on information retention. Implementation has been challenging. The decentralisation of responsibility inherent in a standards-based approach has not been matched by adequate support to local officials and teachers. The curriculum document provided schools and teachers with little guidance, and it lacks common student performance standards to serve as the basis for assessments of students' progress. Thailand will need to conduct a thorough and consultative curriculum review process to address these issues and to provide a grounding for changes to teaching and learning practices in order to improve student outcomes.

Student assessment

A well-balanced, high-quality student assessment framework yields data that allow policy makers to continuously improve the education system, inform teachers' pedagogical strategies and help individual learners improve their own learning. Thailand makes extensive use of standardised tests in its assessment system but these are only useful if they are methodologically sound. It is therefore essential that Thailand add rigour to its test development process. Moving forward, Thailand will need to focus on building capacity to support the effective design and implementation of assessment procedures at all levels of the education system. The country should also balance its use of standardised tests by supporting the development of a broad range of student assessments at the school and classroom level.

Teachers and school leaders

Teachers and school leaders are at the heart of any education reform. Thailand has a large, dedicated teaching workforce. However, Thai teachers are not being prepared well enough through initial teacher education or continuing professional development to support the country's education reform efforts. Thailand should create a nationwide professional development strategy to ensure teachers make effective use of student-centred teaching strategies and formative assessments. To reduce inequities across the education system, Thailand needs to do much more to attract, retain and support educators in disadvantaged rural schools. This will require improvements to ensure labour market planning is based on solid data, and changes to reduce the rigidities of the country's centralised deployment procedures. In rural and urban schools alike, Thailand's teachers need to be able to spend more of their time actually teaching, rather than performing administrative duties. Above all, they require the support of a more professionalised school leadership.

The use of ICT in education

The success of Thailand's education system will increasingly depend on how well it uses the potential of ICT to support students' acquisition of 21st century competencies and, on a system-wide level, better manage schools. Like many countries, Thailand has implemented hardware-focused initiatives that have met with only mixed success. In fact, a recent international assessment revealed that Thai students' ICT proficiency levels were low and that Thai teachers lacked confidence in their own ability to use ICT. Thailand will need to develop a coherent and evidence-based ICT strategy in order to ensure that all key areas, in addition to hardware, are sufficiently addressed. This strategy should focus first on the important role of the teacher by building educators' capacity to use ICT in their teaching repertoire and to foster students' development of computer skills. It should also ensure that schools' Internet access in all regions of the country is more stable and responsive.

A long-term strategy for education reform

In order to make real progress in these four areas of the education system, Thailand should address a number of broad systemic issues. The country needs to make greater use of evidence to inform policy decisions. This should involve the development of co-ordinated statistical-gathering mechanisms to address data gaps and the establishment of a systematic process to evaluate and refine new policies and programmes after implementation. Thailand also needs more coherent, inclusive processes to govern educational administration. At present, the governance system is multi-layered and institutionally complex with a lack of clear roles and responsibilities. Implementing processes to better co-ordinate central and regional bodies will improve the efficiency and effectiveness of the education system as a whole. Finally, the country needs to develop a new long-term strategy for education reform. This strategy should span political cycles and engage stakeholders in working towards the attainment of a small number of key goals connected to student outcomes. Through these efforts, Thailand will help students reach their full potential and strengthen its human capital base to achieve broad social and economic growth.

Assessment and recommendations

Introduction

Over the past several decades, Thailand has moved away from a largely agrarian society, and become a middle-income nation with a relatively diversified economy. Education played an important role in this transformation. In recent years, Thailand has made sweeping reforms to its education system, notably with the 1999 National Education Act, in an effort to adapt to domestic and global changes and to support sustained economic growth. The country has also invested a comparatively large proportion of its national wealth in primary education, resulting in near universal access at that level.

However, Thailand's recent investments in education and its high student participation rates are not resulting in the expected outcomes. The country's results on international tests, such as the OECD Programme for International Student Assessment (PISA), are below those of many peer countries; within Thailand there are significant disparities in student performance between socio-economically disadvantaged and advantaged schools and across rural and urban areas. At the same time, Thailand is facing political uncertainty and the challenges of a shrinking working-age population and slow GDP growth compared to many of its neighbours in the Association of Southeast Asian Nations (ASEAN) Economic Community. Thailand needs to continue to improve the effectiveness, efficiency and equity of its education system to ensure it does not fall behind other countries in this dynamic region.

For this review, OECD-UNESCO analysed four areas of Thailand's education system that are critical for progress: curriculum, student assessment, teacher and school leader policies, and the use of information and communication technologies (ICT) in education. Successful reform in these areas will support a high-quality education system that drives social and economic development:

- A clear and coherent curriculum that sets out what students will learn in school, spells out student performance standards, reflects an overall vision for education, and promotes the acquisition of knowledge, competencies and values that are crucial for success in the 21st century.

- An effective student assessment framework that provides data to inform improvements to teaching and learning in the classroom and across the education system.

- Policies that develop and support teachers, who represent the most important school-related factor that shapes student outcomes, and principals, who play a vital role as instructional leaders in their schools.

- The integration of ICT in education, which is increasingly necessary for the success of individual students and, more broadly, national economies.

This review of Thailand's education system was based on an analysis of the policies, programmes and practices in these four areas. It drew on available data, research literature, and information gathered from interviews with government officials, policy makers and key education stakeholders in the country. This analysis led to the identification of practical recommendations for action in both the short and long term, with emphasis on effective practices in comparable countries. Real progress in each of the four areas depends on Thailand's ability to address a number of broad systemic issues and create an enabling context for reform. This means making greater use of evidence to inform policy decisions, ensuring more coherent, inclusive governance and developing a unifying long-term strategy for education in the country.

Thailand's education curriculum

A good school curriculum is underpinned by a recognised philosophy of teaching and learning, identifies a range of learning areas (i.e. core subjects) and promotes cross-curricular learning on topics considered important for the social, cultural and economic development of a given jurisdiction. It also sets out both "content" standards, describing what students should learn, and "performance" standards, which support teachers' assessment practices (IBE, 2013; UNESCO, 2012; UNESCO, 2015).

A curriculum can be characterised by the fundamental concept underlying its structure and philosophy (e.g. content-based, outcomes-based, or standards-based curricula). In 2001, Thailand replaced its content-based curriculum, which focused on the retention and recall of information, with one that was meant to be more learner-centred and standards-based. The new curriculum outlined predetermined standards for what students should know and be able to do in each subject. This shift in curricular philosophy and structure gave educators a significant amount of responsibility to determine how and what students should be taught – a shift which mirrored the decentralisation taking place across the education system. Teachers found this change confusing. They received inadequate, poorly sustained support to help them with curriculum implementation.

The current curriculum was developed in 2008. It improved upon the 2001 curriculum, but left a number of issues unresolved. Efforts to review the curriculum in 2011 stalled, due in part to a challenging political context. In 2015, Thailand reportedly began to revise the curriculum to better support school-to-work transitions, but the extent to which a clear review agenda has been developed is unclear.

To improve teaching and learning and to align the curriculum with broader social and economic development goals, Thailand should as a first step implement a thorough and consultative curriculum review and revision process. As part of this process, curriculum and student assessment developers should work together, with input from stakeholders, to create common student performance standards. Efforts should then be made to ensure that supports are in place to enable the effective implementation of the curriculum, and to help evaluate its impact through improved student assessments.

Revise the curriculum to improve clarity, consistency and relevance

A standards-based curriculum document (i.e. the written or "intended" curriculum) should provide educators with clear direction about the purpose of the curriculum and how it should be implemented. Thailand's curriculum document lacks this guidance in a number of key areas. For example, it does not provide a clear theoretical underpinning for the curriculum nor does it offer information about what effective pedagogy means in a standards-based environment. This essential information should be added as part of a curriculum review and revision process.

Recommendations

- Resume the process of curriculum reform as soon as possible based on a comprehensive evaluation of the 2008 Curriculum.
- In revising the written or "intended" curriculum:
  - provide clearer direction and advice to teachers about their responsibilities in a standards-based curriculum context;
  - provide a sound and clearly expressed philosophy and theory of learning;

- place increased and more consistent emphasis on the development of key competencies for the 21st century.

Support effective curriculum implementation

A standards-based curriculum allows for greater autonomy in implementation, but this places significant demands on educators. In Thailand, educators have found the implementation of the curriculum confusing. This has led to inconsistencies in teaching and learning across the education system, and it points to the necessity of professional development and supports. Conditions should be put in place to enable all actors to understand the new curriculum paradigm - especially school staff, but also school inspectors, developers of standardized student assessments, and pre-service programme providers.

Recommendations

- Ensure that all parts of the education system with curriculum-related responsibilities (e.g. school inspectors, student assessment developers, providers of pre-service and continuing professional development programs for educators) understand the curriculum and align their activities to support its implementation.

- Provide targeted professional development and support (such as appropriate learning materials) to teachers and school leaders to guide the implementation of the curriculum.

Strengthen capacity to assess how well students are learning

Education systems depend on valid and reliable information to assess whether students are learning successfully. Thailand needs to describe, in the basic education curriculum, common student performance standards at different stages of the learning process, and use these standards as the basis for different types of assessment. This will make assessments more consistent across the education system, and yield data that can be compared and used to inform teaching strategies, policies and programmes.

Recommendation

- Develop common student performance standards to guide assessments at all levels of the education system.

Improve curriculum development procedures

The quality of a curriculum depends to a significant extent on the quality of processes employed to produce it. These need to be carefully planned and administered. In the past, Thailand has implemented robust, systematic curriculum evaluation and development processes. However, the country needs to make strategic improvements to increase the likelihood that the outcomes of these processes – the curriculum itself and, ultimately, student learning – will be of high quality.

Recommendations

- Establish effective, efficient and transparent curriculum review and revision processes that are cyclical, led by experts and informed by research and data as a key strategy within the education reform agenda.
- Optimise opportunities for consultation with all stakeholders, in the interests of equity and transparency.

Student assessment in Thailand

Sound student assessment, guided by a well-designed and implemented curriculum that identifies common student performance standards, is an essential part of any high-performing education system. A good assessment system serves not only to measure but also to improve students' acquisition of skills and knowledge. It provides teachers and policy makers with essential information to support their decisions.

Since the 1999 National Education Act, Thailand has made significant progress in developing an assessment framework. For instance, in 2005 the country established a dedicated assessment body, the National Institute of Educational Testing Service (NIETS), to conduct the majority of the country's standardised student assessments. The most important of these is the Ordinary National Education Test (O-NET), which is taken by students in Grades 6, 9 and 12 (P6, M3 and M6) each year. Despite this progress, it is evident that Thailand faces challenges in the area of assessment.

As an initial measure, Thailand needs to ensure the methodological integrity of its national-level assessments. This is of utmost importance, given the impact these assessments can have on students' academic future, as well as the weight they carry in decisions about policies, programmes and teaching strategies. Thailand should ensure that the curriculum review process produces measureable student performance standards, and that these inform enhancements to the assessment framework to improve student learning. At the same time, Thailand should focus on building capacity to support effective use of assessment procedures at all levels of the system.

Build capacity to develop and use student assessments

Building capacity for an effective student assessment system is a complex, resource-intensive but essential endeavour. Like many countries around the world, Thailand has systemic gaps in capacity, with actors at different levels of the education system unable to make the most effective use of assessments for teaching, learning and policy development. Thailand needs to provide professional development and supports in order to address these gaps and improve the effectiveness of its assessment framework.

Recommendations

- Strengthen teacher training and support in the area of assessment.

- Implement policies and programs to develop professionals in the measurement and psychometric field.

- Strengthen the capacity of policy makers in the Ministry of Education and in local government (i.e. Education Service Areas) to use data and research generated by student assessments to inform decision making.

Ensure student assessments are methodologically sound

In order to yield accurate data that meaningfully contribute to an education system, student assessments must meet standards of methodological rigour. Thailand is not currently taking the necessary steps to ensure its high-stakes tests, including O-NET and the General Aptitude Test and the Professional and Academic Aptitude Test for university admission, meet such standards. This is a significant issue given the importance the Thai education system places on the results of these tests.

Recommendations

- Conduct validity studies for all standardised student assessment instruments, with particular focus on O-NET and the tests for university admission.

- Implement international best practices in equating all forms of an assessment in the same year, as well as year-to-year. This will help ensure, among other things, that students' scores can be compared across testing conditions and over time.

- Develop and analyse assessments and conduct item bank calibration using a modern psychometric methodology, such as Item Response Theory, and implement a rigorous policy that supports the comparability of results for each of the assessment programmes.

Develop the right mix of assessments to meet broad development needs

Education systems need to make use of a diverse range of assessments to accurately monitor and improve student learning. These include formative and summative classroom assessments, local and national assessments (based on common student performance standards), and international assessments. At present, Thailand places too much weight on standardized tests rather than using a broad range of student assessments.

Recommendations

- Examine the education system's overall framework for assessment and evaluation to ensure that its various components, including student, school, teacher and school leader performance assessments, are well balanced, and that they work together effectively to support teaching and student learning.

- Broaden the range of student assessments by supporting the development of school-based and district-based assessments, reducing the weight placed on national assessments.

- Support the development of assessments of greater complexity to enable the sound evaluation of higher-order competencies for the 21st century identified in the curriculum.

- Use international tests as a guide to improving standardised testing in Thailand – including using the results of those tests to gauge concerns surrounding the results of its own standardised tests.

Thailand's teachers and school leaders

Thailand recognises the crucial role teachers play in student learning. Since the early 2000s, the country has implemented a number of reforms to raise the quality of the teaching profession. Key changes have included a longer pre-service teacher education programme, a teacher certification system and, more recently, a new teacher induction programme. While Thailand has worked to reform the teaching profession, the country has also decentralised educational governance. This has significantly increased the administrative and instructional management responsibilities of school leaders.

Thailand's most recent reform agenda has called for additional improvements to the training, development and deployment of teachers. These reforms need to be pursued, with more sustained attention given to improving the pedagogical skills of teachers so that they can help meet Thailand's learning goals. As a priority, Thailand needs to build a holistic professional development strategy that ensures that teachers and school leaders are prepared to effectively implement the basic education curriculum and assessment strategies and work towards system-wide education reform goals. The curriculum review and revision process will inform this work, as will the development of new standards for teachers and school leaders. As a second priority, Thailand needs to reduce inequities across the education system by attracting, retaining and supporting educators in schools serving students from disadvantaged backgrounds.

Strengthen teacher preparation to support education reform

Teacher preparation can be a powerful vehicle for education reform if pre-service education programmes admit the best candidates and prepare them to drive that reform forward. In Thailand, pre-service programmes lack minimum requirements for admission and they do not provide solid preparation in the basic education curriculum or other key areas. Changes in this area will help Thailand build a well-prepared high-quality teaching workforce.

Recommendations

- Establish minimum criteria for entry into teacher preparation in consultation with pre-service programme providers.

- Strengthen teacher preparation in areas key to learning goals (e.g. the basic education curriculum, assessment, teaching students with special needs, 21st century competencies and ICT). Improve the practicum component by, among other things, ensuring that it is conducted throughout the pre-service programme rather than just at the end.

- Streamline and strengthen the pre-service accreditation process by having one organisation take primary responsibility for the process, and by making the accreditation requirements more thorough.

Develop a holistic professional development strategy

Standards describing what teachers should know and be able to do are at the heart of a high-quality teaching profession, which is essential for high-quality student learning. Research recommends that these standards be used to inform and align teacher preparation, performance appraisal and continuing professional development. Thailand plans to update its existing teacher standards. As it does so, it should develop a systematic appraisal process to assess teachers' performance and encourage their participation in ongoing professional development. Training in key reform areas, including the curriculum, assessment and ICT, will be essential.

Recommendations

- Establish a nationwide strategy for professional development to support the country's education reform. It should include a catalogue of professional development opportunities which are:
  - relevant to educators at all stages of their careers
  - aligned with teacher standards
  - focused on the core competencies needed to deliver the curriculum, assess students and support system-wide reforms
  - delivered whenever possible within schools.
- Update and amend the standards for teaching and establish an authentic process to assess whether teachers are meeting those standards and have access to ongoing professional development to support student learning.

Allow teachers to focus on student learning in the classroom

Teacher workload is associated with the quality of teaching and learning. Teachers who feel overburdened are generally less satisfied with their jobs. This has implications for their sense of self-efficacy, which, in turn, can affect student outcomes (OECD, 2014a). In Thailand, teachers' high level of administrative tasks (in particular the paperwork associated with school assessments) prevents them from focusing on student learning. Educators in disadvantaged areas need more support to improve the outcomes of students who are at the greatest risk of falling behind.

Recommendations

- Make efforts to reduce the workload that is taking teachers' attention away from the classroom, notably the paperwork associated with external school assessments.

- Reduce inequities by supporting rural schools in their efforts to improve students' learning outcomes, for example by providing financial and nonfinancial incentives to attract, retain and support staff, and by funding targeted in-service professional development such as mentoring and collaborative inter-school networks.

- Conduct ongoing dialogue with teachers' associations to ensure teachers' voices are heard.

Support and empower school leaders to improve teaching and learning

Like teaching, school leadership is a key factor that policy makers can influence to enhance student learning. In recognition of principals' important role – particularly in driving education reform – high-performing jurisdictions are now developing leadership standards and using them to inform school principals' preparation, performance appraisal and ongoing development. Thailand has developed standards for school leaders but they are based closely on the country's teacher standards, despite differences in the two roles. To better support principals and build their capacity to lead reform, revised standards should be used to develop other key components of a leadership framework.

Recommendation

- Develop a leadership framework to improve and support school leadership in the country, using amended standards for principals as the basis for the development of succession planning procedures, pre-service training, professional development and performance appraisal.

Make teacher deployment procedures more efficient and equitable

There is a clear link between the quantity and quality of teachers in an education system. Subject-matter expertise is one aspect of teaching that improves student learning, and a shortage of teachers is likely to increase out-of-field teaching. In Thailand, out-of-field teaching is also commonly the result of rigid teacher deployment procedures that fail to take into account schools' actual needs. The country is currently producing more new teachers than its education system needs, but there is reportedly a shortage of teachers for certain core subjects, in rural areas and along the country's southern border although gaps in the data make it difficult to accurately gauge its extent. A co-ordinated data management system would allow Thailand to track and respond to teacher supply and demand.

Recommendations

- Develop a co-ordinated data gathering mechanism to support decision making about current and future teacher supply needs.

- Review hiring and transfer processes to ensure their fairness, reduce unnecessary rigidities and enable greater responsiveness to local needs. This could be done, for example, by opening up vacant positions for competition by new or transferring teachers, and by involving schools in hiring decisions.

- Use teacher placement policies as a tool to reduce inequities in the education system. This would involve an evaluation of the impact of existing scholarships and incentive programmes and the development of new policies as needed (e.g. to expand incentives to teachers in more regions of the country).

Thailand's information and communication technology in education

Information and communication technology plays a key role in exchanging knowledge around the world. The ability to use ICT is now vital for citizens' – and countries' – full participation in modern society and a globalised economy. The acquisition of ICT competencies has thus become a major component of education curricula. ICT has also become a valuable teaching tool and a means for education systems to better manage schools.

Over the past ten years, Thailand has enacted a number of measures to promote ICT use to support the country's economic expansion. It has made substantial investments in hardware, software, "people-ware", and infrastructure. It has made significant efforts to improve the ICT skills of both teachers and students through government-initiated programmes, as well as public-private partnerships and ICT initiatives aimed at rural schools and disadvantaged students. Despite Thailand's investment in ICT for education, a recent major International Computer and Information Literacy Study found that Thai students have not yet fully attained the levels of computer, information processing, and communication skills required for the 21st century, and that Thai teachers are less confident than their peers in other countries in their ability to use ICT (Fraillon et al., 2014). All of this suggests the need for improvements in how Thailand's basic education system uses ICT for teaching and learning.

Thailand needs to create a coherent national strategy aligning policies to enhance the use of ICT in education. Informed by a review of the basic education curriculum, this strategy will ensure that all key areas for investment are given sufficient attention. It should focus first on the essential role teachers play in improving students' ICT proficiency by identifying the ICT competencies teachers need, and then developing relevant and effective professional development to help them acquire those competencies. The strategy should also prioritise the expansion and improvement of Internet access in all regions of the country in order to improve equity across the education system and spur Thailand's broader social and economic development.

Provide all schools with a reliable ICT infrastructure and Internet access

In order to make full use of ICT for teaching and learning, educators and students need both digital devices and access to the Internet. Thailand has made significant investments in school hardware in recent years. As a result, the number of computers available to students in Thai schools is high compared to other countries in the region. However, the use of ICT is impeded by a lack of stable high-speed Internet across the education system. Particular attention should be paid to expanding Internet access in rural areas.

Recommendations

- Address the need for a stable, responsive and widely available ICT infrastructure by setting clear, long-term goals to expand Internet access backed by adequate funding to cover devices, connectivity and maintenance.

- Prioritise investments in ICT infrastructure and connectivity in remote areas to ensure equity of access.

Invest in digital learning materials

Digital learning resources (e.g. audio or video files, images or software) are important teaching and learning tools in today's classrooms. They are increasingly used to help students master subject matter and develop 21st century competencies. Thailand has made investments in this area, but has not developed digital learning materials for all subjects and grades of the basic education curriculum. The quality and availability of existing resources is unclear. Their use depends to a large extent on teachers' ability to easily access them. The best way to ensure this is to provide a national repository, or one-stop shop, for digital learning materials.

Recommendation

- Develop a national strategy for developing digital learning materials, and create a common national repository where such materials can be accessed. To reduce costs and improve teachers' digital competency, Thailand should explore the role teachers could play in developing these materials.

Develop teachers' confidence and capacity to use ICT

Teachers' attitudes about ICT and their confidence in their ability to use ICT affect students' own ICT competency (Fraillon et al., 2014). Thailand currently provides teachers with pre-service and in-service training on ICT, but Thai teachers are still less confident and use ICT less frequently than their peers in other countries. To increase Thai students' ICT proficiency, Thailand needs to provide more effective preparation, professional development and support to its teachers. This would represent one essential component of a holistic professional development strategy to help educators work towards system-wide education reform goals.

Recommendations

- Define the ICT competencies teachers need and provide relevant high-quality teacher preparation and professional development based on these competencies.
- Invest in equipment, Internet access and on-line services to support teachers' use of ICT as a pedagogical tool.

Monitor and assess ICT use in schools

Education systems need to gather solid evidence about what is happening in their schools and how initiatives are affecting teaching and learning in order to develop policies that have the greatest chance of improving student outcomes. At present, Thailand's ability to develop evidence-based ICT policies is limited by a lack of sufficient mechanisms to monitor and assess ICT use in schools.

Recommendations

- Put in place a centralised system for periodic (annual or biannual) collection and publication of statistics, fed by school-level data regarding infrastructure, equipment, training and use of ICT.

- Complement the gathering of statistics with evaluations (qualitative data) and continued participation in international surveys to enable a deeper understanding of the issues at hand and a comparative perspective on how Thailand is progressing.

Create a coherent ICT policy strategy

Countries need to develop policies that are aligned towards the attainment of shared goals in order to successfully reform their education systems (see below). Over the years, Thailand's initiatives to integrate ICT in education have been fragmented and have not focused equally on all areas of key importance. To improve the information literacy skills of all students, it is crucial that Thailand develop a coherent and balanced approach to ICT in education.

Recommendation

- Develop a coherent national strategy to further integrate ICT into pedagogy, ensure equity of Internet access for Thai students across the country, improve students' ICT competencies, and use ICT to support educational administration.

Moving forward

Real progress in the four areas explored in this chapter – the curriculum, student assessment, teacher and school leader policies, and ICT in education – depends in large part on three broader enabling factors that Thailand needs to address:

More coherent, inclusive governance of the education system

Thailand's education system is multi-layered and institutionally complex. Policy implementation is challenged by heavy bureaucracy and administrative bottlenecks. Decentralisation, with the creation of over 180 Education Service Areas, seems to have exacerbated this policy-practice gap instead of closing it. Although moves have been made to streamline educational administration, the system is still characterised by multiple offices and agencies with overlapping responsibilities and weak accountability. This has inhibited efficiency and effectiveness. A lack of co-ordination across institutions was an important factor behind the stilted implementation of the 2008 curriculum. Moreover, governance of the education system in Thailand is not inclusive, with teachers, principals and other key stakeholders reportedly feeling disengaged from reform efforts.

There are various means by which Thailand can create more coherent, inclusive governance. Establishing a clear strategic vision for the education system will be an important first step to streamlining the work of different agencies and stakeholders. Education systems also require well-functioning, day-to-day co-ordination mechanisms in order to ensure different actors work together in the design and implementation of policies. In Thailand, this includes, importantly, creating a space for stakeholders to influence policy. Such co-ordination can be established in the form of clear guidelines and mandates for the key agencies involved in the system. The Ministry of Education might also consider ensuring one of its current divisions acts as a co-ordinator to ensure more transparency and efficiency. However, more important than the co-ordination structure itself, is creating the processes and working practices that will encourage actors in the system to collaborate actively and break free from administrative silos (Burns and Köster, 2016).

The complex nature of Thailand's decentralisation calls for particular efforts to improve co-ordination between central and local government, and strengthen the capacity of the Education Service Areas. Lack of local understanding and ownership has impeded progress in implementing the 2008 curriculum and other major reform policies. Each education system must strike its own balance between central leadership and local initiative. However, international experience shows that there is no way around strong local engagement on the path to school improvement and better student outcomes.

Increased capacity for evidence-based policy development

A solid evidence base, including effective mechanisms for data collection and usage, is essential for informed and effective management and timely decision making. It is also critical for accountability, trust and transparency in the education system. Thailand faces significant challenges in this regard. There are data gaps and uncoordinated data gathering mechanisms in critical areas such as the teacher labour market and the availability and use of ICT in schools. There are also serious weaknesses in its standardised student assessments, limiting their potential to drive successful reform efforts. Educational data are not regularly updated, and schools are unable to use the information system as planned. There are only limited efforts to monitor and develop data quality, and to use data in administration and service delivery. Indeed, the capacity of educators and policy makers to use technical assessment appears limited. Thailand also lacks a systematic process to evaluate and refine new policies and programs once they are implemented – a practice which is a hallmark of effective policy development and successful reform.

Addressing these gaps will demand significant increased investment in Thailand's data and information system. As a first step, Thailand should set higher standards for data collection and usage, including protocols for sharing and reporting information. At present, each agency is largely responsible for collecting its own data, according to its own definition and standards, with limited co-ordination and information sharing. Capacity needs to be strengthened across the system and at each stage of the information pipeline, from data collection to analysis and dissemination. To establish its commitment towards more evidence-based policy making, the Thai government should ensure that new policies are grounded in an analysis of available evidence, both national and international, and set clear objectives in terms of expected outcomes and reporting on results.

A long-term strategy for education, aligning reform efforts and uniting stakeholders to work towards the achievement of a high-quality school system

Thailand's 15-year National Education Plan and the Ministry of Education's Four-Year Action Plan are both set to expire in 2016. Since the military took power in May 2014, the government has established several committees and boards to develop a new education reform agenda. Proposed revisions to the curriculum, student assessment and students' classroom hours have been announced, and some new policies are already being implemented. However, without a renewed, comprehensive and broadly endorsed long-term strategy for education, there is a real risk that the policy fragmentation and misalignment highlighted by this review will continue, if not deepen, reducing the scope for improvement that Thailand's education system needs.

An essential component of an effective education strategy is a compelling vision to drive forward change. This is important for any education system, but particularly Thailand's, where a long-term vision could help ensure continuity and prevent unnecessary changes of direction when a new government takes office. Such a vision should provide a galvanising description of how the education system can support Thailand's social and economic development for the benefit of all citizens. To give coherence to reform policies and guide the actions of different stakeholders, this vision needs to be built around a small number of clear objectives.

These objectives should relate to both the quality and equity of the education system and be focused on student outcomes. To ensure the entire system is motivated to attain these objectives, educators, teachers' associations, parents and other key education stakeholders must be engaged in their development (OECD, 2010, 2014b).

Once a coherent long-term vision has been developed, implementation requires an evidence-based strategy that sets out a sequence of coherent initiatives to meet the identified objectives. Such a strategy needs to focus on improving teaching and learning, and not be distracted by reforms to other elements of the education system that may have less impact on student outcomes. This means prioritising revisions to the curriculum and related supports for schools to drive improvements to learning; standards and assessment practices (relating to students', schools' and educators' performance) to align and monitor efforts; and professional development for teachers and school leaders to target areas needed to support the reform. Given that large-scale education reform requires time to take effect, it is important that interim benchmarks are established to steer progress towards the overall objectives over time (OECD, 2010, 2014b). The expiry of current planning cycles provides an opportunity for Thailand to re-focus policy initiatives behind core priorities and bring institutions and stakeholders together behind a united reform effort that delivers real change in Thailand's schools.

Bibliography

Burns, T. and F. Köster (eds.) (2016), *Governing Education in a Complex World,* Education Research and Innovation, OECD Publishing, Paris, hhttp://dx.doi.org/10.1787/9789264255364-en.

Fraillon, J. et al. (2014), *Preparing for Life in a Digital Age: The IEA International Computer and Information Literacy Study International Report,* International Association for the Evaluation of Educational Achievement (IEA), Springer Open.

IBE (2013), *Glossary of Curriculum Terminology*, UNESCO International Bureau of Education, Geneva, www.ibe.unesco.org/fileadmin/user_upload/Publications/IBE_GlossaryCurriculumTerminology2013_eng.pdf.

OECD (2014a), *TALIS 2013 Results: An International Perspective on Teaching and Learning,* TALIS, OECD Publishing, http://dx.doi.org/10.1787/9789264196261-en.

OECD (2014b), *Improving Schools in Wales: an OECD Perspective*, OECD Publishing, Paris, www.oecd.org/edu/Improving-schools-in-Wales.pdf.

OECD (2010), *Improving Schools: Strategies for Action in Mexico*, OECD Publishing, Paris, http://dx.doi.org/10.1787/9789264087040-en.

UNESCO (2015), *Education Policy Review St. Kitts and Nevis*, Draft prepared by UNESCO.

Chapter 1

Thailand's education system

Thailand has made the transition from a largely agrarian, low-income society to an upper-middle income country and now faces the challenge of achieving sustainable growth in the face of a shrinking workforce and regional competition. This chapter outlines its demographics, economy, government and particularly its education system, including recent reform efforts and challenges.

Thailand's basic education has expanded significantly and now encompasses pre-primary and upper secondary schooling. It has been free of charge since 2009 and participation rates are now high, with almost universal pre-primary and primary education. Reform efforts to decentralise administration, and increase the quality of its education to meet broader development goals have had less impact, with challenges of effectiveness, efficiency and equity remaining to be met.

Country overview

The Kingdom of Thailand is located in Southeast Asia. A middle-income country, it is the third largest and fourth most populous in the Association of Southeast Asian Nations (ASEAN).[1] In December 2015, Thailand and its ASEAN neighbours began to form a new economic community, creating a single competitive market of free-flowing labour, trade and investment across the region. Domestically, Thailand has experienced recent political instability, slower economic growth and demographic shifts that will shrink the size of its labour force. A strong education system will be critical to help Thailand respond to these challenges, move beyond middle-income status and achieve inclusive sustainable growth. This chapter provides an overview of Thailand's demographics, economy, government and education system in this period of great transition.[2]

Figure 1.1. Map of Thailand

Source: United Nations (2009), Map 3853, Rev. 2, July 2009, United Nations Geospatial Information Section (formerly Cartographic Section), Department of Field Support, United Nations.

Demographics and economy

Thailand has experienced robust development over the past several decades, but the country is currently facing a number of demographic and economic challenges. Decreases in migration flows and birth rates mean that Thailand will need to rely on fewer workers to reinvigorate the country's economy, which is experiencing slower growth than other countries in the ASEAN region. To face these challenges, Thailand will need to transform its labour market and improve the quality of its education system to ensure that students from all regions of the country are prepared with the competencies, knowledge and values they will need to succeed.

Thailand and its people

Thailand has 67 million inhabitants spread across five regions: the South, the Northeast, the North, the Central Region and Bangkok. Around half of the Thai population live in urban areas, and this number is predicted to climb to over 70% by 2050 (UNDESA, 2014). Thailand's ethnic and religious make-up is relatively diverse, reflecting its geographical position between South and East Asia. Although the majority of people in Thailand are ethnically Thai, significant minority groups include people of Chinese descent and Malay Muslims in the south. There are also various hill tribes in the northern mountainous areas of Thailand, each of which has its own distinct language and culture. Ongoing conflicts between the government and insurgent groups in the southern region have disrupted education provision and left many children out of school.

Thailand went through a fertility transition faster than most countries (Figure 1.2). As a result, the period of its favourable population age structure – the so-called demographic dividend, when the working-age share of the population increases – is coming to an end, and the overall population is forecast to begin to decline within the next decade. The proportion of people over 60 years of age is expected to rise from 13% in 2010 to 23% in 2025, and 37% in 2050.

Figure 1.2. Fertility rates (total births per woman) and life expectancy, 1980-2012

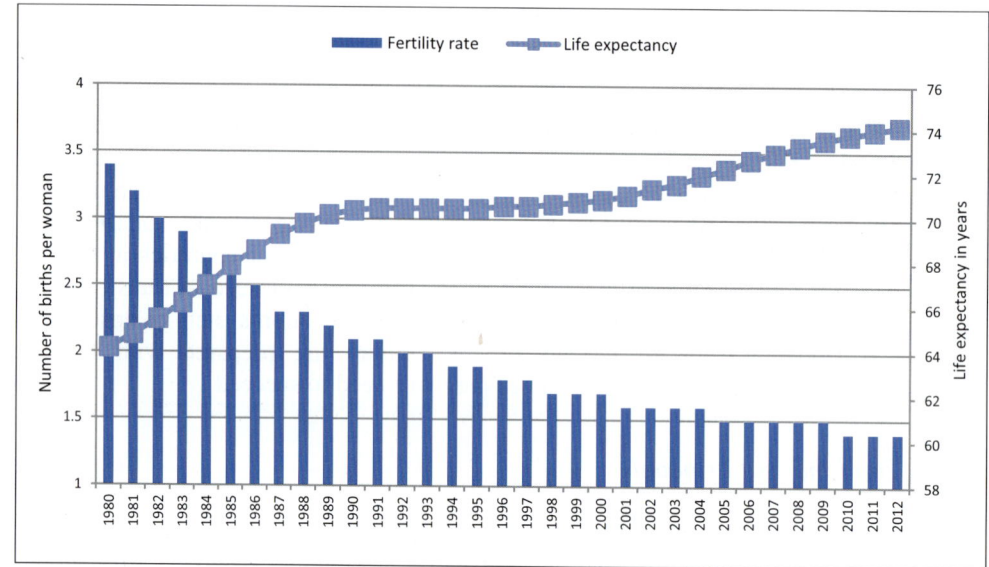

Sources: World Bank (2015a), "Fertility rate, (total births per woman)", http://data.worldbank.org/indicator/SP.DYN.TFRT.IN (accessed 17 December 2015); World Bank (2015b), "Life expectancy at birth, total (years)", http://data.worldbank.org/indicator/SP.DYN.LE00.IN (accessed 17 December 2015).

Faced with these demographic trends, Thailand will need to raise the skill levels of its population, and attract more highly skilled labour from neighbouring countries if it is to boost productivity and sustain growth. However, political changes and an increase in demand for labour throughout the region have slowed immigration rates. Thailand's net migration in 2012 was estimated to be 100 000, a significant decrease from 2002 when net migration was roughly 1.1 million (World Bank, 2012a). These figures suggest that not only have fewer migrants been coming to Thailand in the past decade, but more Thais have been emigrating, further depleting the country's talent pool.

The Thai Office of National Economic and Social Development Board anticipated a labour shortage of nearly 4 million workers in 2015. This gap is expected to reach 5.4 million over the course of the next ten years. It is unlikely that Thailand's current model of low-wage migrant employment will adequately address a growing labour shortage. The Thai government and business owners will therefore need to consider raising wage levels for migrant workers, or restructuring activity towards more technology-driven and high value-added production, further emphasising the importance upgrading Thailand's human capital (Huguet, 2014).

Economy and society

Thailand has risen from a low-income country to upper-middle income status in less than a generation. Between 1985 and 1995, Thailand was one of the world's fastest growing economies, experiencing an average growth rate of 8-9% per year (World Bank, 2014). However, despite a remarkable bounce back after the "Asian crisis" of 1997-98, economic growth has subsequently slowed, in large part due to the fallout of the global financial crisis and the impact of domestic political uncertainty in 2010 and again in 2013-14. Uncertainty continues to affect Thailand's growth prospects. The OECD forecasts an average of 3.6% growth per annum for 2016-20, with this estimate influenced by risks surrounding the country's future economic roadmap, as well as concerns about weak productivity and skills (OECD, 2015). While still fairly robust, growth will likely be significantly below levels in other large ASEAN economies unless Thailand can significantly strengthen its human capital base (Table 1.1).

Table 1.1. Real GDP growth of Southeast Asia, the People's Republic of China and India, annual percentage change

Country	2014	2015	2016	2016-20 (average)	2011-13 (average)
ASEAN countries					
Brunei Darussalam	-2.3	-1.4	0.5	1.8	0.9
Cambodia	7.0	7.0	7.1	7.3	7.3
Indonesia	5.0	4.7	5.2	5.5	6.2
Lao People's Democratic Republic	7.4	6.9	7.0	7.3	8.1
Malaysia	6.0	4.6	4.6	5.0	5.2
Myanmar	7.7	8.2	8.2	8.3	6.9
Philippines	6.1	5.9	6.0	5.7	5.9
Singapore	2.9	2.1	2.4	2.6	4.1
Thailand	0.9	2.7	3.1	3.6	3.2
Viet Nam	6.0	6.4	5.9	6.0	5.6
Two large economies in the region					
China (People's Republic of)	7.3	6.8	6.5	6.0	8.2
India	7.3	7.2	7.3	7.3	5.5
Averages					
ASEAN 10 countries	4.6	4.6	4.9	5.2	5.4
Emerging Asia	6.7	6.5	6.4	6.2	7.0

Note: The cut-off date for data is 2 November 2015. Weighted averages are used for ASEAN and Emerging Asia. The results for the People's Republic of China, India and Indonesia (2016 and 2016 projections) are based on OECD (2016a), "OECD Economic Outlook No. 98 (Edition 2015/2)", *OECD Economic Outlook Statistics and Projections*, (database), http://dx.doi.org/10.1787/bd810434-en.

Source: OECD (2016b), *Economic Outlook for Southeast Asia, China and India 2016: Enhancing Regional Ties*, http://dx.doi.org/10.1787/saeo-2016-en.

Past economic growth has contributed to a significant reduction in poverty and important societal gains. On an aggregate basis, Thailand met most of the United Nations Millennium Development Goals that were set for 2015, including achieving near universal access to primary education. Over the last decade, poverty has been reduced from its peak of 42.6% in 2000 to about 12.6% in 2012 (UNDP, 2015). Maternal and under-five mortality rates have greatly declined. Access to clean water has risen in both urban and rural areas, and is now close to universal (World Bank, 2015c). Access to sanitation has also improved, and contributed to gains in other areas, including girls' enrolment in school (World Bank, 2015d).

Figure 1.3. Annual GDP growth in Thailand, 1980-2014, and proportion of population living below the national poverty line, 2000-14 (percentage)

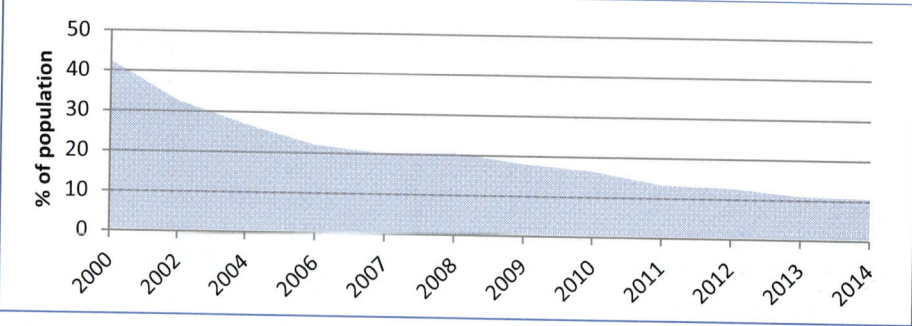

Sources: World Bank (2015e), "GDP growth (annual %)", *World Development Indicators* (database), http://data.worldbank.org/indicator/NY.GDP.MKTP.KD.ZG (accessed March 2016); World Bank (2015f), "Poverty headcount ratio at national poverty lines (% of population)", http://data.worldbank.org/indicator/SI.POV.NAHC (accessed 16 December 2015).

However, progress has not benefited everyone equally, and significant disparities remain across provinces, with the rural northeast, the far north and the far south lagging behind other regions in terms of poverty reduction and meeting other Millennium Development Goals. Although the Gini coefficient decreased from 0.43 in 2000 to 0.39 in 2010, inequality remains a major challenge for the country. The richest 20% of Thais received roughly 50% of the share of income in 2010, while the poorest 20% received only 7%. These proportions have changed little since 2002 (World Bank, 2010). Poverty is increasingly concentrated in rural areas, where some 80% of the country's 7.3 million poor live (World Bank, 2013). Such inequalities are reproduced in the education system, which, as this report shows, tends to reinforce disparities rather than help to overcome them.

Thailand faces challenges in sustaining its export competitiveness, in particular as it comes under increasing pressure from lower-wage nations in Southeast Asia. The World Economic Forum's *Global Competitiveness Report 2014-2015* ranks Thailand 31st out of 144 countries for overall global competitiveness (WEF, 2014). This is well below Singapore and Malaysia, and Indonesia and the Philippines are fast catching up (Figure 1.4). Although primary education participation rates are high, the quality of Thailand's education system is ranked lower than most other ASEAN nations (WEF, 2014). The country's future position is also threatened by its capacity for innovation, which ranks 70th (WEF, 2014). Thailand's gross expenditure on research and development (GERD) in 2009 was 0.25% of gross domestic product (GDP), one of the lowest levels of spending in the region (UNESCO-UIS, 2015). Low private-sector demand for innovation and upgrading contributes to Thailand's brain drain and skills mismatches, constraining growth prospects (OECD, 2013a).

Figure 1.4. Trends in global competitiveness in selected ASEAN countries, 2005-14/15

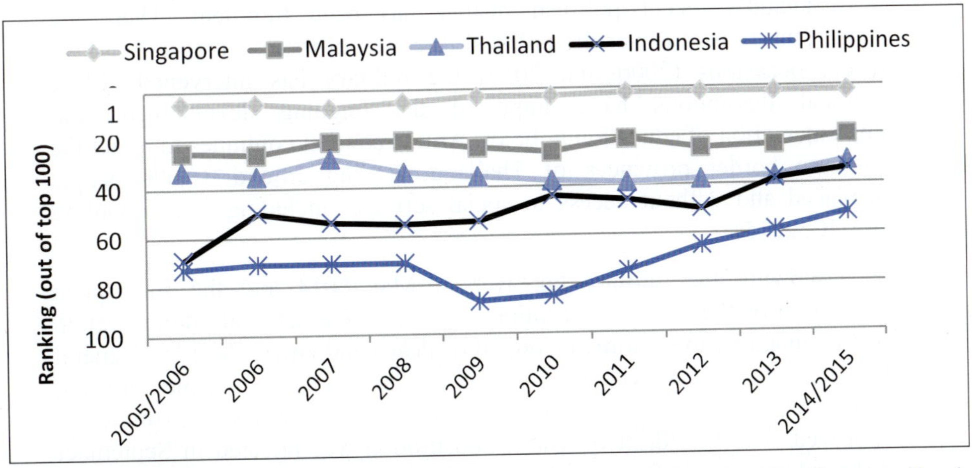

Source: WEF (2014), *Global Competitiveness Report 2014-2015*, www3.weforum.org/docs/WEF_GlobalCompetitivenessReport_2014-15.pdf.

Like many emerging economies, Thailand faces the challenge of creating more high-quality jobs and stimulating greater demand for higher skills. Although the Thai economy is characterised by an official unemployment rate of less than 1% (World Bank, 2014), one of the lowest in the world, there are several signs of weakness in the labour market. Participation rates are low, especially for women: only 62% of women aged 15 and older participate in the labour market, compared to 79% of men (ILO, 2014a). Large shares of workers are employed in labour-intensive activities: the shift in employment away from agriculture and towards industry has stalled (ILO, 2014a). Agriculture still employs 40% of the workforce, compared to 34% in Indonesia and just 13% in Malaysia (ILO, 2014b).

The share of workers in vulnerable employment, defined as self-employment or work done by contributing family members, remains high in Thailand, at 54% for men and over 57% for women in 2013 (ILO, 2014b). Informal employment is even higher, particularly among young Thais. Youths are likely to engage in unpaid family work and face periods of temporary or casual employment during the school-to-work transition (ILO, 2014b). Such high levels of informality constrain both economic and educational development, creating a negative cycle of low skills, low demand and low productivity. Educational attainment also affects unemployment; unemployment rates are almost twice as high for individuals with only a primary education compared with secondary school graduates (World Bank, 2014).

Government and politics

Thailand's recent political history has been turbulent. There are significant divisions over the political direction of the country, and on two recent occasions (2006 and 2014) the military has intervened. These political disruptions have impacted the ongoing development and implementation of education policies. Armed conflict continues to affect the southern border provinces of Thailand, leaving around 35 000 people displaced and without access to social services, including safe schooling (IDMC, 2015).

Following the military takeover of May 2014 and the subsequent revocation of the 2007 Constitution, control of the national administration was assumed by the National Council of Peace and Order (NCPO). General Prayuth Chan-o-cha, who took office as Thailand's 29th prime minister, committed to overseeing a return to democracy once a new constitution is approved. The first draft of a new constitution was rejected in September 2015, with a new draft released in March 2016. A constitutional referendum will be held in August 2016 and general elections are expected to take place by mid-2017.

Thailand's 1997 Constitution introduced significant decentralisation of government services to the country's 76 provinces, or *changwats*, which are overseen by governors appointed by the Ministry of the Interior, and municipalities, governed by elected local officials. A series of decentralisation initiatives ensued, aiming to increase community engagement in local decision making and provide local governments with a larger share of total government revenues (Haque, 2013). These changes are considered important for enhancing social inclusion, improving public sector efficiency and accountability, and furthering the achievement of national development objectives. Their implications for education are discussed below.

The education system in Thailand

Education and literacy development have a long tradition in Thailand (Fry and Bi, 2013). Today's education system aims to build and support practical and academic skills, social competencies, moral and democratic values, and a national identity. Over the years, Thailand has expanded the number of years of free schooling available to Thai youth, and the country now offers a range of schools to meet students' different needs. However, students in remote areas or from disadvantaged backgrounds do not have access to the same quality of education as those in other parts of the country, and there are inefficiencies in the overall governance of the system.

Structure of schooling

Thailand provides three types of education – formal, non-formal and informal. While non-formal and informal education are not the focus of this review, they constitute an important feature of the Thai education system. Both aim to provide basic skills and ensure lifelong learning, and are specifically designed for disadvantaged children and adults in remote areas or from minority communities. At the national level, they are overseen by the Office of Non-Formal and Informal Education (ONIE) within the Ministry of Education (MOE), but other public bodies and private stakeholders also provide education outside the formal programmes. In 2013, over 2.6 million students were enrolled in non-formal learning (Office of the Permanent Secretary, 2014).

Since 1999, formal education has been divided into basic and higher (tertiary) education (UNESCO and IBE, 2011). Basic education is offered free of charge and includes pre-primary, primary and secondary levels (Figure 1.5). Compulsory education starts at the age of six and lasts nine years, consisting of primary schooling (grades P1-6) and lower secondary education (grades M1-3).

Pre-primary education became part of basic education in 2004. It is not compulsory, but has been made free of charge since 2009 in order to facilitate access. State schools typically offer two years of kindergarten (three and four-year-olds) and one year of pre-school classes (five-year-olds). Younger children may attend childcare centres. Participation has increased considerably in recent years. According to international statistics, net enrolment in pre-primary education was nearly universal in 2011 (UNESCO-UIS, 2015).

Students typically begin primary schooling (*prathom*) at the age of six. Primary students make up the largest group in basic education (about 5 million students), and coverage is nearly universal: 95.6% of students within the official age group were enrolled in 2009 (UNESCO-UIS, 2015). Primary is followed by secondary education (*mattayom*), starting at the age of 12. In 2013, 2.4 million students (97% of those of school age) were enrolled in lower secondary education.

Upper secondary education is divided into general and vocational tracks. While not mandatory, it is still considered part of basic education. According to government statistics, about 75% of eligible youth were enrolled in 2013 (Office of the Permanent Secretary, 2014). Students enjoy a certain freedom in choosing their subjects, as upper secondary education aims to prepare them for further studies and working life.

Formal vocational education and training (VET) is offered at the secondary level in specific schools or institutions, or in a dual model based on agreements between schools and companies. After two years of coursework students obtain a diploma, and they may then continue to higher VET at tertiary institutions. The share of upper secondary VET students has been on the decline, and represented roughly one-third (32.7%) of all upper secondary students in 2013 (Table 1.2).

The Thai formal school system is large in terms of enrolments (Table 1.2), but the number of students has been decreasing in the past years. Demographic decline is starting to show in primary and lower secondary education, where net enrolment rates are comparatively high. Upper secondary and higher education on the other hand have recorded a slight increase in enrolment, although rates of participation are much lower (see Chapter 2). The MOE reports that in 2013, roughly 11.2 million children were enrolled in basic education from pre-school to upper secondary level: 1.8 million in pre-primary education, 4.9 million in primary education and 4.5 million in secondary education (Office of the Permanent Secretary, 2014). In 2013, 2.41 million students attended some form of higher education, 90% of them in undergraduate programmes (Table 1.2).

Figure 1.5. The Thai formal education system

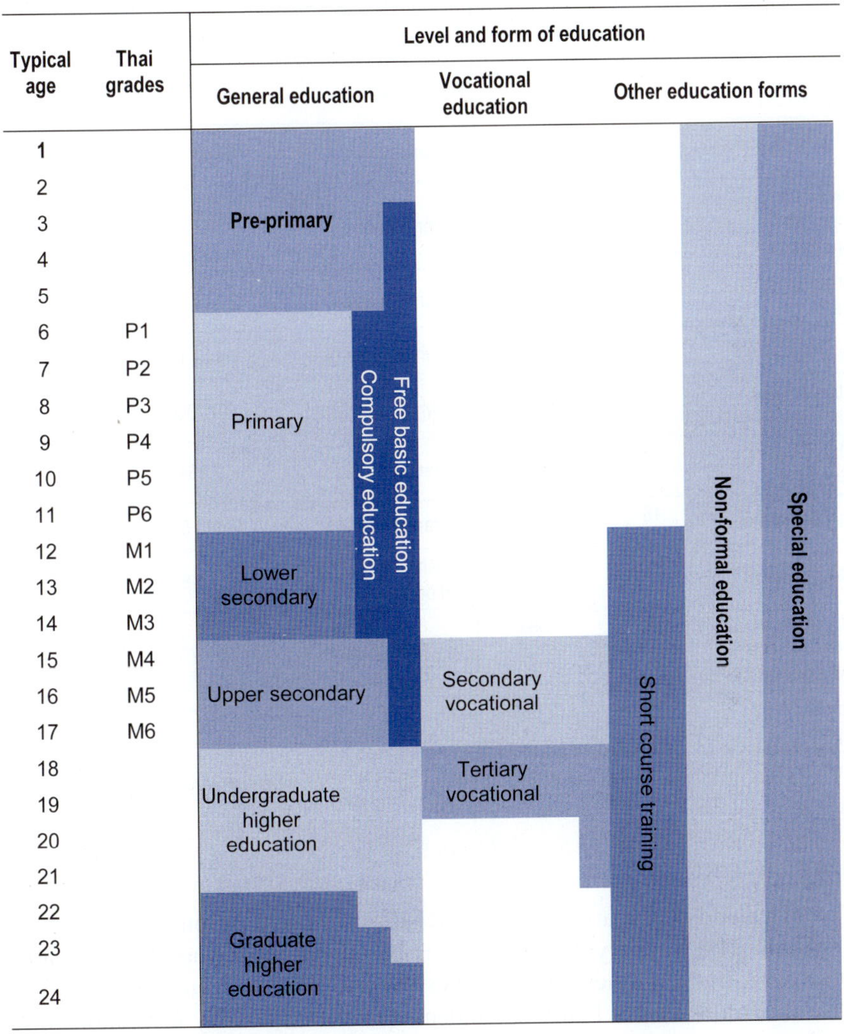

Typical age	Thai grades	Level and form of education		
		General education	Vocational education	Other education forms
1				
2				
3		Pre-primary		
4				
5				
6	P1	Primary		
7	P2			
8	P3			
9	P4			
10	P5			
11	P6			
12	M1	Lower secondary		
13	M2			
14	M3			
15	M4	Upper secondary	Secondary vocational	
16	M5			
17	M6			
18		Undergraduate higher education	Tertiary vocational	
19				
20				
21				
22		Graduate higher education		
23				
24				

Vertical labels spanning groups: *Compulsory education*, *Free basic education*, *Short course training*, *Non-formal education*, *Special education*.

Notes: P = *prathom* (primary level); M = *mattayom* (secondary level).

Sources: Adapted from Ministry of Education (2008), *Towards a Learning Society in Thailand: An Introduction to Education in Thailand*; OECD (2013b), *Southeast Asian Economic Outlook 2013: With Perspectives on China and India*, http://dx.doi.org/10.1787/saeo-2013-en.

Table 1.2. Number of institutions and students in Thai formal education by responsible agency, school type and programme, 2013

Responsible agency	Institutions	Students
TOTAL	38 010	13 606 743
Ministry of Education	35 595	12 482 248
Ministry of the Interior	1 292	677 472
Bangkok Metropolitan Administration	438	307 323
National Buddhism Bureau	405	51 173
Royal Thai Police	178	24 012
Ministry of Public Health	37	18 453
Ministry of Tourism and Sports	28	22 677
Ministry of Defence	16	7 999
Ministry of Culture	16	12 411
Ministry of Social Development and Human Security	3	394
Ministry of Transport	2	2 581

Education level/ programme	All students	Public schools	Private schools
TOTAL	13 606 743	10 852 675	2 754 068
Pre-primary	1 749 196	1 128 040	621 156
Primary	4 905 460	3 866 397	1 039 063
Lower secondary	2 391 390	2 080 249	311 141
Upper secondary	2 144 118	1 738 422	405 696
..of which general	1 442 186		
..of which vocational	701 398		
..other	2 534		
Tertiary education	2 416 579	2 039 567	377012
..of which undergraduate and below	2 186 822	1 838 428	348 394
..of which graduate	229 757	201 139	28 618

Source: Office of the Permanent Secretary (2014), *Educational Statistics in Brief 2013*, www.mis.moe.go.th/mis-th/images/statistic/Statistic/statistics2556.pdf.

School types

Thailand's education system includes a variety of public and private schools. The Ministry of Education is by far the most important education provider, but ten other public bodies oversee their own institutions, which educate more than 1.1 million students (Table 1.2). Many institutions offer primary and secondary education combined, and it is common to attend primary and lower secondary education ("extended primary education") or lower and upper secondary education within a single school (UNESCO Bangkok, 2008). Students with special education needs are currently taught in either mainstream or dedicated facilities, but Thailand is making efforts to expand their opportunities to gain self-sufficiency and integrate into the community.

Roughly 20% of Thai students attend private institutions (Office of the Permanent Secretary, 2014). Under the authority of the 1999 National Education Act, these institutions can be run by individuals, organisations or companies; deliver general, vocational or special education on a formal or non-formal basis (e.g. short or part-time courses, distance learning); and receive public subsidies (Pinyakong, Virasilp and Somboon, 2007). Private school enrolment is highest at the pre-primary and upper secondary vocational levels, where roughly one-third of students attend such schools. However, these proportions vary by region, with more students in the Bangkok Metropolitan Area attending private schools (61% of pre-primary students, 42% of primary students and 36% of upper secondary students). It is also common (especially for children from wealthier families, and in the Bangkok area) to attend private and fee-paying out-of-school tutoring. These so-called "cram" schools aim to prepare students for school or university entrance exams.

The Royal Border Patrol Police maintain roughly 180 schools in remote areas, which serve primarily migrant and hill tribe families. These schools typically offer only pre-primary and primary education. There are also dedicated public or private schools for students of various religious faiths (US Department of State, 2013). For example the National Buddhism Bureau supervises over 400 schools with 52 000 students. Several types of schools offer Islamic education in the southern part of the country: about 270 schools with approved curricula are recognised and subsidised by the government (US Department of State, 2013). There are also about 200 private Islamic schools which are typically registered, a significant number of traditional private and mostly unregistered schools (*pondoks*) with their own curricula, and after-school courses (e.g. in mosques) which are overseen by the Ministry of Education in some regions.

Thailand has a large number of small schools, particularly at the primary level and in disadvantaged and rural areas. Close to 30% of Thai schools are estimated to have an average class size of less than 10 students (Lathapipat, 2015). The World Bank recently suggested that Thailand consider several related options to address this situation: 1) increase expenditure to evenly distribute quality education throughout the country; 2) merge or close approximately 12 000 small schools, while protecting the most remote; and 3) in the long-term, introduce an equitable and transparent demand-side financing mechanism that funds schools on a per-student basis (Lathapipat, 2015). Thailand's results in the OECD 2012 Programme for International Student Assessment (PISA; OECD, 2013c), showed a significant difference in student performance between large and small schools, pointing to the need for action in this area (see Chapter 2 for more information about Thailand's PISA results).

Governance of the formal system

Education in Thailand is governed at national or central, provincial and local levels (UNESCO and IBE, 2011) (Figure 1.6). At the national level, there are many different administrative bodies, some within the government and others at arm's length. A reform in 2003 aimed to improve the quality, democratic responsiveness and efficiency of the country's educational administration, and ultimately resulted in the reorganisation of two ministries and two other bodies under the umbrella of the Ministry of Education (UNESCO Bangkok, 2008). However, educational governance is still characterised by a multiplication of functions across different offices (World Bank, 2011). This institutional complexity is intertwined with issues surrounding the efficient use of financial resources and accountability. Between 2011 and 2015, Thailand implemented a National Education Accounts project with the aim of tracking and analysing education budget flows comprehensively (Quality Learning Foundation Office, forthcoming; UNESCO Bangkok, 2013). The results of this project are pending.

The National Economic and Social Development Board (NESDB) oversees overarching development plans, which include objectives for education. Administrative responsibility for education is shared by the Ministry of Education and the Ministry of the Interior. The MOE, as the lead ministry at the national level, governs all education levels from pre-primary to higher education. It formulates education policies, plans and standards; allocates resources for education; monitors and inspects education provision; and co-ordinates religious affairs, arts, culture and sports in relation to education. The MOE currently has five main offices, each with different responsibilities (Ministry of Education, 2008):

- The Office of the Permanent Secretary (OPS) provides executive guidance. It advises the Education Minister, co-ordinates administrative and management systems and services in the ministry, represents the ministry in public, and acts as a co-ordinating unit for administration and co-operation among government bodies and with international partners. The OPS has several subordinate bodies, including:
    - The Office of Non-Formal and Informal Education (ONIE), established in 2008, supports and co-ordinates all activities outside formal education, makes policy recommendations and manages recognition and equivalency issues between formal and non-formal education.

- The Office of the Private Education Commission (OPEC) inspects and supervises private institutions, approves tuition fees and allocates subsidies.

- The National Institute for Development of Teachers, Faculty Staff and Educational Personnel (NIDTEP), established in 2005, is charged with formulating policies for teacher development, implementing support activities and co-ordinating relevant agencies.

- The Office of the Teacher Civil Service and Education Personnel Commission (OTEPC), established in 2004, supervises all administrative matters concerning public school personnel under the jurisdiction of the ministry (Pinyakong, Virasilp and Somboon, 2007; UNESCO Bangkok, 2011; UNESCO and IBE, 2011).

• The Office of the Education Council (OEC) fulfils an overall planning function, including in areas such as curriculum development and research, legal regulations and education standards. It has traditionally developed the national education scheme, which includes religion, arts, culture and sports, and the five-year national education development plans. Apart from monitoring the plan's implementation in accordance with the national framework, the OEC also proposes policies for the mobilisation of resources for education.

• The Office of the Basic Education Commission (OBEC) is responsible for the entire general basic education sector, including guaranteeing equal access and assisting gifted and special needs students. It oversees basic education policies, standards and curricula, and evaluates education provision. OBEC aims to improve the quality of basic education, develop innovation, and decentralise administrative authority.

• The Office of the Vocational Education Commission (OVEC) provides VET. It assesses the demands of the labour market; implements and standardises VET management and administration; and promotes research, innovation and technology development.

• The Office of the Higher Education Commission (OHEC) establishes funds and monitors higher education institutions, formulates policies and standards, and supports international co-operation around higher education issues.

Several other bodies, although not part of the MOE, fall under its jurisdiction. These include:

- The Teachers' Council of Thailand (TCT), which issues teaching licences and sets out standards for the profession.

- The Committee for Promotion of the Benefits and Welfare of Teachers and Educational Personnel, which offers financial and other assistance to struggling teachers, including accommodation, healthcare, insurance, scholarships, counselling services and support with debt.

- The Institute for the Promotion of Teaching Science and Technology (IPST), which is involved in science, technology, engineering and mathematics (STEM) teaching and learning; conducts research on curriculum development, evaluation and pedagogical materials related to these subjects; and offers training to teachers and students (UNESCO and IBE, 2011; Teachers' Council of Thailand, 2015).

At the local level, basic education is managed primarily by Educational Service Areas (ESAs). These were established following the decentralisation of education administration set out in the 1999 National Education Act. In 2011, Thailand was divided into 185 ESAs, 3 of which are situated in Bangkok (UNESCO and IBE, 2011). The ESAs are responsible for hiring teachers based on central rules established by the MOE's Teacher Civil Service and Education Personnel Commission (World Bank, 2012a).

Schools are responsible for the delivery of education and control their own budget. They do not have authority over teacher salaries, which are determined and paid at the central level (see Chapter 5). Stakeholders and parents are involved in education management through school board committees, and have an advisory function at the local level (World Bank, 2012b).

While the MOE takes the lead on education, other ministries and agencies are also responsible for specialised or local educational institutions, above all the Ministry of the Interior (MOI), which supervises Thailand's local administration organisations (LAOs). Upon meeting MOE criteria, LAOs (including the special administrative entities of Bangkok and Pattaya) may offer education at any or all levels according to local needs. They are supervised and funded by the MOI, while the MOE helps to co-ordinate and provides advice to the local authorities (UNESCO Bangkok, 2008).

Figure 1.6. Governance structure of the education system in Thailand

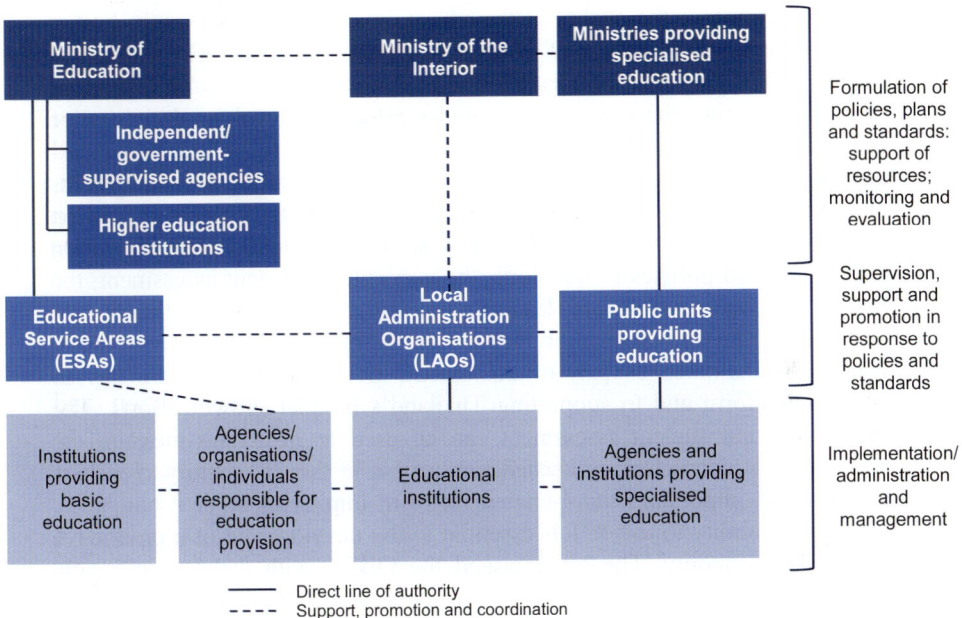

Source: Adapted from UNESCO Bangkok (2008), *Secondary Education Regional Information Base: Country Profile - Thailand*, www.uis.unesco.org/Library/Documents/Thailand.pdf.

Recent education reforms

Education in Thailand has received significant political attention in the past two decades. Thai education reform developed out of the country's recognition that its education system needed to transform to adapt to domestic and global changes and to better support sustained economic growth. This reform can be divided into several phases, the most recent of which began with the 1997 Asian economic crisis and the writing of a new Thai constitution (Fry and Bi, 2013). A major reform was implemented in 1999 under the aegis of the National Education Act. Despite Thailand's progress in increasing overall access to education, translating other reforms into action has been an ongoing challenge. The country will need to establish and effectively implement a new long-term reform agenda in order to improve the quality of the education system and, in turn, meet broader development goals.

The National Education Act and the key reform areas

Thailand's 1999 National Education Act (NEA) introduced sweeping changes to improve the quality of the education system. Moving away from a highly centralised structure of education governance, the NEA called for education financing and administration to be decentralised to ESAs, LAOs and schools, mirroring the government's wider efforts to devolve administrative responsibilities. It established equity and student-centred – rather than rote – learning as guiding principles for the education system, calling for all segments of society to be able to participate in education and for all learners to develop themselves at their own pace and to the best of their potential. The legislation also introduced policies to transform the curriculum, student assessment, the role of teachers and school leaders, and, to a lesser extent, the use of information and communication technology (ICT) in education. These areas, which are examined as part of this OECD-UNESCO review, are key to education reform and to supporting Thailand's broader growth efforts. The curriculum and student assessment can be used to instil and measure the acquisition of competencies needed for success in the 21st century. Teachers are the most important school-related factor in improving student outcomes. Finally, the ability to use ICT is essential to the development of a productive knowledge economy. The NEA tasked the OBEC with developing a new basic education curriculum at the national level, and stipulated that schools would be responsible for developing their own curriculum content to address the needs of their community and "Thai wisdom". It established a quality assurance framework, creating the Office for National Education Standards and Quality Assessment (ONESQA) to inspect public and private schools, and set the stage for the later establishment of a national student assessment body, the National Institute of Educational Testing Service (NIETS). It introduced a number of reforms to enhance the teaching profession and develop educational personnel, including the creation of an independent organisation responsible for establishing standards for teachers and school leaders, which became the TCT, the introduction of a licensing system, and new legislation to ensure educators were sufficiently remunerated. Finally, it listed technological knowledge and skills as a subject to be covered in the formal, non-formal and informal education systems, and encouraged the use of different types of teaching and learning media in schools. Policy issues surrounding the implementation of these reforms, as well as additional changes introduced since 1999, are described in detail in Chapters 3 to 6 of this report.

Access to schooling

The 1997 constitution, as well as later legislative documents, made primary and lower secondary education compulsory. In 1999, the NEA expanded compulsory education from six to nine years to improve students' knowledge and skills, and the 2003 Compulsory Education Act required all children between 7 and 15 years of age to attend a school. Following an NEA amendment in 2002, 12 years of primary and secondary education were made free of charge, including for non-Thai children living in Thailand. However, in addition to issues with equity identified above, research suggests gaps in how the government promotes education among migrant parents, and how it follows up on students who drop out (Arphattananon, 2012). Free schooling was increased to 14 years in 2004 (including 2 years of pre-primary education), and to 15 years in 2009, with the addition of 1 more year at the pre-primary level (UNESCO and IBE, 2011). The provision of three years of free pre-primary schooling represents a significant commitment to ensuring all children get a strong start in learning. Access to non-formal education was regulated in the 2008 Promotion of Non-Formal and Informal Education Act, in line with the principles stipulated by the NEA: lifelong education for all, participation of all parts of society, and continuous development of the learning process (UNESCO and IBE, 2011). Today, overall participation rates are high, but equity of access remains an issue, with fewer students from disadvantaged backgrounds attending school (see Chapter 2).

Education planning instruments and challenges

As mandated by the NEA, Thailand developed a 15-year National Education Plan (2002-16) to promote human-centred development, the knowledge-based economy, continuous learning and the greater participation of stakeholders (UNESCO and IBE, 2011). Although the country has made incremental progress over this time, it has faced persistent difficulties in translating reforms into action at the school level (Hallinger and Bryant, 2013). Research identifies a number of challenges holding back implementation of the reforms, including the political instability of the country, a lack of financial support (see Chapter 2) and, more broadly, the complexity of the sweeping reforms. These have required implementation efforts to go beyond the establishment of a new organisation or new legislation, and to include investments of time, effort and resources to ensure key actors develop a solid understanding of the reforms and acquire the competencies needed to implement them (for example through sustained, effective professional development and information sharing) (Hallinger and Bryant, 2013). Current education priorities are defined through multi-year education planning documents, elaborated by national boards (such as the National Social and Economic Development Plan) or by the MOE (Table 1.3). The National Education Plan and Ministry of Education Four-Year Action Plan both end in 2016, pointing to the need for a new agenda setting out the next long-term vision for education in the country, and for effective policy development to overcome past implementation challenges (as described in the Assessment and Recommendations chapter at the end of this report).

Table 1.3. Education planning instruments in Thailand

National Social and Economic Development Plan	2012-2016	**Overarching development plan for Thailand, integrating education objectives** Promotes lifelong learning and the knowledge-based economy.
Ministry of Education Proposals for the Second Decade of Education Reform	2009-2018	**Mid-term planning document** Principal goals: quality improvement, increasing learning opportunities for all, strengthening stakeholder participation. Measures addressed include evaluation and assessment, governance of small schools and decentralisation, disadvantaged students, qualifications frameworks and curricula, teacher quality, and budget allocation.
Ministry of Education Four-Year Action Plan	2013-2016	**Short-term planning document** Provides vision, mission and strategic targets. Aims at developing education management, lifelong learning, education and teacher quality, and the use of ICT.

Sources: UNESCO and IBE (2011), "Thailand", *World Data on Education*, www.ibe.unesco.org/ileadmin/user_upload/Publications/WDE/2010/pdf-versions/Thailand.pdf; UNESCO Bangkok (2008), *Secondary Education Regional Information Base: Country Profile - Thailand*, www.uis.unesco.org/Library/Documents/Thailand.pdf.

Developments since the 2014 change in government

Following the military coup, the Education and Human Development Reform Committee within the now-defunct National Reform Council (NRC) took responsibility for Thailand's education policy and for developing recommendations for reform. In September 2014, the new government announced several areas of focus for future education policy, including adjusting the education budget; enhancing stakeholder participation, including that of private actors; enhancing equity in education; promoting lifelong learning and vocational education; enhancing the status and training of the teaching profession; and promoting the role of religion and Thai cultural heritage.

After the NRC's dissolution in September 2015, the National Reform Steering Assembly (NRSA) assumed responsibility for developing education policy. The NRSA is currently co-ordinating with the new Constitutional Drafting Committee (CDC) to prioritise national reform efforts – including education – in the new constitution.

While many of the NRSA's education reforms are not likely to be implemented until the next elected government is installed, a "super board" for education, headed by the Prime Minister, has been working to implement immediate changes. A new pilot project to cut classroom hours has been introduced in 4 100 state schools and the government has mandated that English teaching be aligned to the Common European Framework of Reference for Languages (CEFR) (Bangkok Post, 2015a, 2015b).

In an effort to better align education goals with the government's commitment to human resource development, OBEC and OVEC officials have also started drafting a new curriculum for general upper secondary education (Bangkok Post, 2015e; NBT World, 2015). The new curriculum aims to encourage the study of vocational subjects and expand opportunities for work-based learning (Bangkok Post, 2015c; 2015d). Furthermore, a national committee has been appointed to work on a national qualifications framework (NQF) with the ultimate goal of improving Thailand's global competitiveness (Bangkok Post, 2015c).

Conclusions

Thailand has made real efforts over the last two decades to address some of the pressing challenges its education system faces as the country aims to move beyond the "middle-income trap" – economic stagnation due to insufficient performance in global markets. This work continues apace as the country enters the competitive ASEAN economic community, and prepares a new constitution and the next steps for its education reform agenda. It will need to address challenges relating to the effectiveness, efficiency and equity of its education system. Chapter 2 of this review evaluates where the Thai education system stands in terms of student outcomes. This analysis provides a baseline for the subsequent chapters, which address in more detail issues surrounding the curriculum, student assessment, the teaching workforce and the use of ICT in schools – providing recommendations to address challenges in each of these areas, and to support Thai efforts to further reform the education system to better prepare students from all backgrounds for a fast-changing world.

Notes

1. The other ASEAN members are: Brunei Darussalam, Cambodia, Indonesia, Lao People's Democratic Republic, the Philippines, Malaysia, Myanmar, Singapore and Viet Nam.

2. This chapter was updated in January 2016 to reflect recent developments in Thailand.

Bibliography

Arphattananon, T. (2012), "Education that leads to nowhere: Thailand's education policy for children of migrants", *International Journal of Multicultural Education*, Vol. 14/1, pp. 1-15, http://ijme-journal.org/ijme/index.php/ijme/article/view/537/690.

Bangkok Post (5 November 2015a), "Thai English proficiency drops, now 3rd worst in Asia - EF", *Bangkok Post*, www.bangkokpost.com/archive/thai-english-proficiency-drops-now-3rd-worst-in-asia-ef/755560 (accessed 6 January 2016).

Bangkok Post (23 September 2015b), "Govt unveils after-class course details", Bangkok Post, www.bangkokpost.com/archive/govt-unveils-after-class-course-details/703164 (accessed 6 January 2016).

Bangkok Post (31 October 2015c), "Super board raps weak Thai education", *Bangkok Post*, www.bangkokpost.com/archive/superboard-raps-weak-thai-education/749572 (accessed 08 January 2016).

Bangkok Post (21 December 2015d), "Asean countries identifying and filling gaps", *Bangkok Post*, www.bangkokpost.com/business/news/801348/asean-countries-identifying-and-filling-gaps (accessed 7 January 2016).

Bangkok Post (4 March 2015e), "Schools set to offer more trade subjects to students", *Bangkok Post*, www.bangkokpost.com/news/general/487985/schools-set-to-offer-more-trade-subjects-to-students (accessed 20 March 2015).

Fry, G. and H. Bi (2013), "The evolution of educational reform in Thailand: The Thai educational paradox", *Journal of Educational Administration*, Vol. 51/3, pp. 290-319, http://dx.doi.org/10.1108/09578231311311483.

Hallinger, P. and D. Bryant (2013), "Synthesis of findings from 15 years of educational reform in Thailand: Lessons on leading educational change in East Asia", *International Journal of Leadership in Education: Theory and Practice*, Vol. 16.4, pp. 399-418, www.ied.edu.hk/apclc/dowloadables/Publications/2013/Synthesis%20of%20findings%20from%2015years%20of%20educational%20reform%20in%20Thailand.pdf.

Haque, S. (2013), "Decentralizing local governance in Thailand: Contemporary trends and challenges", in C. Rees and F. Hossain (eds.), *Public Sector Reform in Developing and Transitional Countries: Decentralisation and Local Governance*, Routledge.

Huguet, J. (ed.) (2014), *Thailand Migration Report 2014*, United Nations Thematic Working Group on Migration in Thailand, Bangkok.

IDMC (2015), "Thailand IDP figures analysis", Internal Displacement Monitoring Centre, Norwegian Refugee Council. www.internal-displacement.org/south-and-south-east-asia/thailand/figures-analysis (accessed June 2015).

ILO (2014a), *Thailand Labour Market Update*, ILO Country Office for Thailand, Cambodia and Lao People's Democratic Republic, International Labour Organization, www.ilo.org/asia/WCMS_240328/lang--en/index.htm.

ILO (2014b), *Global Employment Trends 2014: Risk of a Jobless Recovery?*, International Labour Organization, 2012 estimates, http://ilo.org/global/research/global-reports/global-employment-trends/2014.

Lathapipat, D. (2015), "Closing the school performance gap through better public resource allocation – The case of Thailand", *World Bank Working Paper*, Preliminary draft (March 2015), World Bank, Washington, DC.

Ministry of Education (2008), Towards a Learning Society in Thailand: An Introduction to Education in Thailand, Bureau of International Cooperation, Ministry of Education of Thailand, Bangkok, www.bic.moe.go.th/newth/images/stories/book/ed-eng-series/intro-ed08.pdf.

NBT World (25 September 2015), "OBEC told to modernize Thai educational curriculum", https://www.youtube.com/watch?v=6-q2UWoIYio (accessed January 2016).

OECD (2016a), "OECD Economic Outlook No. 98 (Edition 2015/2)", *OECD Economic Outlook Statistics and Projections*, (database), http://dx.doi.org/10.1787/bd810434-en.

OECD (2016b), *Economic Outlook for Southeast Asia, China and India 2016: Enhancing Regional Ties*, OECD Publishing, Paris, http://dx.doi.org/10.1787/saeo-2016-en.

OECD (2015), *Economic Outlook for Southeast Asia, China and India 2015: Strengthening Institutional Capacity,* OECD Publishing, Paris, http://dx.doi.org/10.1787/saeo-2015-en.

OECD (2013a), "Thailand: Innovation profile", in *Innovation in Southeast Asia*, OECD Publishing, Paris, pp. 255-280, http://dx.doi.org/10.1787/9789264128712-11-en.

OECD (2013b), *Southeast Asian Economic Outlook 2013: With Perspectives on China and India*, OECD Publishing, Paris, http://dx.doi.org/10.1787/saeo-2013-en.

OECD (2013c), *PISA 2012 Results: What Makes Schools Successful (Volume IV): Resources, Policies and Practices*, PISA, OECD Publishing, Paris, http://dx.doi.org/10.1787/9789264201156-en.

Office of the Permanent Secretary (2014), *Educational Statistics in Brief 2013*, Office of the Permanent Secretary, Ministry of Education of Thailand, Bangkok, www.mis.moe.go.th/mis-th/images/statistic/Statistic/statistics2556.pdf.

Pinyakong, K., P. Virasilp and U. Somboon (2007), "Development of private secondary schools in Thailand", *Research Papers IIEP*, International Institute for Educational Planning, www.unesco.org/iiep/PDF/pubs/Thailand.pdf .

Quality Learning Foundation (forthcoming), *National Education Accounts of Thailand: Methodology and Key Findings*, Quality Learning Foundation.

Teachers' Council of Thailand (2015), "Powers and duties of KHURUSAPHA", Teachers' Council of Thailand website, http://site.ksp.or.th/about.php?site=englishsite&SiteMenuID=13.

UNDESA (2014), *World Urbanization Prospects: 2014 Revision: Highlights*, United Nations Department of Economic and Social Affairs, http://esa.un.org/unpd/wup/highlights/wup2014-highlights.pdf.

UNDP (2015), "About Thailand", United Nations Development Programme website, www.th.undp.org/content/thailand/en/home/countryinfo/ (accessed 16 December 2015).

UNESCO Bangkok (29 May 2013), "National Education Accounts in Thailand", UNESCO Bangkok website, www.unescobkk.org/education/news/article/national-education-accounts-in-thailand/.

UNESCO Bangkok (2011), *Secondary Teacher Policy Research in Asia: Secondary Teachers in Thailand*, United Nations Educational, Scientific and Cultural Organization, Bangkok, www.uis.unesco.org/Library/Documents/secondary-teacher-policy-research-asia-thailand-education-2011-en.pdf.

UNESCO Bangkok (2008), *Secondary Education Regional Information Base: Country Profile Thailand*, UNESCO Bangkok, www.uis.unesco.org/Library/Documents/Thailand.pdf.

UNESCO and IBE (2011), "Thailand", *World Data on Education*, 7th edition, UNESCO and International Bureau of Education, www.ibe.unesco.org/fileadmin/user_upload/Publications/WDE/2010/pdf-versions/Thailand.pdf.

UNESCO-UIS (2015), UIS data centre website, www.uis.unesco.org/Education/Pages/default.aspx (accessed March 2015).

United Nations (2009), Map 3853, Rev. 2, July 2009, United Nations Geospatial Information Section (formerly Cartographic Section), Department of Field Support, United Nations Organisation.

US Department of State (2013), "Thailand", in *International Religious Freedom Report for 2012,* US Department of State, www.state.gov/documents/organization/208482.pdf.

WEF (2014), *Global Competitiveness Report 2014-2015,* World Economic Forum, www3.weforum.org/docs/.

World Bank (2015a), "Fertility rate, total (births per woman)", *World Development Indicators* (database), http://data.worldbank.org/indicator/SP.DYN.TFRT.IN (accessed 17 December 2015).

World Bank (2015b), "Life expectancy at birth, total (years)", *World Development Indicators* (database), http://data.worldbank.org/indicator/SP.DYN.LE00.IN (accessed 17 December 2015).

World Bank (2015c), "Improved water source (% of population with access)", *World Development Indicators* (database), http://data.worldbank.org/indicator/SH.H2O.SAFE.ZS (accessed 3 April 2015).

World Bank (2015d), "Improved sanitation facilities (% of population with access)", *World Development Indicators* (database), http://data.worldbank.org/indicator/SH.STA.ACSN (accessed 3 April 2015).

World Bank (2015e), "GDP growth (annual %)", *World Development Indicators* (database), http://data.worldbank.org/indicator/NY.GDP.MKTP.KD.ZG (accessed March 2016).

World Bank (2015f), "Poverty headcount ratio at national poverty lines (% of population)", *World Development Indicators* (database), http://data.worldbank.org/indicator/SI.POV.NAHC (accessed 16 December 2016).

World Bank (2014), "Thailand overview", World Bank website, www.worldbank.org/en/country/thailand/overview (accessed 8 January 2015).

World Bank (2013), "Poverty Indicators", *World Development Indicators* (database), http://data.worldbank.org/indicator/SI.DST.04TH.20/countries/1W-TH?display=graph (accessed 8 January 2015).

World Bank (2012a), "Net migration", *World Development Indicators* (database), http://data.worldbank.org/indicator/SM.POP.NETM (accessed 13 March 2015).

World Bank (2012b), *Thailand School Autonomy and Accountability: SABER Country Report 2012*, World Bank, Washington, DC, https://openknowledge.worldbank.org/handle/10986/20184.

World Bank (2011), *Thailand: Challenges and Options for 2011 and Beyond*, World Bank, Washington, DC, http://documents.worldbank.org/curated/en/2011/09/15956941/thailand-challenges-options-2011-beyond.

World Bank (2010), "Income share held by highest 20%", *World Development Indicators* (database). http://data.worldbank.org/indicator/SI.DST.05TH.20/countries (accessed 8 January 2015).

Chapter 2

The basic education system in Thailand: A comparative policy perspective

This chapter outlines the basic education system in Thailand and compares it to two groups of benchmark countries – similar middle-income southeast Asian countries and high-income Asia-Pacific ones – on five key policy areas: inputs, access, processes, outcomes and efficiencies.

Thailand invests a significant share of its wealth in education, especially in primary education but is not fully receiving the return it might have expected. Participation is relatively high, particularly at primary and pre-primary level and secondary enrolment is rising but many of the poorest children still do not attend school and less-advantaged children still face unequal opportunities. Teacher qualifications are rising although quality concerns remain an issue. Thai students perform relatively well in international assessments, but there are too few top performing students and too many low performers and wide performance differences suggest a two-tier education system between rural and urban areas, and advantaged and less-advantaged schools.

Introduction

This chapter analyses the basic education system in Thailand based on selected international comparisons in five key policy areas: 1) inputs, 2) access, 3) processes, 4) outcomes and 5) efficiency.

Inputs refer to the financial and human resources invested in education. Access examines student access, participation and progression in education. Processes include the learning environment and the organisation of schools. Outcomes focus on students' results, both in terms of quality and equity.

This analysis uses two groups of countries as international benchmarks (referred to in this chapter as "selected countries"). The first group consists of middle-income southeast Asian countries resembling Thailand in some respects, such as level of GDP, public expenditure on education and learning outcomes: Indonesia, Malaysia, the Philippines and Viet Nam. The second group consists of several high-income Asia-Pacific countries that could potentially serve as a model for Thailand: Australia, Japan, New Zealand, Korea, and Singapore (Table 2.1).

Compared to its middle-income neighbours, the Thai education system is performing relatively well with respect to access to education. However, a paradox of the Thai education system is that substantial financial investments have not translated into expected levels of student achievement (Fry and Bi, 2013). The gap in overall student outcomes between Thailand and high-income countries remains large. International and national assessments indicate that a significant proportion of Thai students are acquiring skills at a low level, and that those in disadvantaged, rural areas of the country are struggling the most. Thailand will need to make strategic improvements if its education system is to be a more effective engine of mobility and social and economic progress.

Inputs

Financial and system inputs

Thailand invests a significant share of its national wealth in education. Public expenditure on education as a percentage of gross domestic product (GDP) rose from 3.8% in 2010 to 4.9% in 2012 (UNESCO-UIS, 2015). Over the last decade, Thailand has consistently allocated around 20% of total government expenditure to education each year, and in some years over 25% (Figure 2.1).

Table 2.1. Development measures, selected countries

Country/ economy	GDP per capita, PPP (current international dollars) (2012)	UNDP human development index (2013)	Public educational expenditure as percentage of GDP (2012)	Average PISA test score (2012)
Viet Nam	3 787.3	121	6.3	516
The Philippines	4 338.7	117	2.7	
Indonesia	4 875.7	108	3.6	384
Malaysia	16 918.5	62	5.9	413
Thailand	9 660.4	89	4.9	437
Korea	30 800.5	15	5.2	542
New Zealand	32 219.4	7	7.4	509
Japan	35 177.5	17	3.9	540
Australia	44 597.8	2	5.1	512
Singapore	60 800.4	9	3.2	556

Note: All data accessed 17 March 2015. Data for Australia and Korea are from 2011.

Countries are ranked using their GDP per capita and presented in two groups, middle- and high-income. Thailand's values are shown between the two groups of countries, to facilitate comparisons.

Sources: GDP per capita: UNESCO-UIS, 2015; UNDP, 2013; UNESCO (2011), *Education for all Development Index*, www.unesco.org/new/en/education/themes/leading-the-international-agenda/efareport/statistics/efa-development-index/; Public spending on education, total (% of GDP): UNESCO-UIS, 2015.

Figure 2.1. Public expenditure on education as a percentage of GDP and of total government expenditure in Thailand, 1999-2012

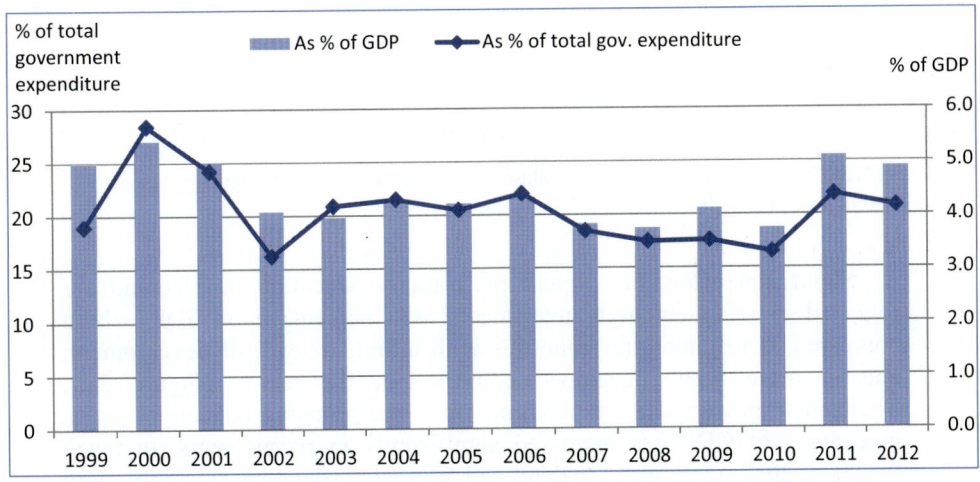

Source: UNESCO-UIS (2015), *Education* (dataset), UIS Data Centre, http://data.uis.unesco.org/Index.aspx?DataSetCode=EDULIT_DS&popupcustomise=true&lang=en.

Overall, the level of spending on education in Thailand is in the mid-range compared with other countries in the region. Relative to GDP, its spending is considerably higher than Indonesia and the Philippines, although below Malaysia and Viet Nam. Only Korea spends a notably greater proportion of its public budget on education (Figure 2.2).

Figure 2.2. Public expenditure on education as a percentage of GDP and of total government expenditure, selected countries, 2012

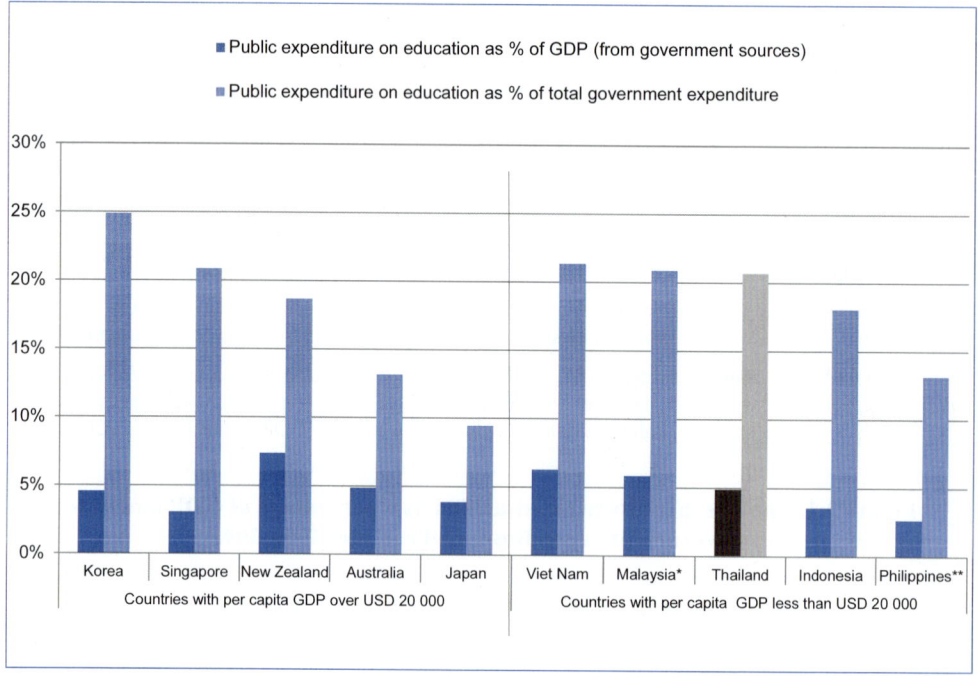

Note: * Data for Malaysia are from 2011. ** Data for the Philippines are from 2009.

Source: UNESCO-UIS (2015), *Education* (dataset), UIS Data Centre, http://data.uis.unesco.org/Index.aspx?DataSetCode=EDULIT_DS&popupcustomise=true&lang=en.

Significant efforts to expand pre-primary education in Thailand are reflected in relatively high investments as a percentage of GDP – both compared to neighbouring countries with a similar level of development, and to more highly-developed countries in the region (Figure 2.3). Thailand's government expenditure on pre-primary education as a percentage of GDP has increased significantly in recent years, to reach 0.32% in 2012. Only New Zealand and Viet Nam spend considerably more on pre-primary education as a percentage of GDP (UNESCO, 2015).

Figure 2.3. Public expenditure on pre-primary education as a percentage of GDP, selected countries, 2012

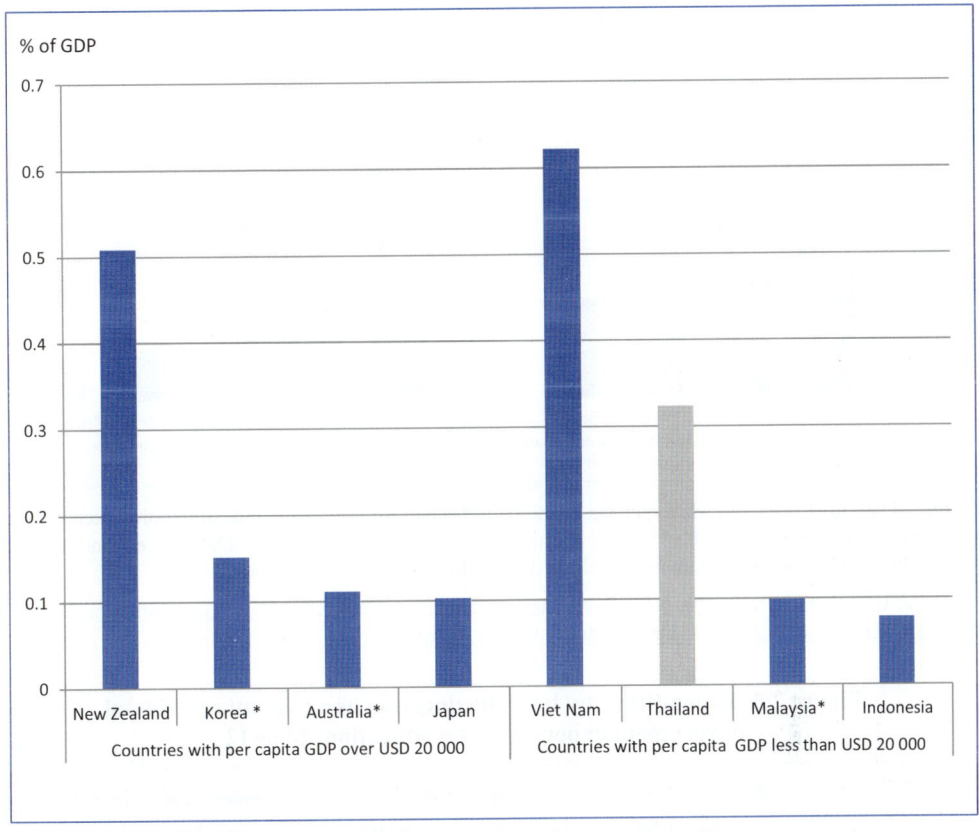

Note: * Data for Australia, Korea and Malaysia are from 2011.

Source: UNESCO-UIS (2015), *Education* (dataset), UIS Data Centre, http://data.uis.unesco.org/Index.aspx?DataSetCode=EDULIT_DS&popupcustomise=true&lang=en.

Thailand's expenditure on primary education is the highest among the selected countries in the region, but it is low at the secondary level. In 2012, Thailand's funding per primary student was 29.4% of per capita GDP, compared to 15.4% in Malaysia (as of 2011) and 11.2% in Singapore (Figure 2.4). In that year, 44.8% of Thailand's government education spending was directed at the primary level, a higher proportion than in any of the other selected countries. At the secondary level, although government expenditure increased from 14.3% of the total in 2008 to 28.6% in 2012 (Figure 2.5), the per-student funding remained low compared to many of the selected countries at 19.7% of per capita GDP.

Figure 2.4. Public expenditure on education per student as percentage of GDP per capita, by level of education, selected countries, 2012

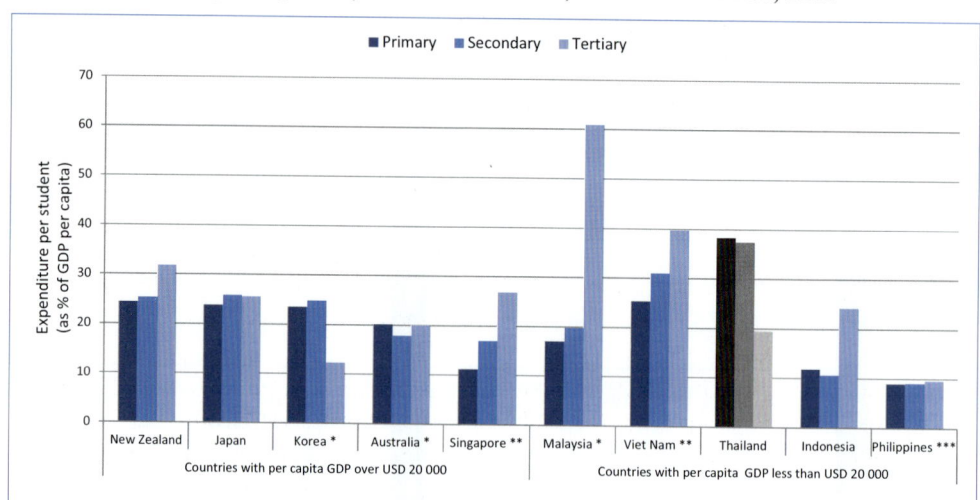

Note: *Data for Korea and Malaysia are from 2011. **Data for Viet Nam and Singapore (except at the tertiary level) are from 2010. ***Data for the Philippines are from 2008. Data on expenditure per secondary student for Viet Nam only include data on lower secondary education.

Source: UNESCO-UIS (2015), *Education* (dataset), UIS Data Centre, http://data.uis.unesco.org/Index.aspx?DataSetCode=EDULIT_DS&popupcustomise=true&lang=en.

Figure 2.5. Expenditure by level of education as a percentage of total government expenditure on education, 2008-12

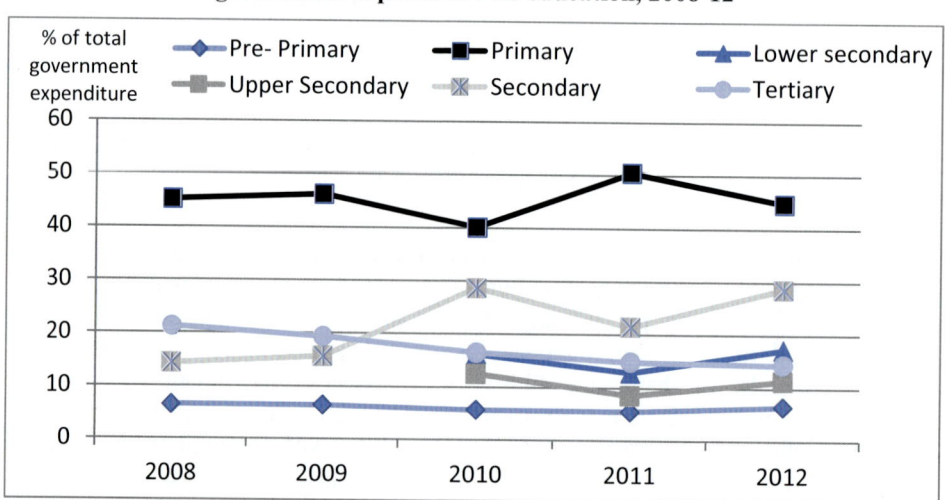

Source: UNESCO-UIS (2015), *Education* (dataset), UIS Data Centre, http://data.uis.unesco.org/Index.aspx?DataSetCode=EDULIT_DS&popupcustomise=true&lang=en.

Human resources

Teachers are the single most important in-school factor affecting student achievement, and teachers' salaries normally represent the largest single item of educational expenditure (OECD, 2013a). The OECD (2013b) has identified the lack of quality teachers and teacher training programmes as a key challenge for the Thai education system (see Chapter 5).

Thailand devotes a comparatively low share of its total educational expenditure to staff compensation. Staff costs formed 50.9% of Thailand's educational expenditure in 2010 (the latest year for which data were available), the lowest proportion among the selected countries for which data are available. In contrast, in 2012 staff costs made up 54.5% of Indonesia's educational expenditure, 64% of Viet Nam's, 66.4% of Japan's and 75% of Malaysia's (2011 figures) (UNESCO-UIS, 2015). The salaries of Thai secondary school teachers relative to per capita GDP are much lower than those of their colleagues in Malaysia – 124% of per capita GDP against 210% – but higher than in Indonesia (40%), as shown in Figure 2.6.

Figure 2.6. Expenditure on education and teachers' salaries, selected countries, 2012

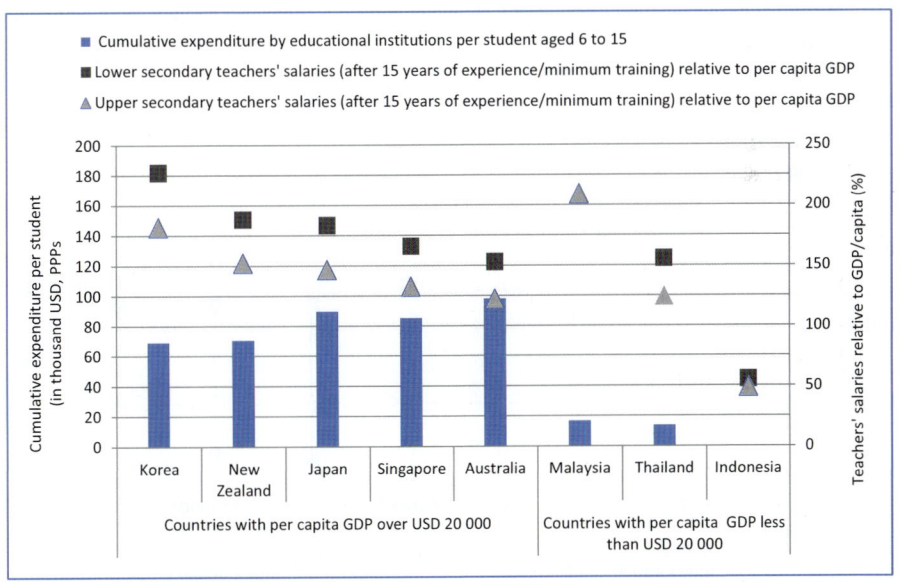

Note: Countries are ranked in descending order of teachers' salaries (average of lower and upper secondary teachers' salaries).

Sources: OECD (2013a), *PISA 2012 Results: What Makes Schools Successful (Volume IV): Resources, Policies and Practices*, http://dx.doi.org/10.1787/9789264201156-en, Tables IV.3.1, IV.3.2 and IV.3.3.

School facilities and resources

The adequate allocation of human and physical resources to schools, as well as functional infrastructure, is crucial for the provision of high-standard education. The availability and distribution of resources across schools in Thailand leaves room for improvement.

The average quality of educational resources in Thai schools is among the lowest of any country participating in the Programme for International School Assessment (PISA), and the uneven distribution of educational resources across schools poses equity challenges. Principals in Thailand also expressed a higher than average concern about shortages of educational resources in schools (OECD, 2013a). Thailand has a larger difference in the quality of educational resources (such as laboratory equipment, instructional materials, computers, Internet connectivity, computer software and library materials) between socio-economically advantaged and disadvantaged schools than many of its peers (Figure 2.7). High-performing countries tend to allocate resources fairly equitably across their schools (OECD, 2013a).

Figure 2.7. Equity in resource allocation, selected countries, 2012

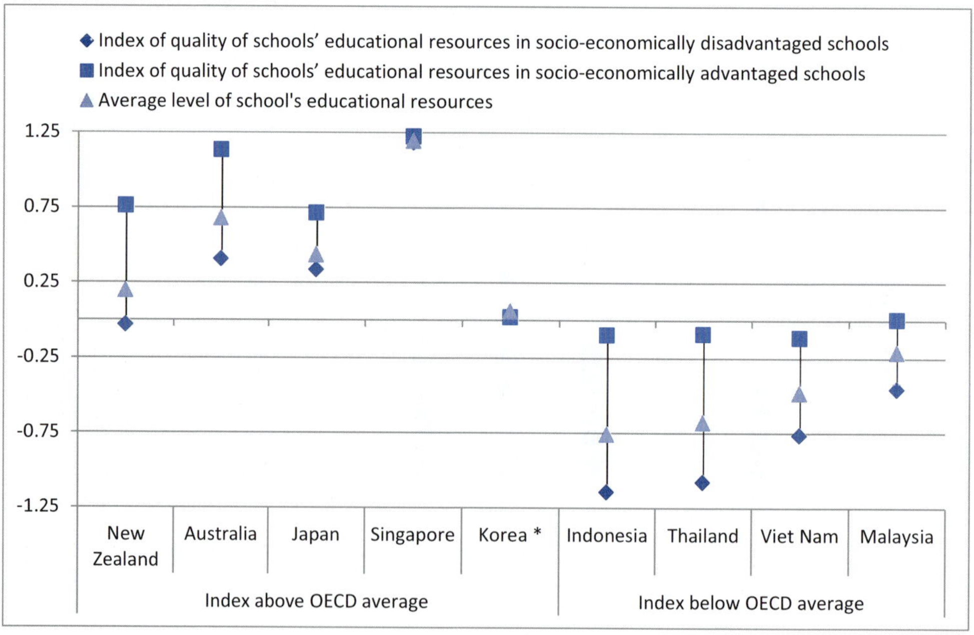

Note: Equity is measured by the difference in the index of quality of schools' educational resources between socio-economically advantaged and disadvantaged schools. *Korea has a negative value (-0.01), which means that disadvantaged schools receive more resources than the advantaged ones.

Source: OECD, (2013a), *PISA 2012 Results: What Makes Schools Successful (Volume IV): Resources, Policies and Practices*, http://dx.doi.org/10.1787/9789264201156-en.

Thailand is one of the few PISA countries where the perceived quality of school facilities has significantly declined in recent years. In 2012, a total of 31.4% of lower secondary students in Thailand were in schools whose principal reported that inadequate facilities and a shortage of instructional space hindered learning "to some extent or a lot" (OECD, 2013a). These figures have increased since 2003, by 16.8 percentage points and 23.3 percentage points respectively.

Access and participation

Overall participation in schooling

Participation in general education in Thailand is relatively high, particularly at the pre-primary and primary levels (Figure 2.8). For example, Thailand's net enrolment rate was close to that of Korea in pre-primary education (92.5% in Thailand versus 89.4% in Korea in 2011) and primary education (95.6% versus 99% in 2010) (UIS, 2015).

Figure 2.8. Net enrolment rates, primary and secondary education, selected countries, 2012

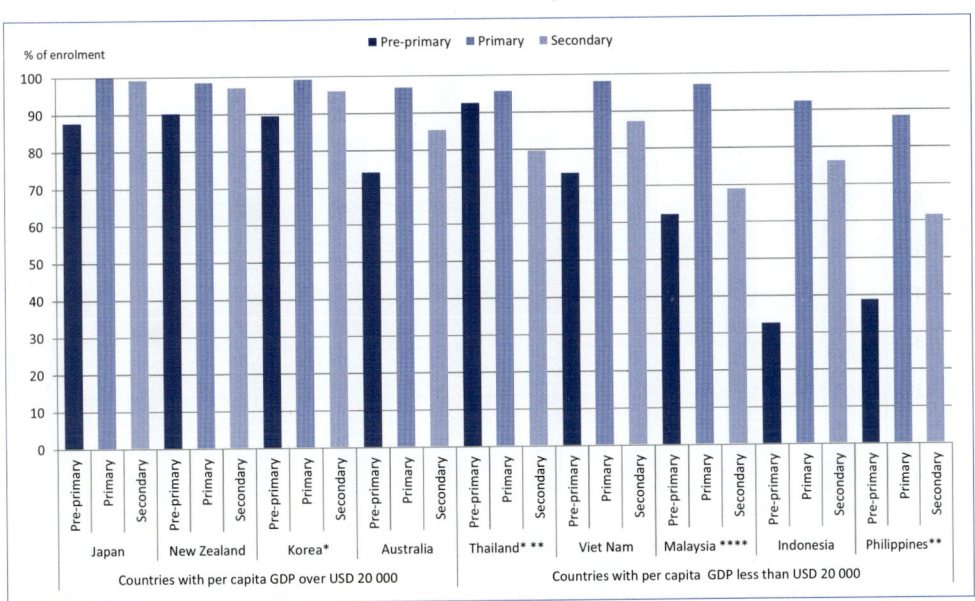

Note: *Data for Korea and Thailand (at the pre-primary level) are from 2011. **Data for the Philippines and Thailand (at the primary level) are from 2010. ***Data for Viet Nam covers lower secondary education only. **** Data for Malaysia at the primary level are from 2005.

Source: UNESCO-UIS (2015), *Education* (dataset), UIS Data Centre, http://data.uis.unesco.org/Index.aspx?DataSetCode=EDULIT_DS&popupcustomise=true&lang=en.

Thailand's primary education participation rate has remained largely stable in recent years, while rates at the pre-primary and secondary levels have increased more substantially. At the pre-primary level, net enrolment increased from 80.9% in 2006 to 92.5% in 2011, the highest rate among the selected countries (Figure 2.9). At the primary level, net enrolment stood at 96.4% in 2009, which is below that of higher-income countries in the region (98.5% on average) and Viet Nam (98%) (Figure 2.10). The secondary net enrolment rate in Thailand rose from 67% in 2006 to 79% in 2012, which is higher than in some of the other middle-income countries in the region, but lower than in countries like Korea and Japan, where participation in secondary education was close to universal (Figure 2.11). At upper secondary level, 35% of Thai students were enrolled in vocational programmes in 2012, compared to 20% in Malaysia and 43% in Indonesia (UNESCO-UIS, 2015).

Figure 2.9. Change in net enrolment rate in pre-primary education, selected countries, 2006 and 2012

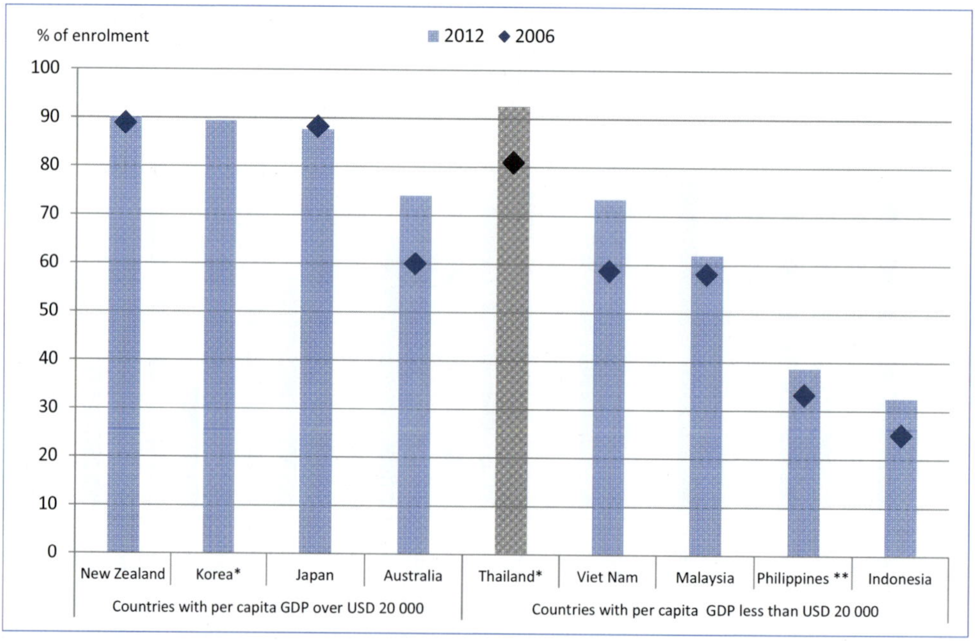

Note: *Data for Thailand and Korea are from 2011. **Data for the Philippines are from 2009.

Source: UNESCO-UIS (2015), *Education* (dataset), UIS Data Centre, http://data.uis.unesco.org/Index.aspx?DataSetCode=EDULIT_DS&popupcustomise=true&lang=en.

Figure 2.10. Change in net enrolment rate in primary education, selected countries, 2006 and 2012

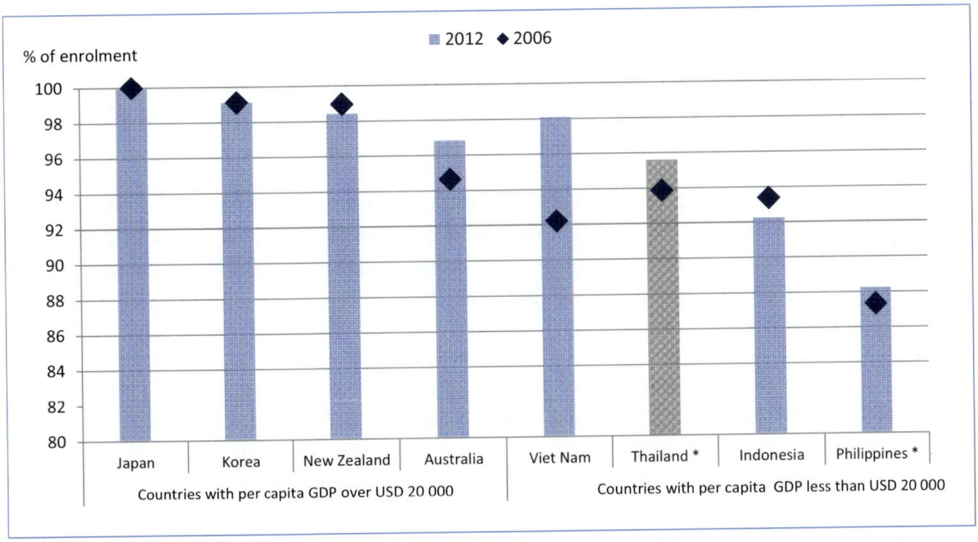

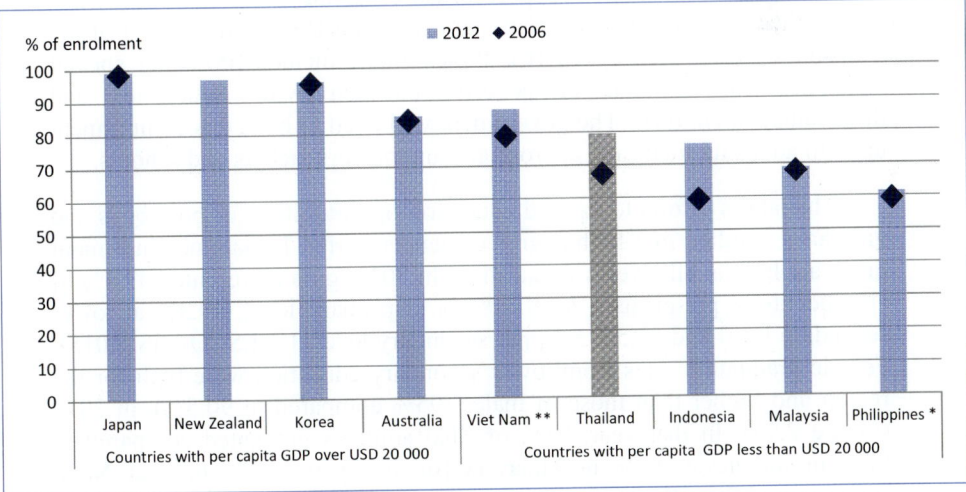

Note: *Data for Thailand and the Philippines are from 2009 instead of 2012.

Source: UNESCO-UIS (2015), *Education* (dataset), UIS Data Centre, http://data.uis.unesco.org/Index.aspx?DataSetCode=EDULIT_DS&popupcustomise=true&lang=en.

Figure 2.11. Change in net enrolment rate in secondary education, selected countries, 2006 and 2012

Note: *Data for the Philippines are from 2009. **Data for Viet Nam are for lower secondary education.

Source: UNESCO-UIS (2015), *Education* (dataset), UIS Data Centre, http://data.uis.unesco.org/Index.aspx?DataSetCode=EDULIT_DS&popupcustomise=true&lang=en.

While the number of out-of-school children has fallen since the turn of the century, many students from the poorest families still do not attend school in Thailand (UIS and UNICEF, 2015). Rates of exclusion are higher in rural areas and among various ethnic and linguistic communities. Despite renewed efforts since the 1990s, access to education for children with disabilities also remains limited in Thailand (Carter, 2006; OEC-MOE, 2014).

Inequalities are particularly pronounced at the upper secondary level, where constraints on access and the opportunity costs of schooling are typically the highest. As Figure 2.12 demonstrates, disadvantaged students aged 15-17 years are twice as likely as their peers from middle- and high-income families to not be in school, although the gap has been narrowing.

To promote enrolment among disadvantaged students, Thailand expanded free education from 12 to 15 years in 2009 and free schooling now extends from pre-primary to upper secondary education. However, the new policy does not cover transportation costs, which are one of the main factors hindering educational access for poor students living at some distance from schools (OECD, 2012).

Those least likely to gain access to upper secondary education, and to complete it, include children living in remote rural areas, children from immigrant families, and those from ethnic communities in the north, northeast and parts of the south. Getting these children into school is a challenge requiring targeted support measures. Achieving greater equity is a central theme of the Eleventh National Education Development Plan of the Ministry of Education (2012-16). Policy goals include providing special assistance for children in poverty, children with disabilities and disadvantaged children. The government will need to back this commitment up with adequate funds and appropriate support for teachers and schools.

Thailand's efforts to expand education opportunities for both boys and girls have resulted in a high degree of gender parity. Female net enrolment ratios are high at all levels of education. In 2012, girls represented 49.3% of all students at pre-primary level, 48.3% at primary level, 49.3% at lower secondary level and 52.5% at upper secondary level (UNESCO-UIS, 2015). Female graduation rates from lower secondary education were high for the region and higher than those of males (95% compared to 90.5%), in 2012 (Figure 2.13). In that year, 93% of Thai students graduated compared to 92% in Indonesia, 85% in Malaysia (in 2011) and 81% in Viet Nam, suggesting higher effectiveness.

Figure 2.12. Trends in the share of children and youth not studying in Thailand, by age and income level, 1990 and 2012

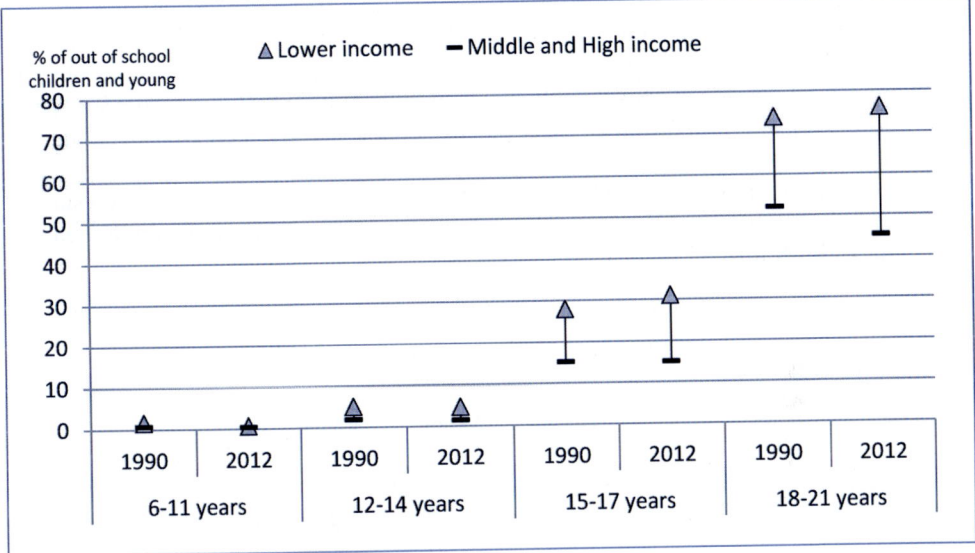

Source: UNESCO (2015), *Education for All 2015 National Review Report: Thailand*, http://unesdoc.unesco.org/images/0022/002298/229878E.pdf.

Figure 2.13. Gross graduation rate from lower secondary education, selected countries, 2012

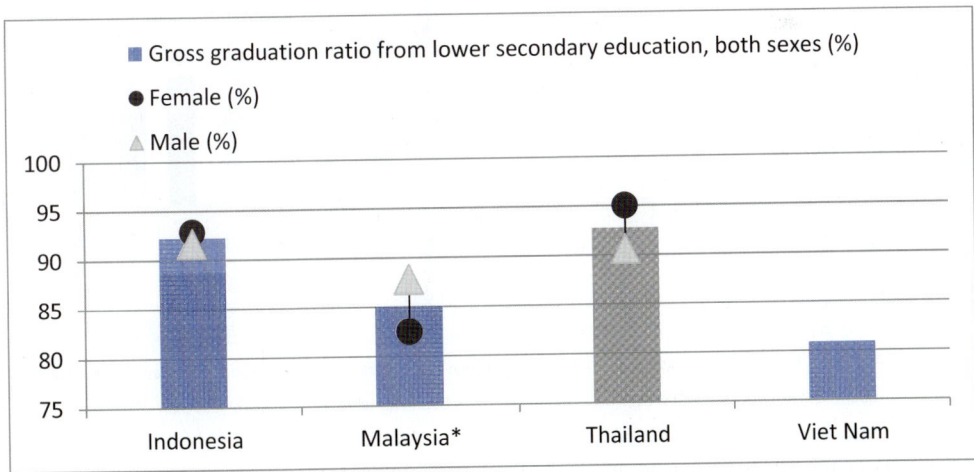

Note: *Data for Malaysia are from 2011.

Source: UNESCO-UIS (2015), *Education* (dataset), UIS Data Centre, http://data.uis.unesco.org/Index.aspx?DataSetCode=EDULIT_DS&popupcustomise=true&lang=en.

However, the out-of-school rate for girls at primary level is higher than for boys: 5.1% of primary-aged girls were not attending school in 2009, compared to 3.8% of boys (Figure 2.14). In 2014, 380 231 children of primary-school age were still out of school, 52% of them girls (UNESCO-UIS, 2015). At the lower secondary level, while the percentage of boys out of school decreased considerably between 2006 and 2009 (falling from 9.1% to 3.9%), the proportion of girls out of school slightly increased over the same period (rising to 3.7% in 2012) (UNESCO-UIS, 2015). These figures compare favourably to some other countries in the region (such as Malaysia and the Philippines), but are above rates in countries such as Japan, Korea and Viet Nam.

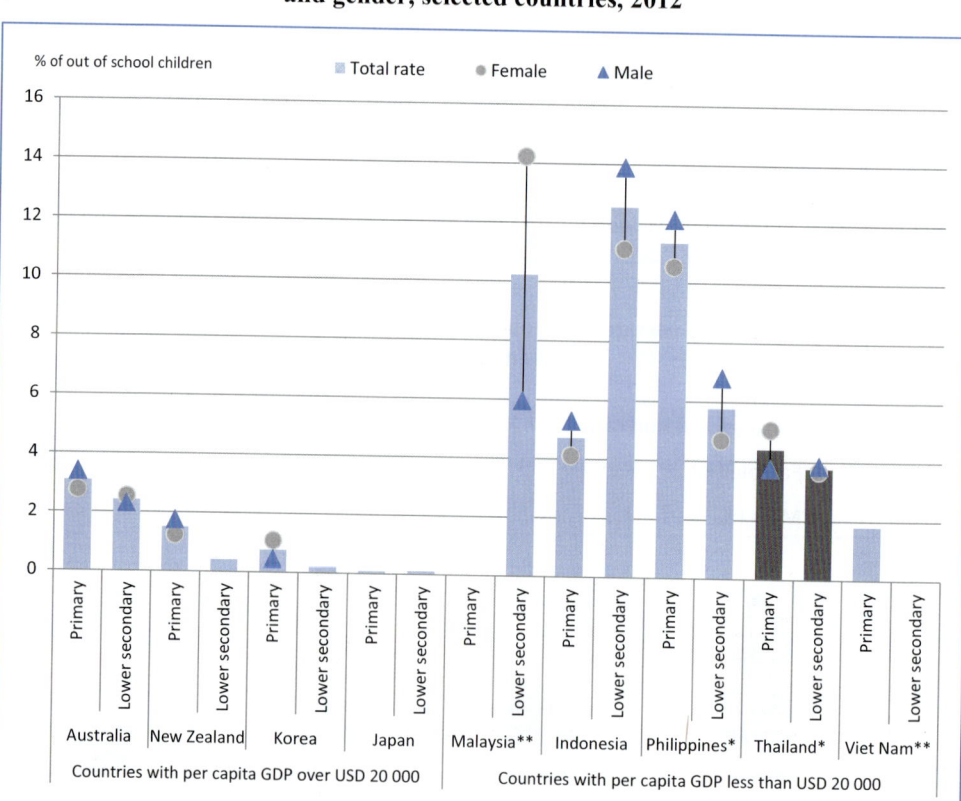

Figure 2.14. Rate of out-of-school children, by level of education and gender, selected countries, 2012

Note: *Data for Thailand and the Philippines are from 2009. **Data missing for Malaysia (at the primary level) and Viet Nam (at the secondary level).

Source: UNESCO-UIS (2015), *Education* (dataset), UIS Data Centre, http://data.uis.unesco.org/Index.aspx?DataSetCode=EDULIT_DS&popupcustomise=true&lang=en.

Tertiary education

Compared to other countries with a similar income level, Thailand has the highest participation rate in tertiary education: a 51% gross enrolment rate in 2012, up from 32% in 1999 (Figure 2.15).

Figure 2.15. Trends in gross enrolment rate in tertiary education, selected countries, 1999-2012 (percentage)

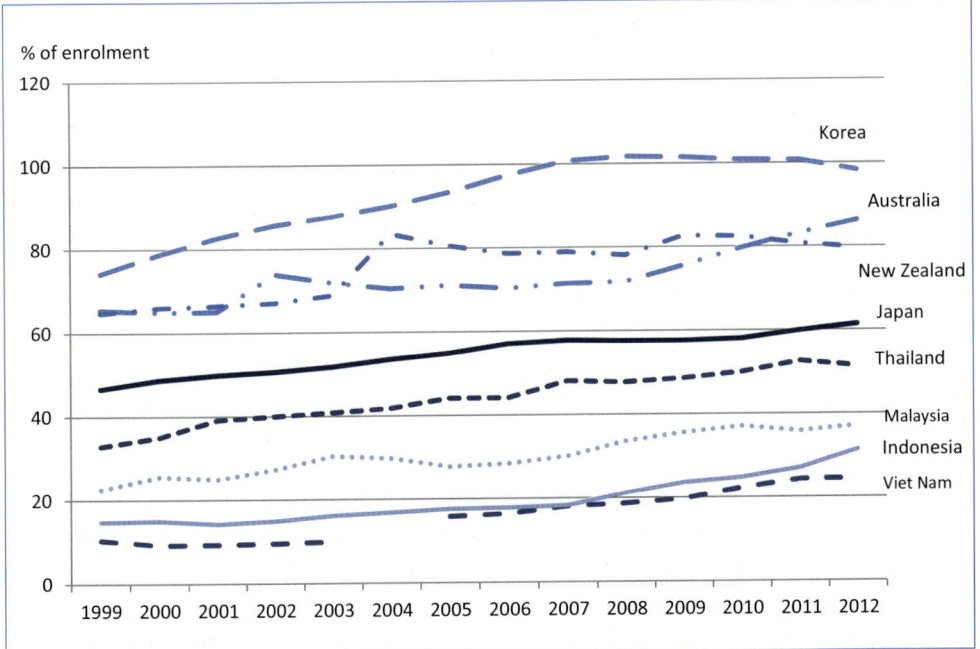

Source: UNESCO-UIS (2015), *Education* (dataset), UIS Data Centre, http://data.uis.unesco.org/Index.aspx?DataSetCode=EDULIT_DS&popupcustomise=true&lang=en.

Despite this expansion, less advantaged students still face unequal opportunities. The gap in tertiary enrolment rates between students from the highest income quartile and those from other quartiles has widened dramatically since 1996, and the gap between young people from the highest and the lowest income quartiles is especially large (Figure 2.16). Such inequality affects skills distribution, access to the labour market and earnings – and thus further widens the gap between rich and poor.

Figure 2.16. Trends in tertiary enrolment rates for 19-25 year-olds in Thailand, by income quartile, 1986-2008

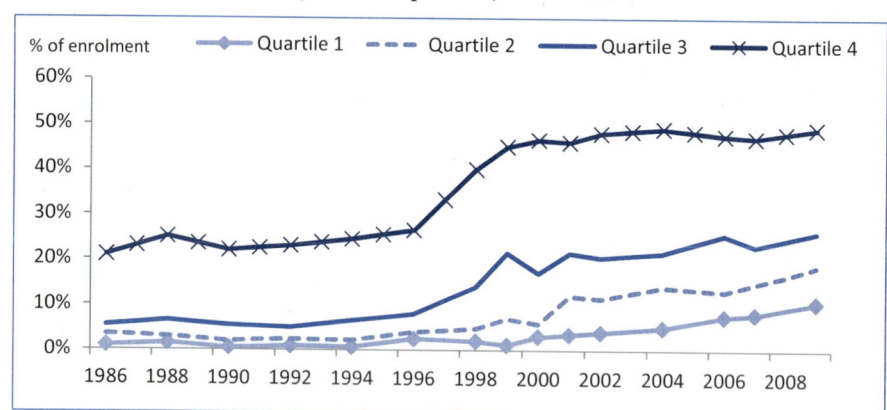

Source: OECD, (2013b), *Southeast Asian Economic Outlook 2013: With Perspectives on China and India,* http://dx.doi.org/10.1787/saeo-2013-en.

Educational processes

Teaching quality and student-teacher ratios

Teachers, and in particular teaching quality, are the most important in-school factor that predicts learning (OECD, 2013a). Teacher qualifications appear to be on the rise in Thailand, as more new teachers attain higher levels of education (Supham and Associates, 2012). In PISA 2012, Thai principals reported that 99.2% of teachers in their secondary schools had a qualification equivalent to the International Standard Classification of Education (ISCED) level 5A (a bachelor's or master's degree); this compares to an OECD average of 84.4% (OECD, 2013c).

Yet several of the stakeholders whom the OECD/UNESCO team met reported a commonly held view that teacher quality has declined. The large number of pre-service programme providers and the lack of minimum requirements for entry to these programmes raise concerns about quality assurance. The adoption of modern teaching methods appears to be slow in most schools, with lectures and rote learning remaining prevalent – especially in upper secondary education, where teaching can be narrowly focused on university entrance examinations (UNESCO Bangkok, 2011) (see Chapters 4 and 5).

Student/teacher ratios are relatively high in Thailand, standing at 20:1 compared to 15:1 in New Zealand and 16:1 in Korea (OECD, 2013a). However there is considerable regional variation across the country, with small schools in rural areas having a much lower ratio than the large urban schools that most students attend. Despite their low student/teacher ratio, these small schools are on average staffed with less than one teacher per grade-level (World Bank, 2015), which can adversely affect educational quality.

There is also evidence of teacher shortages in key subjects such as mathematics, science, foreign languages and Thai. These shortages are associated with Thailand's centralised teacher management system (UNESCO Bangkok, 2011; World Bank, 2012a; Lathapipat, 2015). As a result, large numbers of teachers are expected to teach outside their area of specialty, which can undermine teaching quality. According to PISA 2012, principals reported that approximately 47% of students were hindered by teacher shortages in mathematics compared to the OECD average of 16.5% (see Chapter 5).

Instruction time

The time students spend on effective learning activities is positively related to their performance, even after accounting for the socio-economic status and demographic characteristics of students and schools. In Thailand, students spend less time studying certain key learning areas than students in other countries. For PISA 2012, Thai students reported spending the least amount of time per week on average on language-of-instruction lessons (2 hours and 29 minutes) and mathematics lessons (3 hours and 26 minutes) than all of the other selected countries, except for Malaysia with respect to mathematics (OECD, 2013a; Figure 2.17).

Figure 2.17. Student learning time in school, selected countries, 2012

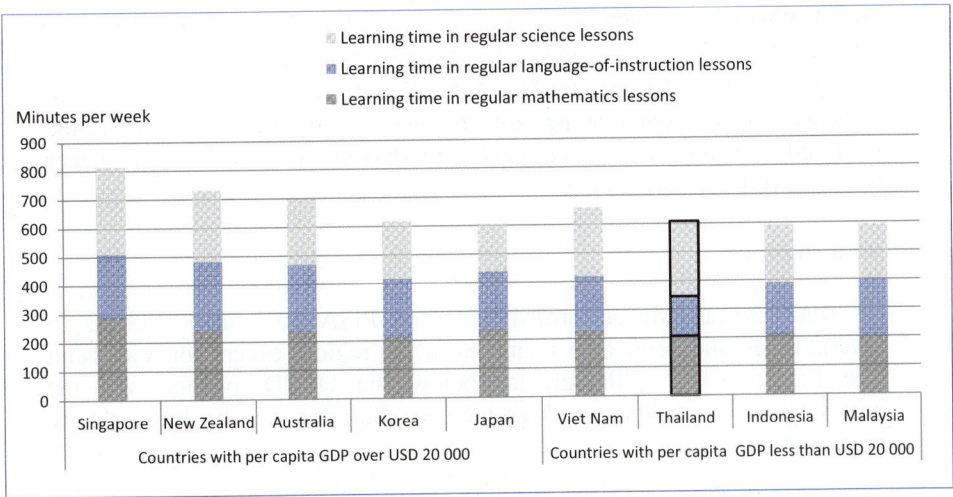

Source: OECD (2013a), *PISA 2012 Results: What Makes Schools Successful (Volume IV): Resources, Policies and Practices*, http://dx.doi.org/10.1787/9789264201156-en.

On average across OECD countries, students in socio-economically disadvantaged schools spend less time in regular mathematics lessons than students in advantaged schools. This is also true in Thailand, where students in advantaged schools spend an average of 46 minutes more per week in regular mathematics lessons than students in disadvantaged schools – the highest differential among countries with a level of income similar to Thailand's. Overall, the time spent per week in regular mathematics, language-of-instruction and science lessons is higher in advantaged schools (670 minutes) than in disadvantaged ones (560 minutes). This may in part explain the performance gap between students attending disadvantaged and advantaged schools.

The learning environment

Results from PISA assessments show that students who are in a school climate characterised by high expectations, classrooms conducive to learning and good teacher-student relations tend to perform better than those who are not (OECD, 2013a). Thai students are happy and have good relationships with their teachers, contributing to a positive school climate conducive to learning. For PISA 2012, over 90% of students in Thailand (as in Indonesia, Singapore and Malaysia) reported that they get along well with most teachers (OECD, 2013a). Almost 94% reported feeling happy at school – close behind Indonesia, which ranks first on this indicator at 95.7%, and above Singapore (87.9%), Japan (85%) and Korea (60%) (OECD, 2013c).

However, a large number of Thai students arrive late to school, which is associated with lower levels of performance. In the two weeks prior to the 2012 PISA test, 34% of Thai students reported that they had arrived late for school at least once, compared to 10% in Viet Nam and Singapore, and 8% in Japan (OECD, 2013a). In Thai schools with a larger concentration of students who reported arriving late, students scored 49 points lower on the PISA 2012 mathematics assessment than students in schools where fewer were late (OECD, 2013a).

Student outcomes

Thai 15-year-olds performed better on PISA 2012 than students in several other middle-income countries in the region, except for Viet Nam (see Figure 2.18). Although far below the OECD average and the performance of students in high-income countries, results have slowly improved over time.

Figure 2.18. Trends in mathematics, reading and science performance, PISA 2000-12

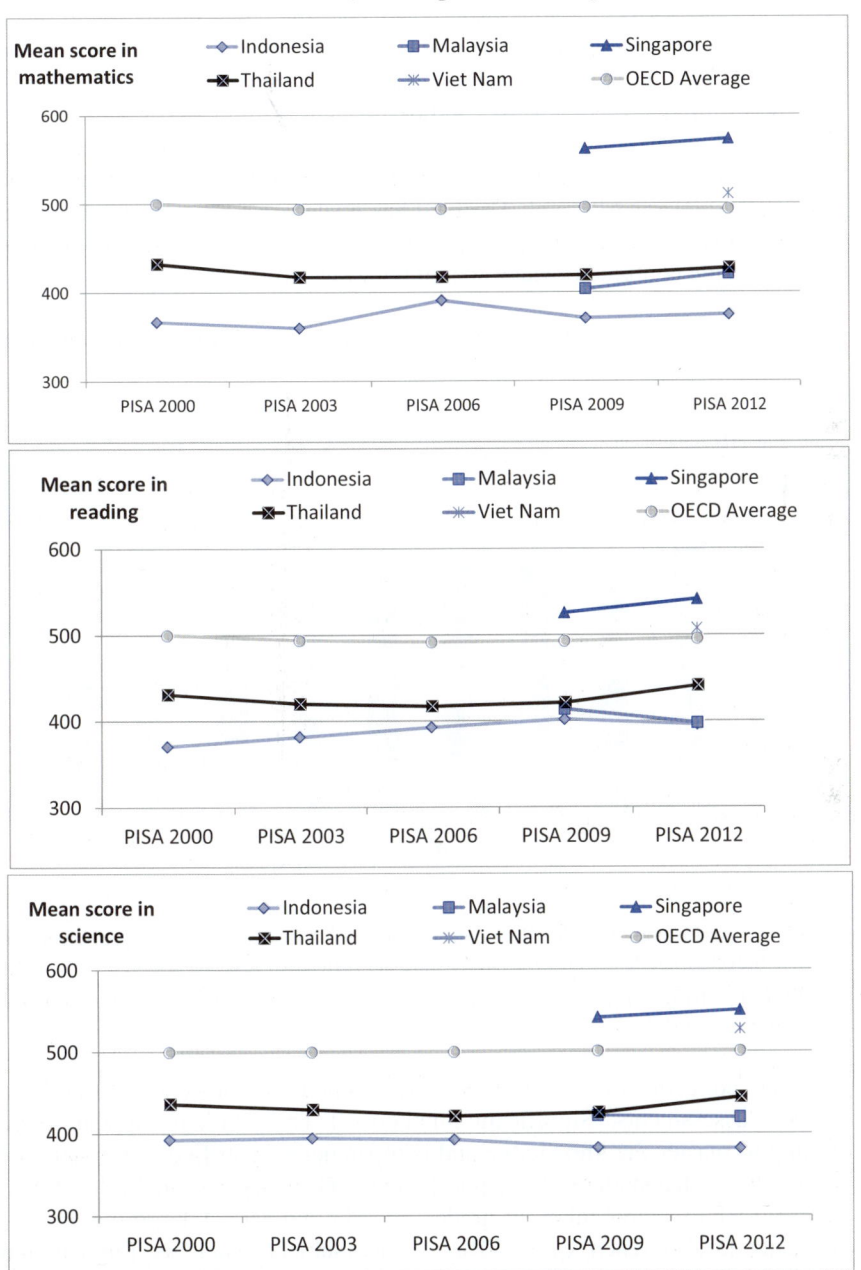

Source: OECD (2013a), *PISA 2012 Results: What Makes Schools Successful (Volume IV): Resources, Policies and Practices*, http://dx.doi.org/10.1787/9789264201156-en.

The core challenge Thailand faces is the very high proportion of students who perform below basic levels, and the small number who reach the highest proficiency levels (Figure 2.19). In PISA 2012, only 2.6% of Thai participants were classified as high achievers in mathematics (i.e. performing at PISA levels 5 and 6), 0.9% in reading, and 1% in science. On the other hand, almost 50% scored below proficiency level 2 in mathematics – compared to fewer than 10% in Korea and Singapore and 14% in Viet Nam. Although Thailand has made some progress over time, it will not be able to enhance productivity and effectiveness if the majority of young people continue to leave school with low skills.

Figure 2.19. Mean mathematics scores, and shares of low and high performers, selected countries, PISA 2012

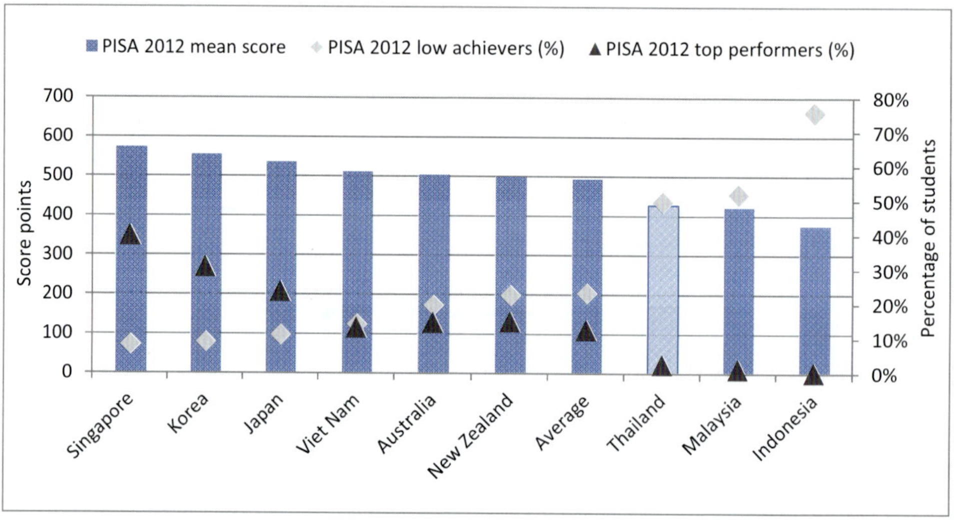

Note: PISA low performers include all students performing below the baseline proficiency level 2. PISA high achievers include all students performing at proficiency levels 5 and 6.

Source: OECD (2013a), *PISA 2012 Results: What Makes Schools Successful (Volume IV): Resources, Policies and Practices*, http://dx.doi.org/10.1787/9789264201156-en.

The concerns raised by PISA are echoed in domestic standardised student assessments. Significant numbers of Thai students appear to be failing to master the knowledge and competencies identified in the national curriculum. Thai students score poorly on the Ordinary National Educational Test (O-NET) exams taken in grades P6, M3 and M6. A large majority of students fail to reach even 50% in core subjects such as English and mathematics (Aramnet, 2014). These scores need to be interpreted with caution; however, since O-NET tests appear to have significant shortcomings (see Chapter 4 for more details).

There are substantial performance gaps between students from different socio-economic backgrounds in Thailand. In PISA 2012, 23.9% of Thai students in socio-economically disadvantaged schools performed significantly below the national average, compared to 2.9% of those in advantaged schools. Only 6.3% of Thai students were "resilient", meaning that they were in the bottom socio-economic quartile but obtained results that placed them in the top quartile of performers. This suggests that the Thai education system is less effective at nurturing high levels of performance from students with low socio-economic status than the systems in Viet Nam, where the proportion of resilient students was 17%, and Singapore, where it was 15% (Figure 2.20).

Figure 2.20. Share of resilient students, PISA 2012

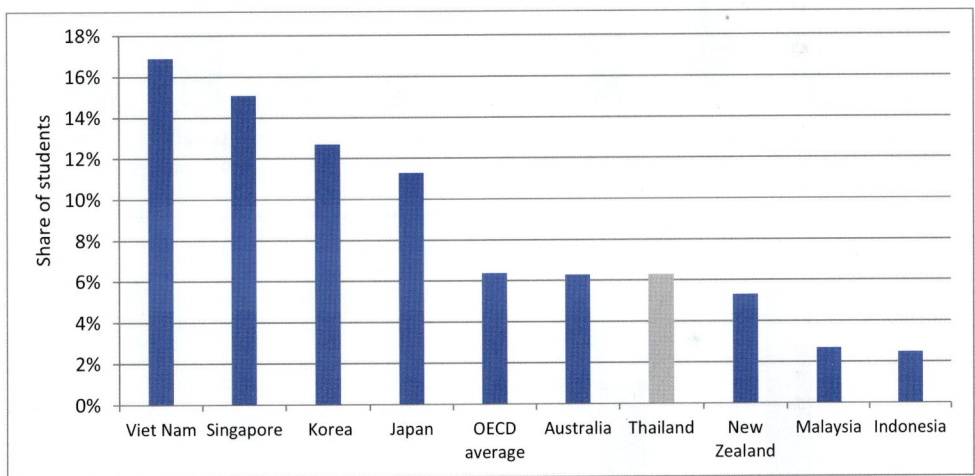

Source: OECD (2013a), *PISA 2012 Results: What Makes Schools Successful (Volume IV): Resources, Policies and Practices*, http://dx.doi.org/10.1787/9789264201156-en.

Student outcomes show significant disparities between urban and rural areas and across regions in Thailand (Figure 2.21). An assessment by Thailand's Office for National Education Standards and Quality Assessment (ONESQA) found that the majority of low-performing schools were in rural areas (ONESQA, 2008: p. 26, note 76). These areas are also home to most of Thailand's approximately 10 000 small schools, which have fewer than 120 students and are experiencing teacher shortages and infrastructure shortfalls. This suggests that Thailand may effectively have a two-tier education system. On PISA 2012, Bangkok students' scores were approximately half a PISA level higher in mathematics than in all other regions of the country except the North where another urban centre,

Chiang Mai, is located. Regional and rural/urban disparities across the country are associated with socio-economic conditions. In the South, they are also related to armed conflict, and in both the North and the South, they may be related to ethno-linguistic differences among the population.

Figure 2.21. Mathematics score by region and locality type, PISA 2012

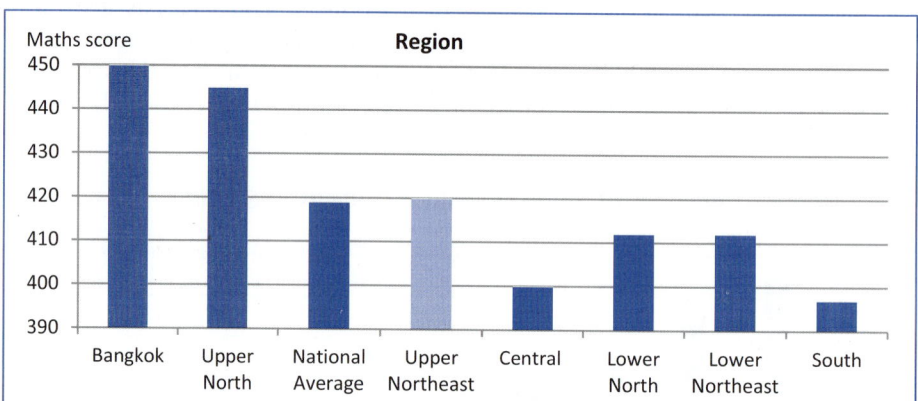

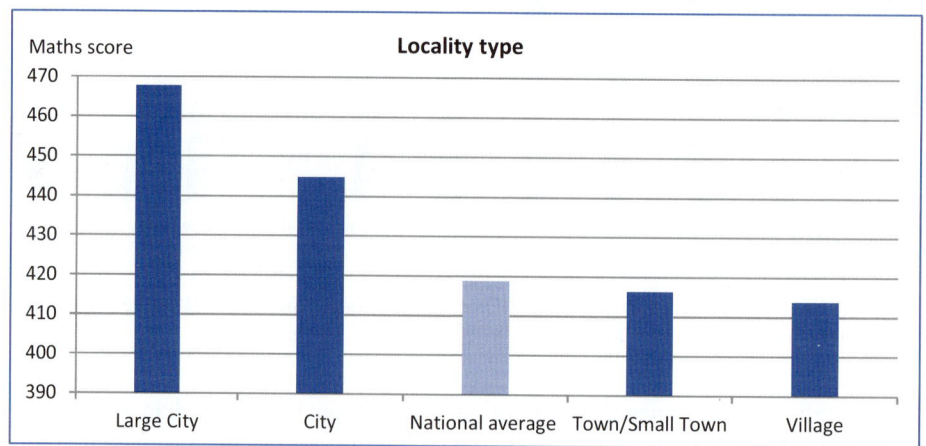

Note: The PISA scale was set so that approximately two-thirds of students across OECD countries score between 400 and 600 points. Gaps of 72, 62 and 75 points in reading, mathematics and science scores, respectively, are equivalent to one proficiency level.

Source: Institute for the Promotion of Teaching Science and Technology (IPST), 2013; www.ipst.ac.th.

Private school students and boys also perform less well in Thailand. Private school students make up 6% of the basic education student population in Thailand (World Bank, 2012b). In PISA 2012, they scored on average 36 points lower in mathematics, 35 points lower in science and 34 points lower in reading than their public school counterparts, the equivalent of one school year (OECD, 2013a). In other countries, it is more usual for private school students to perform better or the same as their public school counterparts. Thailand is also one of the few participating countries where girls outperformed boys in all subjects in PISA 2012: by 14 points in mathematics, 19 points in science and a full 55 points in reading (one of the largest gaps observed in PISA). This gender imbalance may be partly socio-economic in nature in that female students from disadvantaged backgrounds are more likely to drop out of school than those from advantaged backgrounds.

In addition to improving overall student outcomes, Thailand will need to implement a range of strategies to close gaps in educational performance and support greater social mobility. One particularly successful strategy has been the provision of pre-primary education, which first became a part of the Thai basic education system in 2004 and was made free of charge in 2009. In PISA 2003, 15-year-old Thai students who had attended pre-primary education scored on average 27 points more in mathematics than those who had not; by 2012, the difference had grown to 54 points. This is a greater increase than in any of the selected countries for which data is available (see Figure 2.22). To continue this upward trend, Thailand will need to ensure that boys and girls from disadvantaged backgrounds and rural areas have access to high-quality pre-primary education.

Figure 2.22. Relationship between mathematics performance and pre-primary attendance, selected countries, 2003 and 2012

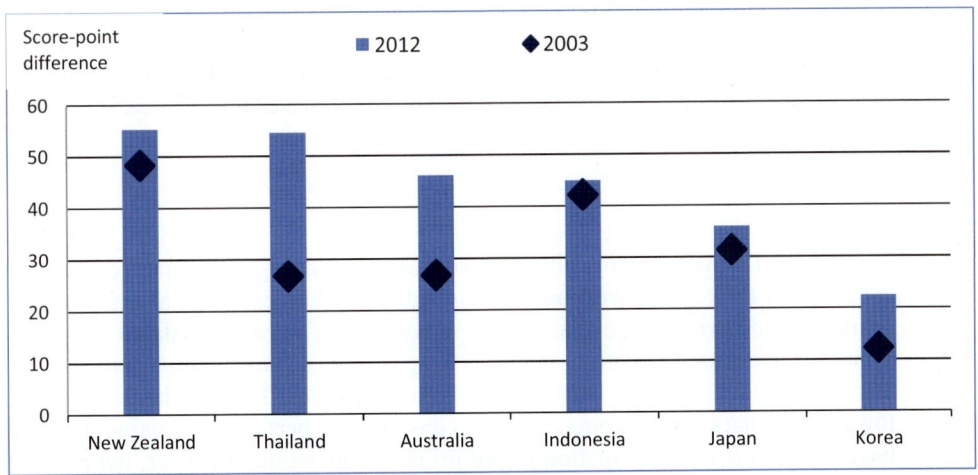

Source: OECD (2012), "Structural policy country notes: Medium-term policy challenges", in *Southeast Asian Economic Outlook 2011/12*, http://dx.doi.org/10.1787/saeo-2011-7-en.

Efficiency

Efficient schools or school systems achieve better outputs, such as student learning outcomes, for a given set of resources, or achieve comparable outputs using fewer resources. Broadly speaking, these resources include not just financial inputs, but also teachers, facilities and other durable and non-durable assets. Thailand devotes a considerable share of its GDP and its public budget to education, but so far it has not fully received the expected returns on this investment. A key factor in explaining this "Thai paradox" appears to be the way in which educational resources are allocated (Fry and Bi, 2013). By improving the efficiency of its resource allocation, Thailand could optimise its investment in education.

Policies on school size might be one area where Thailand could improve its efficiency. As outlined above, the Thai school network is characterised by a large proportion of small schools, mainly in rural disadvantaged areas, which face teacher and infrastructure shortfalls. Teachers in these schools face heavy workloads and administrative burdens, and significant requirements to teach beyond their own field of speciality. Changes to policies like the school funding system could ensure schools of different sizes and in different regions are sufficiently staffed and well resourced.

Thailand should also explore how funds could be reallocated to improve the quality of education at all levels. One of the most efficient educational strategies is to invest early and all the way up through upper secondary education (Woessmann, 2009). PISA shows that investing in high-quality pre-primary, primary and secondary education for all can increase children's chances of completing secondary and, to a lesser extent, tertiary education (OECD, 2013a). By reallocating resources to ensure funding per student is sufficient at all levels, and in particular in the early years, Thailand could increase its citizens' intergenerational mobility in education and in earnings, contributing to overall economic growth.

Conclusions

Thailand's overall expenditure on education is among the highest of the countries in the region, with particularly substantial investments at the pre-primary and primary levels. These investments have translated into improved access to education, which is a significant achievement. There are also encouraging signs in the very positive attitudes Thai students have towards teachers and learning, and the considerable performance gains that have resulted from participation in pre-primary education. However, overall student performance, as measured by international and national assessments, remains low. Almost half of Thai students who participated in PISA 2012 scored at the lowest proficiency level and very few scored at the highest level. Furthermore, a larger proportion of students in the lowest socio-economic quartiles and in rural areas performed poorly. Children from these backgrounds are less likely to participate in the education system, and when they do, they are more likely to attend small schools which lack qualified teachers and sufficient resources.

The gap between inputs and positive student outcomes in the Thai education system suggests that there is room for improved efficiency and greater equity in the allocation of financial resources. For instance, Thailand could explore how funds could be reallocated and the school funding system could be changed to improve access and quality at all levels and in all regions. The remaining chapters of this report present strategies to strengthen the curriculum, student assessment, the teaching workforce and the use of information and communications technology (ICT) in education in order to improve student retention and outcomes. These include strategies to increase the equity of the education system so that children from disadvantaged backgrounds and regions of the country acquire the skills they need to succeed.

Bibliography

Aramnet, C. (12 February 2014), "Mathayom 6 students fare poorly in O-Net", *The Nation*, www.nationmultimedia.com/national/Mathayom-6-students-fare-poorly-in-O-Net-30226655.html.

Arcia, G., K. MacDonald and H. Patrinos (2014), "School autonomy and accountability in Thailand: A systems approach for assessing policy intent and implementation", *Policy Research Working Paper*, No. 7012, World Bank, Washington, DC, https://openknowledge.worldbank.org/bitstream/handle/10986/20347/WPS7012.pdf?sequence=1.

Ares Abalde, M. (2014), "School size policies: A literature review", *OECD Education Working Papers*, No. 106, OECD Publishing, Paris, http://dx.doi.org/10.1787/5jxt472ddkjl-en.

Bangkok Post (21 February 2015), "Pupils fail 6 of 7 uni entry test subjects", *Bangkok Post*, www.bangkokpost.com/news/general/480225/pupils-fail-6-of-7-uni-entry-test-subjects.

Bangkok Post (19 April 2011), "Shockingly low college admission test scores", *Bangkok Post*, www.bangkokpost.com/learning/learning-from-news/232689/shockingly-low-college-admission-test-scores.

Carter, S. (2006), "The development of special education services in Thailand", *International Journal of Special Education*, Vol. 21/2, pp. 32-36, http://files.eric.ed.gov/fulltext/EJ843603.pdf.

Chularat, S. (26 February 2010), "NIETS defends 'ridiculous' Onet questions", *The Nation*, www.nationmultimedia.com/home/2010/02/26/national/NIETS-defends-&039;ridiculous&039;-Onet-questions-30123437.html.

Fry, G. and H. Bi (2013), "The evolution of educational reform in Thailand: The Thai educational paradox", *Journal of Educational Administration*, Vol. 51/3, pp. 290-319, http://dx.doi.org/10.1108/09578231311311483.

Hallinger, P. (2004), "Meeting the challenges of cultural leadership: The changing role of principals in Thailand", *Discourse: Studies in the Cultural Politics of Education*, Vol. 25/1, pp. 61-73, www.tandfonline.com/doi/pdf/10.1080/0159630042000178482.

Hattie, J. (2009), *Visible Learning: A Synthesis of Over 800 Meta-Analyses Relating to Achievement*, Routledge, London.

Hattie, J. and G. Yates (2013), *Visible Learning and the Science of How We Learn*, Routledge, London.

Heckman, J.J. (2011), "The economics of inequality: The value of early childhood education", *American Educator*, Vol. 35/1, pp. 31-35, www.aft.org/pdfs/americaneducator/spring2011/Heckman.pdf.

Ingersoll, R. (2007), "A comparative study of teacher preparation and qualifications in six nations", *CPRE Policy Briefs*, RB-47, Consortium for Policy Research in Education, www.cpre.org/images/stories/cpre_pdfs/RB47.pdf (accessed 14 April 2015).

Institute for the Promotion of Teaching Science and Technology (IPST) (2013), www.ipst.ac.th (accessed April 2015).

Kaewmala (23 February 2012), "Thai education failures – Part 1: Ridiculous O-NET questions", *Asian Correspondent*, http://asiancorrespondent.com/76664/thai-education-part-1-ridiculous-o-net-questions/.

Krueger, A. (1999), "Experimental estimates of education production functions", *Quarterly Journal of Economics*, Vol. 114/2, pp. 497-532.

Lathapipat, D. (2015), "Closing the school performance gap through better public resource allocation – The case of Thailand", *World Bank Working Paper*, preliminary draft (March), World Bank, Washington, DC.

Levtov, R. (2014), "Addressing gender inequalities in curriculum and education: Review of literature and promising practices to inform education reform initiatives in Thailand", *Women's Voice and Agency Research Series 2014*, No. 9, World Bank, Washington, DC, https://openknowledge.worldbank.org/bitstream/handle/10986/21034/927630NWP0Wome00Box385358B00PUBLIC0.pdf?sequence=1.

Lindahl, M. (2005), "Home versus school learning: A new approach to estimating the effect of class size on achievement", *Scandinavian Journal of Economics*, Vol.107/2, pp. 375-394.

Martin, M. et al. (2012), *TIMSS 2011 International Results in Science*, TIMSS & PIRLS International Study Center, Chestnut Hill, http://timssandpirls.bc.edu/timss2011/downloads/T11_IR_Science_FullBook.pdf.

Maxwell, D. (21 November2014), "28 weeks later: Education reform in Thailand under the junta", *Asian Correspondent*, http://asiancorrespondent.com/128438/28-weeks-later-education-reform-in-thailand-under-the-junta/.

Mullis, I. et al. (2012), *TIMSS 2011 International Results in Mathematics*, TIMSS & PIRLS International Study Center, Chestnut Hill, http://timssandpirls.bc.edu/timss2011/downloads/T11_IR_Mathematics_FullBook.pdf.

OEC and Ministry of Education (2014), "Thailand country background report", report prepared in anticipation of OECD-UNESCO pre-mission visit in November 2013 and updated in 2014, Office of the Education Council and Ministry of Education of Thailand, Bangkok.

OECD (2014), *PISA 2012 Results: What Students Know and Can Do (Volume I, Revised Edition, February 2014): Student Performance in Mathematics, Reading and Science*, PISA, OECD Publishing, Paris, http://dx.doi.org/10.1787/9789264208780-en.

OECD (2013a), *PISA 2012 Results: What Makes Schools Successful (Volume IV): Resources, Policies and Practices*, PISA, OECD Publishing, Paris, http://dx.doi.org/10.1787/9789264201156-en.

OECD (2013b), *Southeast Asian Economic Outlook 2013: With Perspectives on China and India*, OECD Publishing. http://dx.doi.org/10.1787/saeo-2013-en.

OECD (2013c), *PISA 2012 Results: Ready to Learn (Volume III): Students' Engagement, Drive and Self-Beliefs*, PISA, OECD Publishing, Paris, http://dx.doi.org/10.1787/9789264201170-en.

OECD (2012), "Structural policy country notes: Medium-term policy challenges", in *Southeast Asian Economic Outlook 2011/12*, OECD Publishing, Paris, http://dx.doi.org/10.1787/saeo-2011-7-cn.

OECD (2007), *PISA 2006: Science Competencies for Tomorrow's World: Volume 1: Analysis*, PISA, OECD Publishing, Paris, http://dx.doi.org/10.1787/9789264040014-en.

OECD (2005), *Teachers Matter: Attracting, Developing and Retaining Effective Teachers*, Education and Training Policy, OECD Publishing, Paris, http://dx.doi.org/10.1787/9789264018044-en.

ONESQA (2008), *Annual Report*, (Thai), Office for National Education Standards and Quality Assessment, www.onesqa.or.th/en/annual/annual.php;%20www.%20unicef.org/thailand/1045_UNICEF_Final_row_res_230911.pdf.

Sakawee, S. (3 February 2014), "Thailand's One Tablet Per Child faces another dead end as a Chinese manufacturer cancels the deal", *Tech In Asia*, www.techinasia.com/thailands-tablet-child-faces-dead-chinese-manufacturer-cancels-deal/.

Sammons, P., J. Hillman and P. Mortimore (1995), *Key Characteristics of Effective Schools: A Review of School Effectiveness Research*, Office for Standards in Education (OFSTED), London.

Scheerens, J. and R.J. Bosker (1997), *The Foundations of Educational Effectiveness*, Pergamon, London.

Supham, V. and Associates (2012), "Thailand K-12 education system: Progress and failure", Report to the Education Knowledge Group, Pico Thailand CSV Institute, May.

Sutherland, D., R. Price and F. Gonand (2009), "Improving public spending efficiency in primary and secondary education", *OECD Journal: Economic Studies*, Vol. 2009, www.oecd.org/eco/growth/46867041.pdf.

Tangkitvanich, S. (2013), "Teach Thais to think", Thailand Development Research Institute website, http://tdri.or.th/en/tdri-insight/10045/.

UIS and UNICEF (2015), *Fixing the Broken Promise of Education for All: Findings from the Global Initiative on Out-of-School Children*, UNESCO Institute for Statistics and the United Nations Children's Fund, Montreal, http://dx.doi.org/10.15220/978-92-9189-161-0-en.

UNESCO (2015), *Education for All 2015 National Review Report: Thailand*, United Nations Educational, Scientific and Cultural Organization, Paris, http://unesdoc.unesco.org/images/0022/002298/229878E.pdf.

UNESCO (2011), *Education for all Development Index*, United Nations Educational, Scientific and Cultural Organization, http://en.unesco.org/gem-report/education-all-development-index (accessed 17 March 2015).

UNESCO Bangkok, (2011), UNESCO *National Education Support Strategy* (UNESS), Thailand: 2010-2015, UNESCO Bangkok, www.unescobkk.org/fileadmin/user_upload/epr/UNESS/uness_thailand_2011.pdf.

UNESCO-UIS (2015), *Education* (dataset), UIS Data Centre, UNESCO Institute for Statistics, http://data.uis.unesco.org/Index.aspx?DataSetCode=EDULIT_DS&popupcustomise=true&lang=en.

Viriyapong, R. and A. Harfield (2013), "Facing the challenges of the One-Tablet-Per-Child policy in Thai primary school education", *International Journal of Advanced Computer Science and Applications*, Vol. 4/9, http://thesai.org/Downloads/Volume4No9/Paper_28-Facing_the_challenges_of_the_One-Tablet-Per-Child.pdf.

Woessmann, L. et al. (2009), *School Accountability, Autonomy, and Choice Around the World*, Ifo Economic Policy series, Edward Elgar, Cheltenham.

World Bank (2015), "Education statistics", *World DataBank*, World Bank, http://databank.worldbank.org/Data/Views/VariableSelection/SelectVariables.aspx?source=Education%20Statistics.

World Bank (2012a), *Leading with Ideas: Skills for Growth and Equity in Thailand*, World Bank, Bangkok, https://openknowledge.worldbank.org/bitstream/handle/10986/2732/672040ESW0P1170hig0res0AW0for0print.pdf?sequence=1.

World Bank (2012b), *Learning Outcomes in Thailand: What Can We Learn from International Assessments?*, World Bank, https://openknowledge.worldbank.org/handle/10986/2723.

World Bank (2008), *Thailand Social Monitor on Youth: Development and the Next Generation*, World Bank, https://openknowledge.worldbank.org/bitstream/handle/10986/8036/428520P09721301WB1SMY20081080305web.pdf?sequence=1.

Chapter 3

Thailand's education curriculum

A clear, coherent and relevant curriculum is at the heart of any good education system. This chapter outlines the impact of Thailand's switch from a content-based curriculum to a modern standards-based approach in 2001 and its revision in 2008. It identifies four policy issues hampering the effective implementation of Thailand's curriculum reforms to improve student outcomes: 1) the quality of the curriculum document itself; 2) a lack of capacity among teachers and schools to implement the curriculum; 3) limited capacity to assess how well the curriculum has delivered its intended outcomes; and 4) weak use of existing review processes.

It recommends Thailand conduct a thorough and consultative curriculum review to address these issues and develop common student performance standards to drive reform in other areas. This should be better communicated to schools and education staff supported in the implementation of curriculum reform.

Introduction

"Curriculum" commonly refers to the intended content of what students will learn, with that content often organised into several distinct disciplines or subjects. The content of each discipline or subject is traditionally described in terms of skills, knowledge and attitudes. More recently, other elements such as cross-curriculum themes, key competencies and values have been added to this simple subject-based paradigm. A curriculum can be characterised by the fundamental concepts underlying its structure and philosophy. Examples include skills-based, content-based, outcomes-based, competency-based and standards-based curricula. There are advantages and disadvantages to labelling curriculum models in this way. The main advantage is that it clarifies the most important teaching and learning priority of the curriculum for readers and users. The most significant shortcoming is that it does not convey the complexity of the curriculum.

In practice, no successful curriculum restricts itself to a single design model. For example, even if a competency-based curriculum consists entirely of identified competencies which are to be developed in learners, those competencies need to be achieved through some content selected and delivered by the teacher. In addition, a student competency – itself a result of a combination of knowledge, skills, values and attitudes that are adapted, combined and applied in a specific context – must also be perceived as an outcome.

Thailand's current Core Curriculum for Basic Education 2008 (the 2008 curriculum), covering the primary and lower secondary education levels, is intended to be standards-based. Traditionally, a standards-based curriculum is directed toward mastery of predetermined standards, which generally include content standards and performance standards (UNESCO-IBE, 2013).

Content standards describe what all students should know and be able to do in each subject and, in many cases, across the curriculum (for example competencies and values that are to be developed by every student and are embedded in every subject). Performance standards specify what levels of learning are expected and assess the degree to which content standards have been met. They can also guide teachers in preparing learning programmes and lessons that might be needed in order for students to be able to reach the prescribed standards.

Thailand's 2008 curriculum is consistent with contemporary international norms for standards-based curricula in several respects. For example, it provides content standards describing what all students should learn at each grade level and places a significant amount of responsibility on educators to determine how the content should be implemented. However, in other ways, the curriculum is atypical, and does not offer Thailand the advantages of a standards-based approach, which generally enables comparability across classrooms, schools and districts. If Thailand's curriculum is to better support the country's education reform efforts and improve student achievement, then the curriculum document needs to be made clearer and more relevant, principals and teachers need to be supported in their implementation of the curriculum, clear student performance standards need to be set out, and a regular curriculum evaluation and review process established.

This chapter starts by describing the recent history of curriculum reform in Thailand. It then reviews four aspects of Thailand's current curriculum: 1) as it was intended by developers; 2) as it is implemented by teachers and principals; 3) as it is attained or achieved by students; and 4) the curriculum processes, particularly those related to development and evaluation (Figure 3.1).

Figure 3.1. The curriculum review

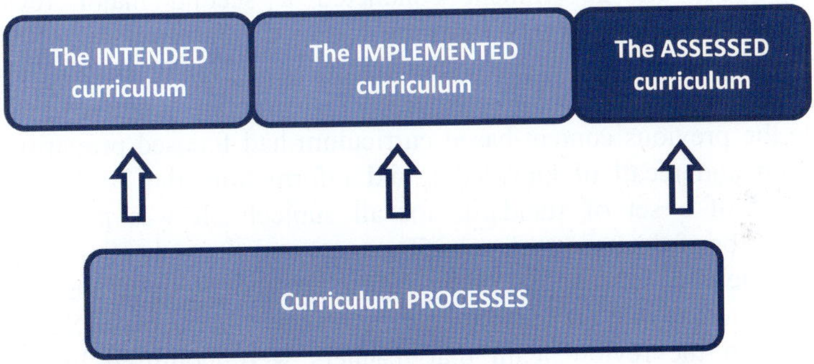

```
┌──────────────┐  ┌──────────────┐  ┌──────────────┐
│ The INTENDED │  │The IMPLEMENTED│  │ The ASSESSED │
│  curriculum  │  │  curriculum  │  │  curriculum  │
└──────────────┘  └──────────────┘  └──────────────┘
       ⇧                 ⇧                 ⇧
┌─────────────────────────────────────────────────┐
│             Curriculum PROCESSES                │
└─────────────────────────────────────────────────┘
```

The Thai school curriculum

After centuries when education in Thailand was provided locally, for instance, by monks in local temples, the 1960s witnessed the beginning of a formal school curriculum intended for nationwide implementation. A system of 7 + 3 + 2 (seven years of primary education, three of lower secondary and two of upper secondary education) was introduced at that time. As Thailand became more open to international influences, foreign languages and vocational subjects were added to the curriculum. During that period, the government administered education through the Ministry of Interior, and increased the period of compulsory education from four to seven years.

In 1978-79, the government undertook a significant review of the curriculum. As a result, it adopted a system of 6 + 3 + 3. The primary curriculum consisted of the following five subjects or learning areas:

1. basic skills for living (consisting of Thai language and mathematics)
2. life experience (consisting of social studies and health)
3. character development (including physical education, art, music and dance)
4. work education
5. extra content as determined by schools (but commonly including English).

Responsibility for both basic and secondary education was moved from the Ministry of Interior to the Ministry for Curriculum and Instruction.

The 2001 curriculum

In 2001, the government conducted a second major review of curriculum, resulting largely from the National Education Act (1999) and forming an integral part of the National Education Plan (2001-2016). A very significant shift in curriculum philosophy and structure occurred at this time. While the previous content-based curriculum had focused primarily on the retention and recall of knowledge and information, the 2001 curriculum consisted of a set of standards for all subjects. It was presented in a relatively brief document of only 58 pages, and the indications are that it lacked a detailed explanation of the shift in the underlying philosophy of the curriculum, as well as advice and guidance to teachers. Stakeholders reported to the review team that teachers were confused by the 2001 curriculum, and did not receive sufficient support to help them interpret and implement it effectively. It is likely that the impact of the shift in philosophy and structure on the role and responsibilities of teachers was significantly underestimated at all levels of the system.

This situation was perhaps exacerbated by the concurrent introduction of a new administrative and support structure in the education system. The government created 225 Education Service Areas (ESAs) at that time, and delegated numerous functions to them under a newly prioritised decentralisation strategy. While no conclusive qualitative evidence is available to measure the impact of this decentralisation, it is likely that the whole education system was under considerable strain at this time, and that support for teachers working in a new curriculum paradigm was inadequate.

The Office of the Basic Education Curriculum (OBEC) conducted evaluative studies of the 2001 curriculum in subsequent years and identified a number of problems, concerns and shortcomings with "the provisions, application process and outcome of the curriculum" (OBEC, 2008). Issues included:

- "Confusion and uncertainty in preparing school curriculums".
- The challenges teachers faced in adapting to new responsibilities in curriculum development without extensive training and support.
- Schools' ambition in prescribing learning areas and expected outcomes.
- Schools' lack of capacity to effectively shape the curriculum and specify learning outcomes to suit the needs of their students and the local environment, which generally requires extensive experience.
- "Measurement and evaluation did not correlate with the standards set, which [sic] effects on preparation of certifying documents and transferring of learning outcomes".
- Assessment processes did not effectively measure curriculum outcomes, rendering assessment information unreliable (see Chapter 4).
- "Issues of learners' quality resulting from acquisition of essential knowledge, skills, capacity and desired characteristics and attributes were quite disconcerting"[1].

It is clear from these findings that the introduction of a standards-based curriculum had not achieved the outcomes expected and that, in very important ways, the quality of student learning was significantly compromised during this period. The government attempted to address these issues with its next iteration of the curriculum.

The 2008 curriculum

The most significant change incorporated into the 2008 curriculum was the addition of very detailed "grade-level indicators" and "interval indicators" (for Grades 10-12) to guide teachers in their selection of content needed to achieve the standards. In essence, these provided a range of instructions to teachers, each commencing with a verb, such as "record", "explain", "present" or "express". This was probably intended to assist teachers in interpreting the standards at classroom level, but it may have instead reversed the progress towards a contemporary standards-based curriculum, leading the education system back to a content-based curriculum and reducing the likelihood of schools developing their own content.

Many of the issues identified in the evaluation of the 2001 curriculum still compromise the implementation of the 2008 curriculum. The government continued its decentralisation strategy across all sectors, and so the curriculum itself continued to rely heavily on local-level decision making and capacity. At the same time, policy makers continued to underestimate how deep and broad the impact of a standards-based curriculum would be, and of the degree to which training and other support would be needed to ensure the curriculum was implemented effectively.

The 2011 curriculum review

Since 2011-12, Thailand has been preparing a new curriculum and an instruction reform, with a vision of fostering core values and skills required by today's Thai society open to an international world. The plan is to move from a standard-based curriculum to an outcome-based one. As part of the revision process, a range of stakeholders has been mobilised.

It is difficult to gauge the true intent and scale of the changes to the curriculum that are being proposed, although it could be assumed that the primary purpose of the revision is to address the deficiencies identified in the 2008 curriculum. The review team were given little information about the new curriculum during the consultation mission, and consequently had no opportunity to discuss, for example, what was meant by an "outcome-based curriculum".

However, we understand that if it is implemented, the new curriculum will have the following features:

- The curriculum will contain ten generic skills, six values and attitudes, six learning experiences, and six key learning areas.
- It will be "learning outcomes based" with measurable learning outcomes (both knowledge and skills).
- There will be horizontal alignment among subjects and vertical alignment across levels.
- An assessment data management system for formative and summative assessment and for internal quality assurance will be included.
- There will be a "triangle of reform" with greater co-ordination between curriculum, instruction, and assessment. (Magee, 2013).

However, the decision to halt or postpone the reform process interrupted the consistent line of revision and the very important commitment to systematic and continuous improvement of the intended curriculum. While there is a broadly held view that the structure and contents of the current curriculum need to be improved, no real action to achieve this improvement appears to have taken place, as the regular meetings of the standing National Education Reform Steering Committee have not yet produced any tangible outcomes.

Policy Issue 1: Thailand's intended curriculum lacks clarity, consistency and relevance

In general terms, Thailand's 2008 curriculum compares well with the curricula in high-performing countries in the region, such as Singapore and Korea. These curricula take as their primary focus the standardised knowledge and skills which students are expected to achieve, and devolve a very significant degree of autonomy to teachers and schools. The onus is on teachers to select topics and related content, to plan and teach lessons and sequences of lessons, and use assessment strategies and "student-centred" teaching methodologies in such a way as to help students achieve the standards. For this reason, the curriculum document (i.e. the written or "intended" curriculum) should provide educators with clear direction and advice about the purpose of the curriculum and how it should be implemented without being prescriptive about the contents to be taught. Thailand's 2008 curriculum document is more comprehensive than the 2001 iteration, but issues remain regarding its structure, contents and alignment with education reform priorities.

The structure and contents of the 2008 curriculum document

The 2008 curriculum document improves upon its 2001 equivalent by providing more detail about the different interconnected components of the curriculum (Figure 3.2). An introductory section provides statements of the vision and goals and a range of information and advice regarding, among other things, the rationale for changes to the 2001 curriculum, the importance of learners' key competencies and desired characteristics, time allocations, and learning management. In each of the eight learning area sections devoted to the subjects studied by students in grades P1 to M6 (primary to upper secondary), there are designated strands, clear descriptions of the learning standards, and grade-level indicators. However, the curriculum is still lacking in several areas essential to its effective implementation. It does not articulate a clear theoretical underpinning or student performance standards, or clarify what effective pedagogy means in a standards-based environment, and provides little to no guidance or direction on how to meet the needs of different learners, support the acquisition of 21st century competencies and allot instructional time.

Figure 3.2. Key components of the 2008 Curriculum document

Relationships in the development of learners' quality according to the Basic Education Core Curriculum

Vision

The Basic Education Core Curriculum is aimed at enhancing capacity of all learners, who constitute the major force of the country so as to attain a balanced development in all respects – physical strength, knowledge and morality. They will fully realize their commitment and responsibilities as Thai citizens and members of the world community. Adhering to a democratic form of government under a constitutional monarchy, they will be endowed with basic knowledge and essential skills and favourable attitude towards further education, livelihood and lifelong learning.

Goals

1. Morality, ethics, desired values, self-esteem, self-discipline, observance of Buddhist teachings or those of one's faith, and applying the principles of Sufficiency Economy Philosophy.
2. Knowledge and skills for communicating, thinking, problem-solving, technological know-how, and life skills.
3. Good physical and mental health, hygiene and preference for physical exercise.
4. Patriotism, awareness about a democratic way of life and form of government under a constitutional monarchy
5. Awareness of the need to preserve all aspects of Thai culture and Thai wisdom, protection and conversation of the environment, and public-mindedness with dedication to public service for peaceful and harmonious coexistence.

Learners' key competencies	Desired characteristics
1. communication capacity 2. thinking capacity 3. problem-solving capacity 4. capacity for applying life skills 5. capacity for technological application	1. love of nation, religion and the monarchy 2. self-discipline 3. avidity for learning 4. applying principles of sufficiency 5. dedication and commitment to work 6. cherishing Thai nationalism 7. public-mindedness

Learners' quality at basic education level

Learning standards and indicators	Learner development activities
1. Thai language 2. Mathematics 3. Science 4. Social Studies, Religion and Culture 5. Health and Physical Education 6. Art 7. Occupations and Technology 8. Foreign Languages	1. consulting activities 2. student activities 3. activities for social and public interest

Source: OBEC (2008), Basic Education Core Curriculum, B.E. 2551, Ministry of Education of Thailand, Bangkok.

The theoretical underpinning of the curriculum

Elaborating a curriculum's philosophy contributes significantly to the effectiveness of its implementation. As part of this process, education policy makers articulate their beliefs in a specific learning theory. Curriculum developers then use that theory consistently as the reference point for determining and arranging content, and setting out requirements for teachers to put these beliefs into practice in their classrooms. The theory is also reflected in teacher training and professional development programmes, and serves as the basis for evaluating textbooks.

In Thailand, the shift in curriculum philosophy and structure first undertaken in 2001, and revised in 2008, marked a very significant turning point for the Thai education system. Thailand moved away from a knowledge-based, centralised curriculum characterised by didactic teaching and minimal opportunities to contextualise the curriculum to reflect local needs, and towards a standards-based curriculum incorporating a high degree of local curriculum decision making.

While the 2008 curriculum document makes a number of statements that suggest an underlying theory and philosophy (such as numerous references to "child-centred learning", and even a direction to observe "the principles of development of the brain and multiple intelligence"), it provides no cohesive framework of learning theory or accepted approaches to curriculum construction. There is no obvious hierarchy of skills and knowledge, with reference to how teachers should gradually extend the thinking capacities of their students. Box 3.1 gives an example of one such framework, Bloom's taxonomy (Anderson and Krathwohl, 2001).

Box 3.1. Learning theories and Bloom's taxonomy

Learning theories develop hypotheses that describe how the process of acquiring, enriching or modifying one's knowledge, skills, values, attitudes, behaviour or worldview takes place. The scientific study of learning started in earnest at the dawn of the 20th century.

The major concepts and theories of learning include behaviourism, cognitive psychology, constructivism, social constructivism, experiential learning, multiple intelligence and situated learning theory and community of practice.

Bloom's taxonomy, originally developed in the 1950s by researchers working under Benjamin Bloom of the University of Chicago, has its roots in behaviourism, and in its current form, also relates to other learning theories, including constructivism and the acquisition of 21st century competencies.

> **Box 3.1. Learning theories and Bloom's taxonomy** *(cont.)*
>
> Bloom's taxonomy comprises three learning domains: cognitive, affective and psychomotor (i.e. motor or behavioural skills). Each domain describes learning objectives at increasing levels of difficulty, with examples of activities and keywords to indicate mastery at each level. The cognitive domain, in particular, has provided an influential model for classifying learning objectives and activities in school curricula.
>
> Revised in the 1990s, this domain currently describes six progressively complex levels of thinking:
>
> 1. remembering (retrieving, recognising and recalling)
> 2. understanding (constructing meaning by interpreting, exemplifying, classifying, summarising, inferring, comparing and explaining)
> 3. applying (carrying out, executing or implementing)
> 4. analysing (breaking information into parts, differentiating, organising and attributing)
> 5. evaluating (making judgements, checking and critiquing)
> 6. creating (putting elements together to form a whole, generating new ideas).
>
> The latter three cognitive processes are commonly known as high-order thinking skills, which are often cited as competencies needed for success in the 21st century.
>
> *Source*: UNESCO-IBE (2013), *Glossary of Curriculum Terminology*, www.ibe.unesco.org/fileadmin/user_upload/Publications/IBE_GlossaryCurriculumTerminology2013_eng.pdf.

Student performance standards

While the 2008 curriculum may, at least in its intent, be defined as a standards-based curriculum, it does not indicate the expected standards of student performance or achievement (see Box 3.2 for more detail on what performance standards should provide). It provides teachers with no criteria to assist them in judging and distinguishing between various levels of student achievement. Instead, the Criteria for Learning Assessment section of the curriculum requires that schools determine their own criteria for assessment.

This is problematic for principals and teachers, who need guidance to develop effective criteria, and for the education system as a whole. A lack of consistent standards renders system-wide assessments and comparisons of student performance across schools and regions unreliable (Chapter 4 explores student assessment practices in Thailand in further detail).

> **Box 3.2. Student performance standards**
>
> Within the context of a standards-based curriculum, performance standards – sometimes known as achievement standards – specify what levels of learning are expected and assess the degree to which content standards have been met in various subject areas. They are intended to provide:
>
> - teachers with targets for instruction by specifying what, and how much, learners must be able to do in order to demonstrate mastery of content standards and the achievement level that is called for
>
> - test developers with clear directions about the kinds of performance situations and tasks that will be used to make judgements about learner proficiency
>
> - the public with a sense of what it means for a learner to be classified at a particular level.
>
> *Source*: UNESCO-IBE (2013), *Glossary of Curriculum Terminology*, www.ibe.unesco.org/fileadmin/user_upload/Publications/IBE_GlossaryCurriculumTerminology2013_eng.pdf.

Pedagogy

The 2008 curriculum makes some reference to pedagogy and assessment but offers little in the way of practical advice to teachers about how to plan and deliver learning programmes and lesson plans in a standards-based environment. The curriculum document provides detail about the content standards organised into "strands", "standards" and "grade-level indicators", reflecting an organisational structure relevant to the subject or discipline, but no guidance on how to integrate material across strands and standards, or about how to effectively sequence material in ways that facilitate effective learning (Box 3.3). For example, the curriculum has no section devoted to sequencing learning programmes and activities. Similarly, while the curriculum makes a number of references to "projects", it gives no clear guidance as to why projects are important and what they can achieve.

The 2008 curriculum document added a large amount of information to each of the learning areas in the form of grade-level indicators. This was probably intended to address the confusion that followed the introduction of the 2001 curriculum by providing teachers with assistance in interpreting the standards at classroom level. However, the real effect appears to have been to reverse the progress towards a contemporary standards-based curriculum, and return to a content-based curriculum. The impression that emerged from school visits during the review is that most teachers may be interpreting the additional information as an invitation to teach this traditional content and ignore the primary focus of the curriculum – the standards. What many teachers perceive as a renewed emphasis on content may even discourage them from devising new and challenging cross-disciplinary projects, and limit schools' efforts to develop an engaging curriculum which is grounded in the local context and is characterised by student-centred, experiential learning.

Box 3.3. An example of pedagogical guidance provided in the 2008 curriculum

For each of the eight learning areas studied by every student from grades P1 to M6 in Thai schools, the 2008 curriculum provides the following guidance to educators: a rationale (i.e. why it is necessary to learn the learning area), a summary of the content (i.e. an overview of the learning strands), a statement of "learners' quality" (i.e. student outcomes at the end of grades P3, P6, M3 and M6, the years of national assessment) and a description of the standards and grade-level indicators for each strand.

For example, the Thai language learning area encompasses five strands:

1. reading (e.g. pronouncing words; reading to oneself for comprehension and for acquiring thinking skills in analysing and synthesising knowledge to apply in daily life)

2. writing (e.g. writing various kinds of communications, compositions, synopses and reports)

3. listening, viewing and speaking (e.g. speaking to express opinions and feelings; speaking on various matters in logical sequence)

4. principles of usage of the Thai language (e.g. accurate linguistic usage appropriate to different occasions and persons)

5. literature and literary works (e.g. learning and comprehension of chants, children's rhymes and folk songs representing valuable Thai wisdom).

Within the reading strand, there is one standard (Standard TH1.1): application of the reading process to build knowledge and thoughts for decision making and problem solving, and encouraging the acquisition of reading habits. For this standard, there are eight to ten grade-level indicators for each of grades P1 to M3 and interval indicators for grades M4 to M6.

> **Box 3.3. An example of pedagogical guidance provided in the 2008 curriculum** *(cont.)*
>
> The grade-level indicators for P6 (grade six) are:
>
> 1. accurately read aloud prose and verse
> 2. explain meanings of words, sentences and idiomatic expressions
> 3. read short stories, setting time limits, and ask questions about what has been read
> 4. differentiate between facts and opinions
> 5. apply knowledge and thoughts from what has been read for decision-making to solve problems in life
> 6. read explanatory paragraphs, instructions and suggestions and then follow them
> 7. explain meanings of data from diagrams, maps, charts and graphs
> 8. regularly read valuable books with interest and explain benefits obtained from what has been read
> 9. have good reading manners.
>
> *Source:* OBEC, (2008), Basic Education Core Curriculum, B.E. 2551.

Flexibility to meet the needs of different learners

The 2008 curriculum document lacks clear guidance over ways to adjust the curriculum to address the widely varying needs of students who enrol in Thai schools. This is a critical issue for curriculum inclusiveness and equity. Differentiation or adjustment needs to be able to accommodate students with learning difficulties, gifted and talented students, and a range of other priority groups, including ethnic minorities and non-Thai speaking migrants. One paragraph in the curriculum document, under the heading Educational Provision for Special Target Groups refers briefly to this issue (OBEC, 2008: p. 28). However, if Thailand is to achieve its policy goal of "increasing education opportunities" for all Thai people, this aspect of the curriculum needs to be strengthened considerably.

Key competencies for the 21st century

The 2008 curriculum introduced the concept of competencies and named five key competencies all students were expected to achieve: 1) communication capacity; 2) thinking capacity; 3) problem-solving capacity; 4) capacity to apply life skills; and 5) capacity for technological application. This is consistent with the approach taken in a number of contemporary curricula (Box 3.4).

Box 3.4. Curricula and key competencies for the 21st century

It is increasingly common for modern curricula to describe the knowledge, skills, behaviours and dispositions that students need to live and work successfully in the 21st century. These competencies, also called transversal skills, generally bridge all subjects of the curriculum, pointing to the interdisciplinary nature of learning in today's world. The 2013 National Curriculum of Australia describes these cross-curricular competencies in the form of seven "general capabilities":

1. literacy
2. numeracy
3. information and communication technology (ICT) capability
4. critical and creative thinking
5. personal and social capability
6. ethical understanding
7. intercultural understanding.

Source: ACARA (2013a), *General Capabilities in the Australian Curriculum*, www.australiancurriculum.edu.au/generalcapabilities/pdf/overview.

Developing students' 21st century competencies will be critical for a competitive, secure and prosperous Thailand. Teachers need to understand the nature of such competencies and be provided with clear examples of the relevance of competency development to particular subjects, strands and standards, and how competencies can be developed through teaching programmes and classroom activities.

While the 2008 curriculum includes key competencies, it does not consistently apply the development of these competencies in students. The document remains unclear about what "competencies" actually are, how they fit into the curriculum structure and how they are to be assessed. Most significantly, competencies do not appear to be important to the standards and grade-level indicators for each subject, and the curriculum provides insufficient advice to teachers about how important they are and how they can be incorporated into teaching programmes. For example, it does not map competencies to the standards or indicators as an illustration of how they might be taught in the various learning areas.[2] Stakeholders also mentioned to the review team that the key competencies and the eight desired characteristics of learners (listed in Figure 3.2), needed to be revised to be more compatible with and reflect the current Thai national and regional context.

The 2008 curriculum does not support cross-curriculum learning to acquire 21st century competencies. While subjects or learning areas are no doubt the most popular ways of organising curricula, the 2008 curriculum provides little advice to schools and teachers about other approaches. In the curriculum document, the eight subject-based learning areas and associated strands are highly segregated, with limited guidance to teachers about how to connect learning across disciplines.

An alternative methodology would be to organise content into cross-curriculum learning areas (such as sustainability, media literacy or human rights education), which would break down perceived barriers between subjects and make students' learning more relevant and meaningful. Stakeholders in Thailand also called for the learning areas to be redefined, combined and reduced to focus on 21st century competencies.

Instructional time

One strategy used by the curriculum to encourage decentralisation is to allocate minimum hours to subjects, leaving some time for each school to develop a local curriculum (the school-based curriculum – 160 hours out of 1 000 hours (or 16%) at the primary level and 320 hours out of 1 200 hours (or approximately 27%) at secondary level. There are two types of school-based curriculum time:

- Learner development activities, such as counselling, student associations and voluntary service.

- "Additional courses/activities provided by schools, depending on their readiness and priorities" (OBEC, 2008).[3]

While the learner development activities component of this school-based curriculum is relatively clear, there is little guidance on how the time allotted to additional courses or activities should be used. At the upper secondary level, this component accounts for "not less than 1 600 hours" from Grades 10 through 12 (M4 to M6).

The review team heard different reports about how schools exercise their discretion in this area. Some stakeholders stated that the time is simply used to "cram" for the Ordinary National Educational Test (O-NET). Others claimed that the time is used to make the curriculum more relevant and offer diverse pathways to respond to the different interests and capabilities of upper secondary school students. It was clear that schools would benefit from more guidance in how to design their own curricula and manage learning time effectively. Consideration could also be given to making the time for each learning area more flexible so that schools have more space to connect disciplines, and can ensure that adequate time is allocated for students to acquire core competencies.

The 2008 curriculum and government policy objectives

The Second Decade of Educational Reform (OEC, 2009) and other government policy documents set out Thailand's education policy priorities. These include: 1) further decentralising the education system; 2) supporting school-to-work transitions; 3) integrating the country with the Association of Southeast Asian Nations (ASEAN) economic community; and 4) conserving Thai culture and traditions. The 2008 curriculum does not align with all of these priorities, and the curriculum document lacks guidance to schools and teachers to help them work towards them.

Decentralisation and increased local decision making

The 2008 curriculum provides support, at least in principle, for the government's decentralisation strategy by shifting responsibility for some curriculum-related decisions to the local level. A standards-based curriculum, by its nature, sets standards of content and achievement to be taught and learned in all schools, thus devolving to schools and teachers the responsibility for planning the annual / semester / term teaching programme and developing lesson plans and classroom activities. As mentioned above, the 2008 curriculum purposefully devolves to schools a number of hours for the development of "school-based" curriculum.

This does not mean, however, that the decentralisation of the curriculum has been successful, and it could be argued that the inclusion of elaborately detailed grade-level indicators in fact reduces the potential for decentralisation. Suggestions for how this could be addressed are detailed in the section on the "implemented" curriculum below.

School-to-work transitions

The "[p]roduction and development of high-quality manpower endowed with knowledge, skills and competencies" is one of the proposals for action described in the Second Decade of Educational Reform in Thailand (OEC, 2009). However, the 2008 curriculum does not mention the importance of learners' key competencies to the workplace. Its descriptions of the competencies do not mention how they might apply to situations in students' future careers. It also fails to distinguish between generic competencies, like the competencies that are important in the 21st century, and the occupation- or work-related competencies that are frequently used by industry. The curriculum should clearly articulate the context in which the term "competency" is being used.

In addition, the curriculum contains very few direct references to vocational skills. Although there is a vocational pathway after Grade 9 (M3), it was reported to the team that this option is viewed as being of lower status than the academic pathway. In any event, the goal should be to provide all students, regardless of the chosen upper secondary school pathway, with the knowledge, skills and understanding needed to support their school-to-work transition.

The curriculum lacks examples about how the standards and other elements of content can be contextualised to the workplace. Such examples would encourage teachers to demonstrate how knowledge, skills and attitudes can be developed in a simulated workplace-related situation. Among the curriculum's 67 content standards, only one is devoted to occupation-related learning within the Occupations and Technology learning area:

Strand 4: Occupations

Standard OT4.1: Understanding and acquiring the necessary skills and experiences; proper perception of future career; the technological application for occupational development; possessing morality and favourable attitude towards careers (OBEC, 2008).

At the upper secondary level, where significant attention would presumably be devoted to preparation for post-school pathways such as employment, the indicators that elaborate this standard are expressed at a very low level, with verbs such as "discuss", "choose", "have (experiences...)" and "have (the desired characteristics...)".

The 2008 curriculum could be better aligned to the important government priority of producing high-quality manpower by:

- providing a rationale for including learners' key competencies in the curriculum, making specific reference to their applicability in the contemporary workplace

- strengthening the occupations and technology learning area

- including a reference to employment and the world of work in the rationale for every learning area

- developing new subjects or learning areas, such as "business studies" or "work studies", particularly in the upper secondary curriculum, with equal status in terms of time allocated.

These changes would increase alignment with the government's manpower policy, preparing Thais to participate in the "knowledge economy" and to benefit from future economic opportunities.[4]

ASEAN integration

The emergence of the ASEAN Economic Community creates a range of challenges and opportunities. One of the Ministry of Education's policy priorities is to prepare for ASEAN integration, establishing a link between Thailand's education system and its future economic, political and socio-cultural partnerships.

Despite this, the 2008 curriculum makes only one reference to ASEAN, in the history learning area (rather than, say, economics or geography) in the SO4.2 standard for the grade-level indicator for Grade 6 (P6): "Tell in brief the relationship of the ASEAN Group".

Standard SO4.2:

Understanding of the development of mankind from the past to the present; realising the importance of the relationships and the continuous changes of events, and ability to analyse their effects (OBEC, 2008).

There is anecdotal evidence that teachers understand the importance of this issue and that the government has promoted the agenda directly to schools. As a consequence many schools incorporate ASEAN issues in students' work and activities, however the expected learning about ASEAN in the current curriculum is clearly inadequate and out of date. It needs to be both broadened and deepened.

A revision of the curriculum is even more timely, given the publication of an extensive curriculum support document, the ASEAN Curriculum Sourcebook, in August 2012 (Box 3.5).

> **Box 3.5. ASEAN Curriculum Sourcebook**
>
> The ASEAN Curriculum Sourcebook (ASEAN, 2012) was developed jointly by the ASEAN Secretariat, the Southeast Asian Ministers of Education Organization (SEAMEO), and ASEAN member states, including Thailand, with funding provided by USAID. The sourcebook is a resource guide for teachers at the basic and upper secondary education level. It covers five themes:
>
> 1. knowing ASEAN (e.g. the structure, membership, purpose, accomplishments and future challenges)
> 2. valuing identity and diversity
> 3. connecting global and local
> 4. promoting equity and justice
> 5. working together for a sustainable future
>
> In July 2012, all ASEAN member states agreed to launch the sourcebook according to their context and readiness. In Thailand, OBEC published a pamphlet that related the five themes in the sourcebook to 21st century skills acquisition and encouraged schools to establish working committees to plan and develop units, lesson plans, learning activities, and other projects (such as assemblies or excursions) that cover the sourcebook's contents.
>
> *Sources*: ASEAN (2012) *ASEAN Curriculum Sourcebook*, http://library.stou.ac.th/sites/default/files/ASEAN_Curriculum_Sourcebook.pdf; OBEC (2012), *ASEAN Curriculum Sourcebook*, http://academic.obec.go.th/web/doc/d/1235.

Conserving Thai culture and tradition

Of the four policy objectives considered in this section, the 2008 curriculum addresses "Thai-ness" most comprehensively. The first principle underpinning the curriculum states: "The ultimate aim is attainment of national unity; learning standards and goals are therefore set with a view to enabling the children and youths to acquire knowledge, skills, attitudes and morality to serve as a foundation for Thai-ness and universal values" (OBEC, 2008: p. 4). Similarly, Goal 5 in the curriculum is "Awareness of the need to preserve all aspects of Thai culture and Thai wisdom" (OBEC, 2008: p. 5).

These statements are reinforced in various parts of the curriculum, including in the Thai language Strand 4, "... preservation of Thai language as a national treasure", and various strands within the social studies, religion and culture, health and physical education and arts learning area. It could therefore be argued that there is a high degree of alignment between this government policy and the 2008 curriculum. However, it could also be claimed that, given the emergence of strong, intra-regional (ASEAN) influences, teachers need to balance the emphasis on "Thai-ness" with the need to create global citizens and the curriculum should provide teachers with guidance on achieving this balance.

Recommendations

The review team recommends that Thailand:

1. Resume the process of curriculum reform as soon as possible based on a comprehensive evaluation of the 2008 curriculum.

In an era of rapid and multi-faceted global change, it is very important that all countries keep their curricula as up-to-date as possible. It is therefore common for curriculum authorities to view curriculum development as part of a continuous cycle through which curriculum or particular facets of curriculum are monitored and, if necessary, improved. The curriculum review cycle can be defined as:

> A systematic approach to evaluating, reviewing and revising curricular areas and programmes within a specific timeframe which aims to identify gaps and weaknesses with a view to increasing curriculum effectiveness and continually improving student learning experiences. Normally it involves several phases including: research and selection; revision and development; implementation; and evaluation and monitoring. (UNESCO-IBE, 2013)

It is regrettable that the review cycle in Thailand appears to have stalled, and that no progress has been made towards a revised curriculum in recent years. It is important that Thailand resumes the cycle in order to ensure that the curriculum is contemporary, of high quality and supports overall education priorities, and that all stakeholders have confidence in the process and its management. Confidence and credibility remain at serious risk as long as there is a high level of uncertainty about the process. It is therefore critical for Thailand to reinitiate a systematic, evidence-based curriculum review and reform so its curriculum can contribute effectively to its education goals and regional and global competitiveness.

The government should investigate ways to restart and accelerate the process to avoid the kind of interruptions that have occurred in the past (see also recommendations related to Policy Issue 4).

2. **Revise the written (or intended) curriculum to:**

- **provide clearer direction and advice to teachers about their responsibilities in a standards-based curriculum context**
- **provide a sound and clearly expressed philosophy and theory of learning**
- **place increased and more consistent emphasis on the development of key competencies for the 21st century.**

While considerable progress has been made in the transition from a content-based curriculum to a standards-based one, a number of challenges remain. The most urgent of these is the need for clear advice to teachers, a sound philosophy and theory of learning, and increased emphasis on competency development.

Policy Issue 2: Education staff need more training and support to implement the standards-based curriculum

The implemented curriculum – the curriculum as it is interpreted and applied by principals and teachers – includes the planning and delivery of programmes, lessons and classroom activities to facilitate learning effectively. A standards-based curriculum allows educators greater autonomy in implementation, but places significant demands on them. In Thailand, there are indications that teachers and principals have found the implementation of the curriculum confusing and challenging, leading to inconsistencies in teaching and learning across the education system and pointing to the need for greater support.

Implementation responsibilities and challenges

In Thailand, the shift from a content-based curriculum to a standards-based one transferred very significant implementation responsibilities to school staff. With a standards-based curriculum, teachers are in effect responsible for determining how students achieve the standards. At a minimum, they must therefore:

- understand the standards well
- be able to develop programmes, learning plans and lessons that enable students to achieve these standards

- be familiar with and use a range of teaching strategies consistent with the intended curriculum
- be familiar with, have access to, and be able to use a range of resources to enhance learning
- be able to judge how well students have achieved the standards.

Given the amount of instructional time now determined by schools, principals and teachers must:

- be familiar with the exact requirements and intent of the intended curriculum
- be able to evaluate the needs of students so that the school-based curriculum they develop targets needs and provides enhanced learning opportunities
- be able to design and develop appropriate courses and activities that are purposeful and well sequenced
- evaluate the products which they develop in a structured and systematic way.

Research on the past curriculum reform and recent discussions with stakeholders in Thailand reveal a number of curriculum implementation challenges (OBEC, 2008). There was widespread confusion among teachers about how to implement the 2001 curriculum. This situation must inevitably have compromised the quality of student learning, and to some extent would have undermined confidence across the system. It is also highly likely that the students most affected were those in isolated and poorly resourced schools.

Gaps in key areas in the 2008 curriculum are likely to be continuing to cause some confusion. For example, the absence of an articulated theory underpinning the curriculum means that teachers must develop programmes and lesson plans based on their own experiences, their own professional reading and their intuitions. This is likely to have led to a varied approach to pedagogy across Thailand, and to a very inconsistently implemented curriculum.

A number of teachers told the review team that they did not understand their responsibilities as curriculum developers and designers. They reported feeling confined by the standards to plan and teach in a methodical way to ensure they covered all of them. Related to this, stakeholders reported that the dominant teaching style in Thailand continues to be very conservative and focused primarily on the transfer of knowledge, frequently to the exclusion of the development of students' real-life skills, appropriate values and useful competencies. Some expressed the opinion that the main obstacles to quality education lie in teaching practices rather than in the content that is taught.

Enabling and supporting implementation

Thailand's shift in curriculum paradigm continues to have significant implications for the entire education system. Implementing a standards-based curriculum means creating the conditions to enable the new paradigm to be understood by all actors. Teachers and principals, in particular, need to feel confident and empowered to implement the curriculum. However, the Office for National Education Standards and Quality Assessment (ONESQA), which inspects schools, the National Institute of Educational Testing Service (NIETS) and pre-service programme providers also need to understand the new curriculum.

Preparation, support and continuing professional learning

It is doubtful that teachers and principals have the capacity to effectively implement a standards-based curriculum that is consistent and systematically assessed across the country. They would need a large and targeted investment in their preparation and continuing professional development to ensure they understand the new curriculum and appreciate their responsibilities in delivering it (see Box 3.6 below). While principals in Thailand appear to be familiar with the notion of the school-based curriculum and know that they must develop programmes and activities to fill in the time available, no evidence was presented that this is being done in a consistent and professional way. Principals would particularly benefit from guidelines and continuing professional development to support the delivery of high-quality and targeted courses and activities. Teachers would benefit from targeted training devoted to content selection, sequencing, instructional design, assessment strategies and techniques, and the development of effective learning environments.

Consultations, interviews and discussions during the review mission found no sign that this enabling context has been achieved. The review team saw no evidence of strategies to support teachers and principals in their responsibilities as curriculum developers and designers. It thus seems reasonable to conclude that the implemented curriculum is of inconsistent quality due to, among other things, teachers and principals not being confident and effective in their implementation roles.

Learning materials

To support implementation, it is important that the education system assure the quality of the curriculum products being developed at the school level (for example by providing programme templates or course approval processes). In particular, learning materials should focus on the standards (rather than the indicators), and should provide teachers with a range of activities and approaches on which they can base their pedagogical decisions. In other words, they should reflect the spirit of a standards-based curriculum, rather than present teachers with a single approach to achieving the standards. Existing textbooks would in most cases need to be reviewed to ensure that their contents and approaches are aligned or mapped in some meaningful and helpful way to the standards.

Monitoring and data gathering

Other enablers of effective curriculum implementation in Thailand include the individuals who monitor schools: the ONESQA inspectors, as well as regional and district education officers (see Chapters 4 and 5 for further information and recommendations relating to school inspections).

It is not known whether the halted 2011 curriculum review had begun to gather information about whether the release of the 2008 curriculum had addressed the confusion, poor-quality teaching and learning, and inequality across schools that followed the implementation of the 2001 curriculum. Such research, along with a review to determine how well teachers understand the current intended curriculum, would allow Thailand to make evidence-based decisions about future curriculum reforms.

Recommendation

The review team recommends that Thailand:

- **Communicate the nature of the standards-based curriculum and support its implementation across the education system in a targeted and systematic way in order to create a true enabling environment for its use.**

Full commitment to the standards-based curriculum will be critical if Thailand is to create a truly enabling environment for its implementation in schools. Everyone in the education system with curriculum-related responsibilities (including initial teacher education, continuing professional development, school inspection and textbook development) needs to understand the curriculum paradigm and concentrate their efforts towards its successful implementation. Teachers and principals must have greater and more targeted support in order to gain the knowledge, skills and confidence they need to fully implement the intended curriculum. All of the curriculum support and related activities, including professional development programmes, development of learning media, assessment methodologies (see Chapter 4) and related training, should be consistently focused on creating the enabling environment to improve the quality of teaching and learning and increase confidence in the education system. Data gathering should also be used to enable the development of evidence-based revisions to the curriculum, as part of the curriculum review recommended in the preceding section.

This aligns with the recommendations in Chapter 5 that Thailand add training in the curriculum as a pre-service programme requirement and establish a nationwide professional development strategy to support the country's education reforms. For example, Hong Kong, China introduced a Continuing Professional Development Framework to support the implementation of a new curriculum, as well as related assessment procedures (Box 3.6; see also Box 4.2 in Chapter 4).

Box 3.6. Professional development in Hong Kong, China

One jurisdiction that has introduced professional development practices to support capacity building in the face of a new curriculum and system-wide education reform is Hong Kong, China. Since the reform began in 1999, the Hong Kong Education Bureau has introduced the following:

- a Continuing Professional Development Framework designed strategically to provide training to educational personnel before each new reform is introduced in schools
- the publication of professional development activities four months before the start of the school year to give schools enough time to plan their participation in advance
- a Curriculum Development Institute to provide professional development specifically focused on implementing new curriculum and assessment mechanisms
- collaborative in-school support, provided by Education Bureau staff, to assist individual schools with delivery of the new curriculum, including group lesson planning, research and development, seminars and workshops
- altered teaching and working time to allow for increased mentoring, collaboration and classroom observation.

Source: Jensen et al. (2012), Catching Up: Learning from the Best School Systems in East Asia, https://grattan.edu.au/report/catching-up-learning-from-the-best-school-systems-in-east-asia/.

Policy Issue 3: Thailand has limited capacity to assess how well the curriculum has delivered its intended outcomes

It is crucial for any education system to have valid and reliable information to assess whether students are learning successfully (the achieved curriculum). Internationally, it is becoming increasingly common for common national curricula to describe clear student performance standards at different stages of the learning process, and to use these standards as the basis for different types of assessment (Box 3.7).

This alignment allows for consistent assessment across the education system, yielding data that can then be used to compare regional and school results and inform the development of policies, programmes, curriculum changes and teaching strategies to support improvements locally and nationally. It also ensures that school- and classroom-based assessments are designed in ways that encourage students to aspire to equally high standards across all schools. Thailand's current curriculum provides some guidance to teachers about their assessment responsibilities (OBEC, 2008). However, it does not otherwise support alignment or provide clear direction about assessment.

The "criteria for learning assessment" in the 2008 curriculum document are not clear and do not effectively support assessments conducted by individual schools and teachers. They refer to learners being assessed "on all indicators and pass all criteria prescribed by the educational institutions". The reference to students needing to "pass all criteria" seems completely inconsistent with the philosophy of criterion-referenced assessment, in which students demonstrate their achievement on a continuum, rather than complying with some notion of passing or failing. In addition, the criterion that is mentioned first, at both primary and secondary levels, relates to attendance, stating that "Learners must have an attendance record of not less than 80%". In other words, the criterion is about amount of instructional time, not about the effectiveness of the learning.

Most significantly, the absence of common student performance standards in the curriculum has resulted in a lack of consistency in assessment across the education system. As mentioned above, content standards are determined nationally (through the Curriculum Standards in the Basic Education Curriculum), but performance standards (or "indicators" and "criteria") are the responsibility of individual schools. The "criteria for learning assessment" section of the curriculum requires that teachers "base their judgement on learners' individual development". While it is not clear what this means precisely, it would seem that teachers are to pay no attention to broader norms of student achievement as determined by larger cohorts across the region or country. This means that what is considered to be a satisfactory standard of achievement in one school may be unsatisfactory in another school or more than satisfactory in still another, resulting in highly unequal expectations for students. Thus, although curriculum content is standardised across the country, judgements about how well students have achieved learning outcomes are not. This is a significant concern, particularly given that Thailand currently makes comparisons across students and schools, and teachers are expected to act on these comparisons without the necessary guidance (see Chapter 4 for more detail about this issue).

The lack of system-wide student performance standards and the confusing and inconsistent criteria for learning assessment have significant implications regarding how well the system can ensure that:

- the implemented curriculum follows the intended curriculum

- assessments conducted at each systemic level reflect the intended curriculum, including assessing the full range of outcomes (notably, competencies)

- the policy requirements related to assessment contained in the intended curriculum are being implemented consistently across the country

- the assessment regime in place in Thailand generates data about student achievement that is comprehensive and reliable, and can accurately inform curriculum-related policy decisions.

As described more fully in Chapter 4, stakeholders reported to the review team that assessment policy and practice in Thailand still focus on traditional learning outcomes related to knowledge and information retention and repetition. It is critical that assessments not be confined to the measurement of these knowledge outcomes alone. Common student performance standards, and related indicators and criteria, should be used to support assessment methods that, instead, measure skills and knowledge application and a full range of outcomes, notably competencies for the 21st century.

Box 3.7. Student performance standards and supports for assessment in New Zealand

Performance standards for student assessment may relate to a country's education reform priorities and the acquisition of 21st century competencies, as well as other specific student learning objectives.

In New Zealand, schools make most decisions about what is taught to students. These decisions are based on the common New Zealand Curriculum and national standards of expected student performance in reading, writing and mathematics in years 1 to 8. Teachers are responsible for choosing the appropriate assessment methods and using their professional or overall teacher judgment (OTJ) to determine whether the standards have been met.

To support teachers with these responsibilities and reduce the possibility that they will misinterpret the standards, each national standard includes a description of what is required to meet the standard at different grade levels and exemplars illustrating what this looks like in practice. This is supplemented by a range of online resource material and tools (such as a glossary of curriculum terminology and Literacy Learning Progressions, which describe the knowledge, skills and attitudes students draw upon to read and write at different levels of the curriculum).

For example, the description of the writing standard at one grade level is: "By the end of Year 5, students are required to create a variety of texts in order to think about, record, and communicate experiences, ideas, and information across the curriculum. To meet the standard, students draw on the knowledge, skills, and attitudes for writing described in the Literacy Learning Progressions for students at this level".

The exemplars for this description include writing samples showing how students are demonstrating the quality required to meet the standard. Other supports provided to teachers to ensure strong competencies in assessment and an understanding of the national standards include mentoring and induction for new teachers and continuing professional development programmes.

Sources: OECD (2013), *Synergies for Better Learning: An International Perspective on Evaluation and Assessment*, http://dx.doi.org/10.1787/9789264190658-en; Chamberlain (2010), "Blueprint for National Standards", www.edgazette.govt.nz/Articles/Article.aspx?ArticleId=8187; New Zealand Ministry of Education (2010), "National Standards", http://nzcurriculum.tki.org.nz/National-Standards.

Recommendation

The review team recommends that Thailand:

- **Develop common student performance standards to guide assessments at all levels of the education system.**

This work should be undertaken as part of a resumed curriculum reform process, as recommended above, and would inform broader efforts to revise assessment policies and practices in Thailand, as recommended in Chapter 4.

Adopting common student performance standards would provide Thailand with a national framework for the development of appropriate assessment strategies and would allow policy makers and educators to reliably compare student achievement within or between classes, schools and regions. The standards would also guide teachers preparing effective learning programmes and lessons to improve student achievement.

Student performance standards should support the country's education reform priorities and the acquisition of 21st century competencies, and outline the expected outcomes for each defined level of performance across the various elements of the curriculum. They should also support a movement away from assessments of traditional learning outcomes related to knowledge and information retention and repetition.

While inconsistencies in assessment practice are at the core of this issue, the reason many students fail to make satisfactory progress is also closely related to principals' and teachers' understanding of and capacity to implement a standards-based curriculum (as discussed above). Preparation, continuing professional development and support focused on assessment, as well as other aspects of curriculum implementation, are essential.

Policy Issue 4: Thailand's curriculum review processes need to be put into practice

The quality of the curriculum in any country depends to some extent on the quality of processes employed to produce it. It is therefore important that Thailand carefully plans and implements the process of evaluating the current curriculum and developing a new one. Thailand appears to have a very robust, systematic process of curriculum evaluation and development, as illustrated in Figure 3.3. However, the review team was not able to make evidence-based judgments about how, and how well, these processes are implemented.

Figure 3.3. Roadmap for curriculum development

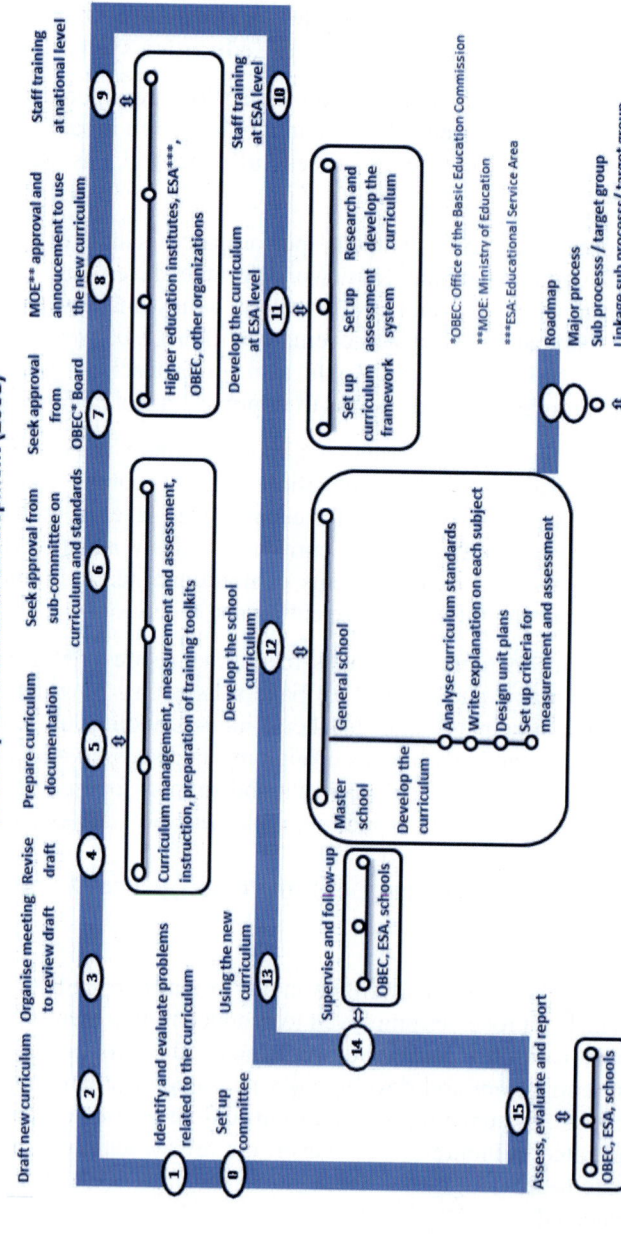

Source: OBEC (2015), "Basic Education Reform", Office of the Basic Education Commission, Bangkok.

While Thailand's curriculum review cycle process appears to be well documented, it could consider a number of improvements. One such improvement is the timing and extent of consultations with stakeholders. The review team heard that consultations consist of a national public forum to consider and respond to an advanced draft of the curriculum. This approach excludes stakeholder consultation during the development of the draft itself.

Some stakeholders reported to the review team that curriculum processes in Thailand are not consultative enough and that, in particular, teachers are not well informed about planned changes to the curriculum, why they have been considered and what the impact on the role of teachers will be. Stakeholders also reported that employers are not necessarily consulted in a systematic way. Overall, there was a lack of clarity regarding which stakeholders were or should be consulted.

The International Bureau of Education (IBE) advocates that, at a minimum, a wide range of stakeholder groups be consulted and listened to during curriculum processes. These groups and the rationale for their involvement are summarised in Table 3.1 (UNESCO-IBE, 2016).

Table 3.1. Stakeholders in the curriculum development process

Curriculum is important to …	Because they have a right to …
Students and their families	… a curriculum that will provide them with life opportunities.
Teachers	… contribute to a process in which they are among the acknowledged experts, and to know what is expected of them and their students.
Employers	… know that students are being prepared to enter the world of work.
Tertiary education institutions	… know that students are well prepared for post-school study.
Communities	… know that students will be aware of their social and community responsibilities.
Governments	… know that schools are contributing to the development of a national consensus on economic, political and social goals such as equity, inclusion and sustainable development.

Source: UNESCO-IBE (2016), *What Makes a Quality Curriculum?*, UNESCO International Bureau of Education, Geneva, www.ibe.unesco.org/en/document/what-makes-quality-curriculum.

No information was provided to the review team about the evaluation of the 2008 curriculum, although it is understood that plans for a revision of the curriculum were well advanced in 2011 before it was postponed. It is unclear whether appropriate consultations were held to help determine the aims, objectives, structure and contents of the new curriculum.

Research recommends that curriculum processes be:

- **Planned and systematic:** the development of curriculum should follow a transparent and public process and be well managed in terms of focusing on the curriculum vision, conducting effective development activities and adhering to timelines and budgets.

- **Inclusive and consultative:** curriculum documents should reflect broad social values and aspirations. A range of groups have a legitimate interest in these documents and therefore should have a voice in their development; curriculum documents should not be developed by education experts "behind closed doors". Good-quality curriculum development processes not only acknowledge legitimate stakeholder interests, but also seek their insights in an open-minded manner and a spirit of plurality. This is particularly important to ensure that the principles of equity underpin the curriculum.

- **Led by curriculum professionals:** curriculum development is a specialist field within education, and so the process should be led and managed by qualified and experienced professionals (Box 3.8).

- **Cyclical in nature:** good quality curriculum development is an ongoing and continuous process, not least because curricula constantly need to respond to change. Curricula need to keep pace with a world in which knowledge is rapidly expanding, communication technologies are broadening access to information, and, as a result, the skills needed by students are constantly changing or emerging. A well-planned and systematic curriculum development process should therefore be conceived as a dynamic cycle of development, implementation and evaluation, which leads to and informs the next cycle.

- **Sustainable:** because of the dynamic nature of curriculum development, education systems should ensure that they provide the leadership, resources and expertise to ensure that the curriculum can be regularly evaluated and improved (UNESCO-IBE, 2016).

Regular curriculum evaluation processes should be conducted by suitably qualified and experienced people in a systematic and planned way:

- based on a clear purpose and scope
- using valid and reliable data
- within a clear quality framework (UNESCO-IBE, 2016).

> **Box 3.8. International examples of curriculum development bodies**
>
> Internationally, curriculum development is commonly the responsibility of government departments or autonomous agencies that are accountable to the government. In both cases, stakeholder involvement is a crucial element of the development process. In most OECD countries, education experts tend to contribute to the curriculum development, while teachers, principals, parents and other community representatives play a consultative role.
>
> In Singapore's small, highly centralised education system, the Ministry of Education's Curriculum Planning and Development Division is responsible for designing curricula, as well as developing teaching approaches and assessment strategies, and instructional resources to support curriculum implementation. In Korea, the Ministry of Education, Science and Technology is responsible for developing a national curriculum framework and revising it every five to ten years. However, a major overhaul of the curriculum in the 1990s was conducted by an arm's length body: the Korean Educational Development Institute.
>
> The Curriculum Development Council (CDC) of Hong Kong, China is a freestanding advisory body appointed by the government to develop curriculum and also work with the territory's student Examinations and Assessment Authority (HKEAA). It consists of:
>
> - A council of approximately 25 members, including teachers, principals, parents, quality assurance inspectors, and representatives of the HKEAA, universities and businesses.
>
> - Five functional committees, dealing with topics like gifted education and special education needs.
>
> - Nine key learning area committees, one for each area (such as Chinese language or mathematics).
>
> - Joint CDC-HKEAA committees for each key learning area.
>
> The Australian Curriculum Assessment and Reporting Authority and the Board of Studies, Teaching and Educational Standards in the Australian state of New South Wales are autonomous advisory bodies that bring together stakeholders to develop both curriculum and national or state-wide student assessments.
>
> *Sources*: ACARA (2013b), "About us", www.acara.edu.au/about-us; BOSTES (2015), "About BOSTES", www.boardofstudies.nsw.edu.au/about/; Curriculum Development Council (2015), "Background", http://cd1.edb.hkedcity.net/cd/cdc/en/page01.htm; Kärkkäinen (2012), "Bringing about curriculum innovations: Implicit approaches in the OECD area", http://dx.doi.org/10.1787/5k95qw8xzl8s-en; NCEE (2015), *Instructional Systems: South Korea*, www.ncee.org/programs-affiliates/center-on-international-education-benchmarking/top-performing-countries/south-korea-overview/south-korea-instructional-systems/; Singapore Ministry of Education (2016), "Curriculum planning and development", www.moe.gov.sg/about/org-structure/cpdd/.

Recommendations

The review team recommends that Thailand:

- **Establish effective, efficient and transparent curriculum review and revision processes as a key strategy within the education reform agenda.**

As in any country, the quality of Thailand's curriculum will be influenced by the processes by which it is developed. It is not sufficient for the education reform agenda to focus on the end product only. The way in which the curriculum is reviewed and revised also needs to be addressed.

Internationally, a variety of different bodies, both within and outside government, can be responsible for curriculum development (Box 3.8). Given the already institutionally complex nature of Thailand's education system, it may not be advisable for it to establish a new curriculum development agency separate from government at this time. However, to assure educational quality, Thailand should ensure that curriculum development is in the hands of experienced professionals who understand the nature of both curriculum processes and curriculum products and who are highly respected and credible. These professionals should be accountable to the government (through the appropriate minister), but free from direct political influence. They should work in consultation with the NIETS to align the curriculum and assessment, notably through the establishment of common student performance standards. Stakeholders need to be engaged in meaningful ways throughout the process to enrich the finished product.

- **Optimise opportunities for consultation with all stakeholders, in the interests of equity and transparency.**

In particular, the timing and nature of stakeholder inputs should be reviewed, and more intensive and more frequent consultations should be conducted early in the curriculum development process. These consultations should be conducted in good faith, based on the view that, although every stakeholder opinion cannot be accepted, they can all be valued. Comprehensive stakeholder consultations would help to ensure that:

- the curriculum reflects both government priorities and the competencies employers value
- teachers understand the rationale for, and the nature of, the curriculum reforms
- regional and district education officers who monitor the curriculum are equipped to accurately evaluate its implementation.

The ultimate aim of these consultations is to enrich the curriculum and to ensure that it is inclusive.

Conclusion

This chapter has provided an overview of the basic education curriculum in Thailand, defining the curriculum in broad terms to encompass the written or intended curriculum (what the education system intends students to learn); the implemented curriculum (as it is interpreted and applied by teachers in their classrooms); the achieved curriculum (the extent to which the curriculum delivers the outcomes sought); and the processes for reviewing and revising the curriculum.

Thailand's decision in 2001 to move away from a traditional content-based curriculum to a standards-based one was a necessary and laudable one. In making this change, Thailand moved to a flexible national curriculum with, at least in theory, a high degree of local input and greater flexibility. This transformation was an important achievement that should not be underestimated but significant issues remain, particularly with the implementation of the curriculum and the resulting lack of progress in student performance. In developing policies to address these issues, it is critical that Thailand gathers solid evidence about where problems are occurring in translating curriculum intentions into high-quality learning.

Of the recommendations proposed in this chapter, Thailand should first implement a thorough and consultative curriculum review and revision process. This should involve the development of common student performance standards to improve teaching and learning in the country. This process would serve as a key driver for reform in other areas, including student assessment, teacher and school leader policies and the use of ICT. It would also have broad implications for the future of education in Thailand, providing the country with an opportunity to consider what students should learn as part of a new long-term vision for education to support social and economic development.

Notes

1. The original data and reports on which these statements were based were not examined by the review team. As a result, specific examples of "issues of learners' quality" encountered during the implementation of the 2001 Curriculum are not known but it is clear that significant problems were identified.

2. Australia's new national curriculum provides an example of this type of mapping at www.australiancurriculum.edu.au/generalcapabilities/overview/general-capabilities-in-the-australian-curriculum.

3. It is not clear in this context whose readiness is being referred to: the readiness of schools to deliver and implement particular content, or the readiness of students to learn particular content.

4. In 2015, Thailand reportedly began to revise the curriculum to better support school-to-work transitions, but the extent to which a comprehensive review agenda has been developed is unclear.

Bibliography

ACARA (2013a), "General Capabilities in the Australian Curriculum", Australian Curriculum, Assessment and Reporting Authority, www.australiancurriculum.edu.au/generalcapabilities/pdf/overview.

ACARA (2013b), "About us", Australian Curriculum, Assessment and Reporting Authority website, www.acara.edu.au/about-us.

Anderson, L. and D. Krathwohl (eds.) (2001), *A Taxonomy for Learning, Teaching, and Assessing: A Revision of Bloom's Taxonomy of Educational Objectives*, Longman, New York.

ASEAN (2012), *ASEAN Curriculum Sourcebook*, Association of Southeast Asian Nations, http://library.stou.ac.th/sites/default/files/ASEAN_Curriculum_Sourcebook.pdf.

BOSTES (2015), "About BOSTES", Board of Studies, Teaching and Educational Standards website, www.boardofstudies.nsw.edu.au/about/.

Chamberlain, M. (11 October 2010), "Blueprint for National Standards", *New Zealand Education Gazette*, New Zealand Ministry of Education, www.edgazette.govt.nz/Articles/Article.aspx?ArticleId=8187.

Curriculum Development Council (2015), "Background", Curriculum Development Council website, http://cd1.edb.hkedcity.net/cd/cdc/en/page01.htm.

Jensen, B., A. Hunter, J. Sonnemann and T. Burns (2012), *Catching Up: Learning from the Best School Systems in East Asia*, Grattan Institute, Carlton, Australia, http://grattan.edu.au/wp-content/uploads/2014/04/129_report_learning_from_the_best_main.pdf (accessed 23 January 2015).

Kärkkäinen, K. (2012), "Bringing about curriculum innovations: Implicit approaches in the OECD area", *OECD Education Working Papers*, No. 82, OECD Publishing, Paris, http://dx.doi.org/10.1787/5k95qw8xzl8s-en.

Magee, R. (2013), "2013 Thailand curriculum reform: FAQs", presented at the Centara Grand and Bangkok Convention Center, 25 June 2013.

NCEE (2015), "South Korea: Instructional systems", National Center on Education and the Economy website, www.ncee.org/programs-affiliates/center-on-international-education-benchmarking/top-performing-countries/south-korea-overview/south-korea-instructional-systems/.

New Zealand Ministry of Education (2010), "National Standards", Ministry of Education website, http://nzcurriculum.tki.org.nz/National-Standards.

OBEC (2015), "Basic Education Reform", Office of the Basic Education Commission, Bangkok.

OBEC (2012), "ASEAN Curriculum Sourcebook", Office of the Basic Education Curriculum, http://academic.obec.go.th/web/doc/d/1235.

OBEC (2008), "Basic Education Core Curriculum", B.E. 2551, Ministry of Education of Thailand, Bangkok.

OEC (2009), "Proposals for the Second Decade of Education Reform (2009-2018)", Office of the Education Council, Ministry of Education of Thailand, www.onec.go.th/onec_backoffice/uploads/Book/694-file.pdf.

OECD (2014), *PISA 2012 Results: What Students Know and Can Do (Volume I, Revised Edition, February 2014)*: *Student Performance in Mathematics, Reading and Science*, PISA, OECD Publishing, Paris, http://dx.doi.org/10.1787/9789264208780-en.

OECD (2013), *Synergies for Better Learning: An International Perspective on Evaluation and Assessment*, OECD Reviews of Evaluation and Assessment in Education, OECD Publishing, Paris, http://dx.doi.org/10.1787/9789264190658-en.

Singapore Ministry of Education (2016), "Curriculum planning and development", Ministry of Education website, www.moe.gov.sg/about/org-structure/cpdd/.

UNESCO-IBE, (2016), *What Makes a Quality Curriculum?*, UNESCO International Bureau of Education, Geneva, www.ibe.unesco.org/en/document/what-makes-quality-curriculum.

UNESCO-IBE, (2013), *Glossary of Curriculum Terminology*, UNESCO International Bureau of Education, Geneva, www.ibe.unesco.org/fileadmin/user_upload/Publications/IBE_GlossaryCurriculumTerminology2013_eng.pdf.

Annex 3.A1

Summary of the structure and contents of the Basic Education Core Curriculum (2008)

- A number of introductory parts which detail the background to the curriculum, the vision for the curriculum, the principles which underlie the curriculum and the goals of the curriculum.

- Five learners' key competencies which the curriculum aims to "inculcate" in all students.

- Eight desired characteristics which "enable learners to enjoy their lives as Thai citizens and global citizens".

- A summary of learning areas, strands and learning standards.

- Advisory sections on the following issues:

  - **learner development activities** (one component of a school-based curriculum)

  - **educational levels**, which describe primary, lower secondary and upper secondary levels of education

  - **learning time allotment**, which describes the methodology of allocating time to the various learning areas at each school level

  - learning time structure

  - **educational provision for special target groups**, which provides some guidance on addressing equity

  - **learning management**, which describes in brief the principles of learning on which the curriculum is based and the classroom processes which are consistent with these principles, as well as the roles of teachers and learners within the curriculum

  - **learning media**, which "serve as tools for promoting and supporting management of the learning process"

- **learning assessment** at classroom, school, local and national levels
- criteria for learning assessment
- documents showing evidence of education
- **transfer of learning outcomes**, which relates to students moving between schools or systems
- **curriculum implementation and management**, which describes the various roles of the education system and local level institutions and schools in curriculum development and implementation.

- A section devoted to each of the following eight learning areas which are to be studied by every student in grades P1 to M6:
  - Thai language
  - mathematics
  - science
  - social studies, religion and culture
  - health and physical education
  - art (including visual arts, music and dramatic arts)
  - occupations and technology
  - foreign languages.

- Each learning area section comprises:
  - rationale: why it is necessary to learn [learning area]
  - summary of content: what is learned in [learning area]
  - statement of "learners' quality" which appear to be student outcomes at the end of Grades 3, 6, 9 and 12
  - a number of "strands". The information provided for each strand consists of 1) standards and 2) grade-level indicators.

Chapter 4

Student assessment in Thailand

A well-balanced, high-quality student assessment framework yields data that can be used to improve the education system, inform teaching practices and help individual learners. This chapter describes Thailand's extensive national standardised testing regime as well as assessments at classroom, school and local level. It identifies three policy issues impeding the effective use of assessment to improve student outcomes and fairness: 1) weak assessment capacity right across the education system; 2) the validity and comparability of Thailand's national assessments; and 3) the narrow approach to assessment which fails to address the full range of the skills its students need.

It recommends Thailand build on its existing national assessment infrastructure to add rigour to its test development process and broaden its assessment mix, and build capacity to support the effective design and implementation of assessment procedures at all levels of the education system.

Introduction

When effectively linked to a well-designed and well-implemented curriculum, sound student assessment lies at the heart of any high-performing education system. A balanced system of assessment provides feedback to students on how well they are mastering a defined set of skills and knowledge, and points them to ways in which they can improve. A good system can let teachers know how well they and their students are doing, and help identify ways to better deliver and tailor instruction. It can tell parents and other caretakers how well students are performing, and enable them to better support children at home and in other settings outside of school. It can help administrators and education officials to understand the strengths and weaknesses of their schools and school systems, as well as in the performance of individual teachers – and to take actions that help build student success. It can inform policy makers about challenges in their education system, allowing them to develop policies that reinforce performance, and to situate these interventions in a broader policy context. And finally, a sound system of student assessment can ensure accountability to members of the general public, providing assurance that investments are being well spent and providing a sense of where, as concerned citizens, they may need to intervene.

A good assessment system serves not only to measure but also to improve students' acquisition of skills and knowledge. Given the deepening and broadening demands for skills that modern societies make on individuals, as well as the additional responsibility that has been vested in individual schools to monitor their own progress, it is not surprising that much attention has been paid in recent years to improving student assessment. The OECD recently directed a multi-year study, *Synergies for Better Learning*, which situates student assessment in the broader frame of evaluation and assessment within school systems (OECD, 2013a). Other studies have focused on assessment practices in specific regions, such as UNESCO's work on the Asia-Pacific (UNESCO, 2012a). Still others have focused on the more technical issues of assessment, such as the recently revised guidelines by the American Psychological Society, the American Educational Research Association and the National Council on Measurement in Education on standards for educational and psychological testing (AERA, APA and NCME, 2014). The latter is an important reference work for good assessment practice both in terms of technical quality and as regards fairness and ethical testing.

A variety of frameworks have been proposed to support the development of strong student assessment. One of the most useful and concise, published by the American Academy of Arts and Sciences (Braun et al., 2006), encourages the development of assessment systems that ensure:

- **clarity** of "the goals of education at each level, as well as the links between those goals and the relevant assessments, must be explicit, and [the] results must be meaningful to all interested parties"
- **coherence**: "assessments at different levels must articulate properly with each other"
- **consistency**: "the development, implementation, and evolution of the assessment system must be carried out over a substantial period of time".

Good assessment must be diversified (OECD, 2013a). An overall approach to student assessment needs to effectively combine summative assessment (which measures the level of student success or proficiency that has been obtained at the end of an instructional unit, comparing it to some standard or benchmark) with formative assessment (which is a lower-stakes assessment whose goal is to gather feedback that can be used by the instructor and the students to guide improvements in the ongoing teaching and learning process, and to modify and validate instruction). Additionally, good assessment needs to deploy a wide range of tools. Classical tests should themselves be varied in content, ranging from multiple-choice to more open-ended approaches. But other kinds of products, such as written essays or lab reports; other kinds of performance, such as role plays, experiments and presentations; and holistic tools such as student portfolios all have an important role to play in a robust student assessment system (OECD, 2013a). Increasingly, new technology can be used to enrich all these various forms of assessments.

Assessment also needs to be well balanced by level. Most student assessment will occur in the classroom and within the school. But external large-scale assessment has an important role to play – helping schools compare themselves to others, and informing administrators and policy makers about the overall state of schools, school districts and school systems. Such assessment can take two forms: 1) instruments that provide information but have low stakes for students even if they potentially have higher stakes for teachers and schools; and 2) examinations, which have higher stakes for students. The number of large-scale external assessments has been growing throughout the world at regional, national and international levels. As well as contributing to the accountability of education systems, research evidence shows that countries with external examinations tend to perform better than those without (Bishop, 1997, 2006; Luedemann, 2011; OECD, 2013a).[1]

The OECD/UNESCO review team has identified three broad priority action areas that Thailand might focus on to build an assessment system which supports strong student achievement:

- strengthening the capacity of actors throughout the education system to conduct and use high-quality, fair student assessments
- paying special attention to the quality (the validity, reliability and comparability over time) of measurement in the national external assessment system, as this measurement has major consequences for students, teachers and schools
- developing a more diverse range of assessments to measure the full range of skills students need.

This chapter provides an overview of current assessment policies and practices in Thailand, and then explores each of these three themes, paying special attention to measures to improve large-scale national assessments – an area where, in the opinion of the review team, Thailand faces particularly pressing challenges.

The Thai context

The current assessment framework

The 2008 Basic Education Core Curriculum outlines the framework principles behind the current student assessment system in Thailand, building on the broad expectations for student assessment laid out in the 1999 National Education Act B.E. 2542 (NEA). The 2008 curriculum identifies two overarching objectives for student assessment: helping learners develop their capacity and measuring their achievements. It points to four main levels of student assessment:

- classrooms, where teachers are to regularly and continuously measure and evaluate learners' performance
- schools, where annual - or semester-based assessment seeks to determine whether the education programme has enabled learners to reach learning goals, and to identify any gaps that need to be addressed
- the educational service area (ESA) or local level, which monitors student learning through instruments including standard examination papers and data obtained from schools
- the national level, where assessment of students in Grades 3, 6, 9 and 12 (P3, P6, M3 and M6) provides data to compare educational quality "at different levels". The results of national tests are meant to support planning efforts to raise education quality and inform policy making more broadly.

Overall responsibility for assessment in the public basic education system lies with the central commissions described in Chapter 1 of this report – primarily the Office of the Basic Education Commission (OBEC) and the Office of the Vocational Education Commission (OVEC).

Assessment at the classroom, school and local level

As described in Chapter 3, Thailand's current standards-based curriculum (the 2008 curriculum) requires schools to determine their own criteria for student learning assessment. Teachers are responsible for identifying, designing and employing assessment techniques in their classrooms, and using these for both formative and summative purposes. They do so with assistance from their schools, their local ESA, the central commissions and other agencies such as the Institute for the Promotion of Teaching Science and Technology (IPST). Reforms stemming from the 1999 NEA have emphasised implementing assessments that gauge student progress and achievement in a variety of ways. For instance, the central authorities have actively promoted portfolio-based assessment. However, the 2008 curriculum gives teachers only scant concrete guidance on how to assess students in ways that contribute to them achieving the curriculum's goals, and principals and teachers may not receive the training and support they need to use classroom assessment to better enable student learning (see Chapter 3 for more details).

The results of classroom and school-based assessment are reported up to the ESA and central levels. From our interviews in Thailand, the review team understands that the data are not analysed at regional or national levels, except on an ad hoc basis – for instance, Thailand compared school data to national assessment data soon after the Ordinary National Educational Test (O-NET) was introduced, in attempt to see whether the O-NET was generating scores that made sense compared to existing data.

Assessment at the national level

Thailand operates a large-scale national level assessment system. Created in 2005, the National Institute of Educational Testing Service (NIETS) is responsible for managing testing systems and methods, developing tools to measure and assess educational standards, and assessing educational management and national education tests. NIETS also provides assessment support to local and regional educational institutions and agencies, as well as to educators. NIETS assessments (Table 4.1) are administered to primary Grade 6 (P6) students, as well as to secondary school students in Grades 9 (M3) and 12 (M6) (NIETS, 2013). They are census-type tests, applied to the whole student cohort, not samples.

Table 4.1. National student assessments in Thailand

Test name		Target group	Content
Ordinary National Educational Test	O-NET	Students at the end of general primary, lower secondary and upper secondary levels (P6, M3 and M6).	Eight subject groups:* Thai language; social studies, religion and culture; foreign languages; mathematics; science; health and physical education; arts; and occupations and technology.
Vocational National Educational Test	V-NET	Students in 2nd or 3rd year of a vocational certificate course (M5/6).	- M5 level: Three subjects: fundamental abilities, learning abilities and occupational abilities - M6 level: Twelve possible subjects (depending on the area of specialisation): learning abilities, mechanics, construction, civil engineering, textiles, commercial studies, arts, fabrics and apparel, beauty, tourism, agriculture, and aquaculture.
Non-Formal National Educational Test	N-NET	Students in the final year of in non-formal education at secondary level.	Five learning areas: learning skills, basic knowledge, occupational skills, life skills and social development skills.
Islamic National Educational Test	I-NET	Students following the Islamic curriculum in the final year of study at primary, lower or upper secondary Islamic education level.	Eight subjects at each level: Al-Qur'an-explanations, words from the Prophet, principles of faith, religious commandments, Islamic history, Islamic ethics, Bahasa Melayu and Arabic.
Buddhism National Educational Test	B-NET	M3 and M6 students in general Buddhist scripture schools under the National Buddhism Office.	Three subjects: Buddhist history and disciplines, religious practices, and Pali.
General Aptitude Test / Professional and Academic Aptitude Test (since 2009)	GAT / PAT	Secondary school graduates wishing to be admitted to higher education within the national admissions system.	GAT: reading, writing, critical thinking, and English. PAT: Seven common subjects: Thai language, social studies, English, mathematics, chemistry, biology and physics.

Note: * For the 2015/16 school year, the number of subjects has been reduced to five, removing health and physical education, arts, and occupations and technology (NIETS, 2015a).
Source: NIETS (2015a), www.niets.or.th/en/catalog/view/2211.

NIETS does not develop the tests at Grade 3 (P3), which are also mandated by the 2008 curriculum. Rather, these fall under the responsibility of OBEC's Bureau of Educational Testing. The Grade 3 test focuses on skills in reading, writing and reasoning.

Of the tests administered by NIETS, the O-NET has by far the greatest significance for the Thai education systems. O-NET exams are administered to over 2 million students per year: approximately 800 000 Grade 6 (P6) students, 720 000 Grade 9 (M3) students and close to 450 000 Grade 12 (M6) students in 2014 (NIETS, 2015b). The O-NET accounts for roughly 80% of all students taking the NIETS "NET" assessments. In contrast, the vocational V-NET accounts for about 10% of assessments, the non-formal N-NET for roughly 8% (concentrated at the M6 level), the I-NET for around 3% and the B-NET for less than 0.5%.

The O-NET covers a broad range of content areas – as do the other "NET" tests, although this coverage varies by test (Table 4.2).

Table 4.2. Subjects tested in the Ordinary National Educational Test (O-NET), 2015

Subject	Content/areas of assessment
Thai language	Reading, writing, listening, observation, and speaking; principles of language application, literature, and literary outputs.
Mathematics	Numbers and numerical work, measurement, geometry, algebra, data analysis and probability, mathematic skills and procedures.
Science	Living beings and life processes, life and environment, properties of matter, force and mobility, energy, earth studies, astronomy and space, the nature of science and technology.
Social science, religion and culture	Religion, morality, and righteousness; civil responsibility, culture, and life in society; economics; history; geography.
Foreign languages	Language and communication; language and culture; the relationship between language and other subject groups; the relationship between language, community and work.

A large number of students who take the O-NET fail to obtain good scores, and results tend to vary substantially across geographical regions. For instance, at all three different grade levels in 2010, far fewer than half of all students scored above 50% in mathematics and science – indeed, at Grade 12 (M6) level, only around 5% of students did (World Bank, 2015). NIETS reports significant variation in O-NET scores year over year. This is a key issue which will be raised in a subsequent section of this chapter.

As is readily apparent, inconsistency affects some subject areas more than others. The scores of the Thai language test, for instance, show some variation between years but there are much more dramatic swings in mathematics and social science results (Figure 4.1). These likely reflect serious challenges facing the tests. There is also substantial variation in scores at the Grade 6 (P6) and Grade 9 (M3) levels from year to year (Figures 4.2 and 4.3).

Figure 4.1. Results from the Ordinary National Educational Test in %, Grade 12, 2008-14

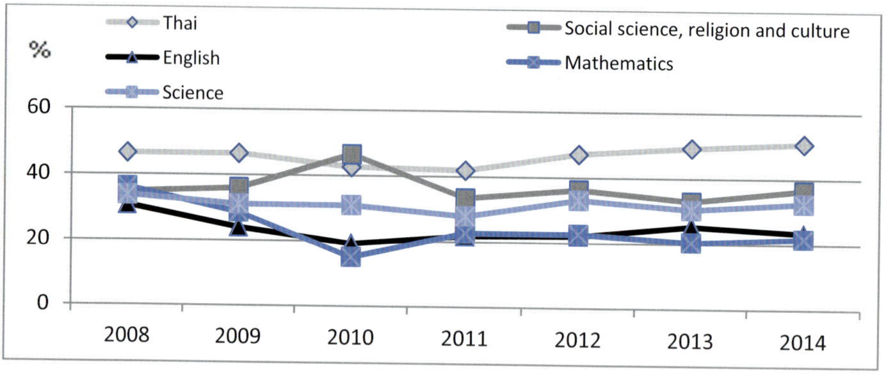

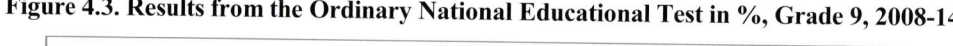

Source: NIETS (2015b), "Country report on National Educational Testing and Assessment: Thailand", Powerpoint presentation to the OECD/UNESCO Review Team, February 2015.

Figure 4.2. Results from the Ordinary National Educational Test in %, Grade 6, 2008-14

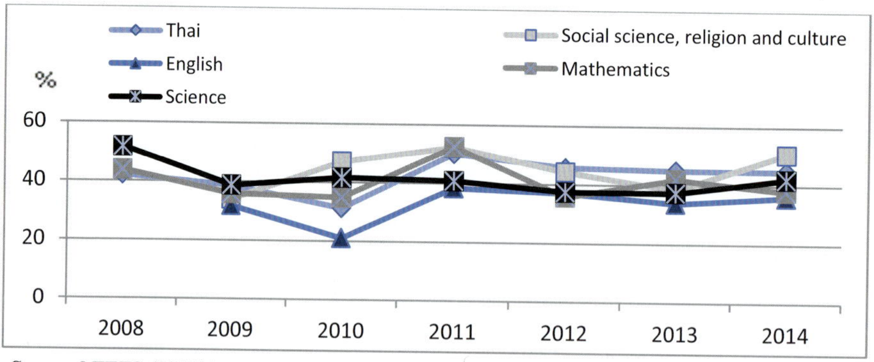

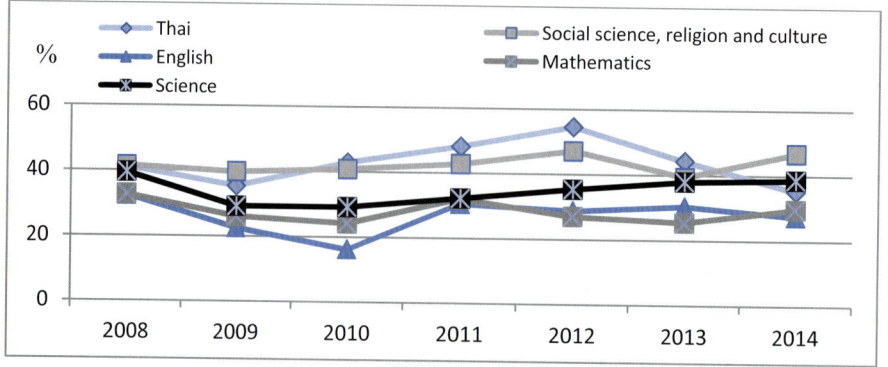

Source: NIETS (2015b).

Figure 4.3. Results from the Ordinary National Educational Test in %, Grade 9, 2008-14

Source: NIETS (2015b).

Apart from the "NET" test series, NIETS also administers the General Aptitude Test (GAT) and the Professional and Academic Aptitude Test (PAT) which also partly measure the outcomes of secondary education. They are used, alongside O-NET and local university tests, to determine students' aptitude to enter higher education. The GAT measures the ability to read, write and solve problems, as well as ability to communicate in English. The PAT is a suite of assessments which assess knowledge considered fundamental to study a specific subject at university. Each of these tests lasts three hours. In 2014, 340 000 students took either the GAT or the PAT assessments.

Uses of student assessment in Thailand

From a comparative international perspective, Thailand makes great use of its assessment data. The data are used to 1) inform decisions about student retention and promotion, and grouping of students for instructional purposes; 2) to compare individual schools against district or national performance, or against the performance of other schools; 3) to monitor schools' progress from year to year; 4) to make judgements about teachers' effectiveness; 5) and to identify aspect of the curriculum that could be improved. On the School Questionnaire for PISA 2012 (OECD, 2013b), Thai principals representing over three-quarters of the Thai school population answered reported using assessment results for 15-year-olds for each of these purposes. The average in OECD countries is nowhere near as consistent: for some purposes (e.g. grouping students, making judgments about teachers' effectiveness or comparing a given school with other schools), only about 50% of students in OECD countries are in schools where principals report using assessment data for these purposes.

In addition, nearly all Thai students are in schools whose principals report that student achievement data are tracked over time by an administrative authority, compared to an OECD average that is roughly 30 percentage points lower. This is consistent with practices in Thailand's nearest Asian neighbours who participate in the Programme for International Student Assessment (PISA), Viet Nam, Indonesia and Singapore; many Asian countries have traditionally made extensive use of national-level exams (UNESCO, 2012a). But practice in Thailand does not as closely reflect trends in other Asian countries such as the People's Republic of China, Japan and Korea. For instance, in Japan, it is uncommon to use assessment results to compare schools to each other, or to compare them to the national level performance.

O-NET's examination role has direct consequences for students. Unlike the other "NET" tests, O-NET informs decisions about whether students have successfully completed their programme up to Grades 6 (P6), 9 (M3) and 12 (M6) – and it also plays a role in university admission decisions (NIETS, 2015b). Initially, O-NET made up 20% of the exit decision at Grade 12 (i.e. the decision for high school completion and certification), but this rose to 30% in 2014, and it was reported to the OECD/UNESCO team that this may soon further rise to 50% (with the remainder of the decision being based on school assessment).

Aggregated national O-NET results are released publicly but more disaggregated levels get less wide release. ESA administrators receive the data (password protected) for schools and students in their area and individual schools receive data about their own school, but only aggregated data about other schools. Students may have access to their own results, but not to the results of other students. Parents can see their children's scores but do not have access to a written report on the results of their children's school. They may be briefed at annual meetings on their children's school's ONET results, although apparently not on the Grade 3 (P3) test results. Some schools that do particularly well, such as elite private schools in Bangkok, may seek to make their results more widely known: the team observed the school score level displayed prominently outside one school. Finally, some researchers in Thailand appear to be able to access data at the school level upon special request.

ESAs make use of O-NET data to compare the performance of schools in their area against the average of all schools in the country. For instance, one ESA administrator whom the team met demonstrated a colour-coding system, in which schools are assigned a green, yellow, blue or red coding depending on whether they score in the top, second, third or lowest quartile nationally for their student results. Such analysis is shared with schools, giving school administrators a sense of where their institution stands comparatively. It is used by ESAs working with schools to plan interventions to address gaps that show up at individual institutions, such as academic camps or tutoring programmes in areas of particular weakness. Students might also be given access to practice tests based on previous year's national assessments – for instance, using computerised interfaces. Schools and teachers have access to the results of their own students and can use these to design tailored interventions. While results from O-NET and other national assessments are not available as quickly as those from classroom summative or formative assessment, they can potentially be useful in addressing issues affecting the learning pathways of individual students. The OECD/UNESCO review team was not able to identify evidence about the extent and the effectiveness of interventions based on student (or school) scores on national assessments – although it has been suggested to us that when interventions are made, they may not be sustained over time.

Assessment data from NIETS also serves an evaluation purpose. The Office for National Education Standards and Quality Assessment (ONESQA) reviews all educational institutions in Thailand every five years (see Box 4.1). It uses a variety of criteria to determine whether an individual school meets minimum quality standards, but ONESQA informed the team that by far the most common reason why schools fail to meet the quality threshold is their low standardised test scores: about one-quarter of schools failed to pass the initial evaluation in the most recent review round. If these schools are subsequently able to demonstrate O-NET score improvements, though, this spares them from having to go through a full reassessment. O-NET scores are also used as part of teacher evaluations for career advancement (see Chapter 5).

At the national level, NIETS assessment data can play an important part in the policy process. Low scores, unevenly distributed scores, as well as perceived changes in scores over time, are all pieces of evidence that inform public policy discussion. NIETS data are also used in third-party research, such as that of the Quality Learning Foundation and the World Bank to enable independent checks on national performance and support deeper analysis of trends in learning outcomes.

O-NET tests have been the object of some criticism in recent years. The release of national level scores, coupled with comments made by students and other stakeholders on the Internet and on social media, has led to doubts with regard to the meaningfulness of some O-NET results. This issue – in addition to the concerns of some parents with whom the review team spoke – is further examined later in this chapter.

> **Box 4.1. External quality assurance of schools**
>
> Educational institutions' responsibility for assessment and evaluation is directly linked to Thailand's educational quality assurance system, which consists of both an internal and an external quality assurance programme. All affiliated agencies and schools are required to have an internal quality assurance system as part of a continual educational management process, and they must submit an annual report to the local education authority; local education authorities report up to the Ministry. As part of its external assessment system, in 2000 Thailand established a quality assessment process that falls under the responsibility of the Office for National Education Standards and Quality Assessment (ONESQA) (ONESQA, 2015).
>
> Although each educational establishment is responsible for the quality of the education outcomes of its students, quality assurance functions such as those of ONESQA respond to the need for the government to ensure the overall quality of education. This is achieved through monitoring the quality of learning outcomes and of the systems and processes that the educational institutions have in place to achieve those learning outcomes. Other countries that have institutions like ONESQA, such as the United Kingdom and New Zealand, offer particularly good examples of quality control in the educational process.

Assessment at the international level

While this is not required under the terms of the NEA, over recent decades, Thailand has actively participated in international educational assessment programmes such as PISA and the Trends in International Mathematics and Science Study (TIMSS). This makes a number of datasets on the performance of children aged 10 to 15 available. Given their scope, these international tests have their own particular requirements, characteristics and limitations. As sample-based tests, they cannot provide the same level of detail as NIETS assessments nor assess performance against national curriculum goals. They do, however, provide a good insight into the performance of the various cohorts and the evolution of performance in the country as a whole with respect to the knowledge and competencies they assess – especially in comparison to peer countries, as outlined in Chapter 2.

Policy Issue 1: Thailand needs to build assessment capacity right across its education system

Building capacity for an effective assessment system is a complex, resource-intensive endeavour. It requires a strong initial foundation, as well as regular efforts to maintain and improve the functioning of the system. The intensity of these demands lead to frequent gaps in assessment systems across the world. Even countries with very high-performing education systems can still lack technical expertise for the continuous assessment of learning. Systemic gaps affect assessment at the classroom level in particular, where teachers often lack the training and the tools to use assessment results to inform practice, but national assessment agencies also face challenges in areas such as human resources.

Thailand's assessment system has made strides forward in the last few decades. For instance, the design of the 2008 curriculum has the potential to facilitate assessment through its identification of key competency levels to be attained, although does not yet identify the relevant performance standards, as recommended in Chapter 3. The creation of NIETS in 2005 was also an important step forward. If fully implemented and adequately resourced, NIETS has potential to help develop and disseminate the information resources and practical expertise required for an effective system that covers all stages of assessment.

Despite these recent developments, the OECD/UNESCO review team has identified concerns about the capacity of Thailand's assessment system to deliver the results needed. These concerns are partly tied to the resources available for assessment, including for the interpretation of assessments. There are shortfalls at all key levels: in schools themselves, in agencies that support assessment and amongst the wider users of the assessment system (in particular teachers, principals and policy makers).

Teachers and schools

To improve education outcomes and increase the impact of assessment results, teachers and school leaders need both a theoretical and a practical understanding of the learning and assessment processes. Such an understanding empowers them to design and implement the right kinds of assessment activities and, in particular, to make full use of the information they collect to improve their teaching practice and tailor it to the needs of students. This in turn requires rigorous teacher training programmes, continued in-service training for all practitioners and other forms of ongoing support such as peer mentoring. Ongoing support builds teacher capacity to apply good practices in their classrooms under many different conditions, in ways that are adapted to the realities of their students, their school and their region.

Evidence presented to the review team suggests that these types of support are inadequate in Thailand, and that teachers do not always have the training they need. For instance, although the Teachers' Council of Thailand's list educational measurement and evaluation as one of the contents of pre-service programmes in their standards of knowledge, the Office of the Higher Education Commission makes no reference to assessment or evaluation in its outline of the skills and knowledge that student teachers are meant to acquire (Office of the Higher Education Commission, 2015). This suggests that training in assessment may not be receiving the full weight it needs. During a visit to the faculty of education at one of Thailand's many Rajabhat universities (regional universities that historically have a strong focus on teacher education and continue to account for a large share of pre-service teacher training), the review team was informed that students are required to take a single course in measurement and assessment, where they learn basic assessment techniques. The training programme provides only limited exposure to the kinds of statistical analysis good assessment procedures are built on, for instance.

The extent of ongoing support for teacher assessment is unclear. Different stakeholders reported varying kinds of support, including professional development activities provided by OBEC and ESAs, and targeted support from agencies such as the IPST and NIETS. For example, education councils and the IPST provide teachers with assessment guidebooks, and some teachers who receive formal training return to their schools as "master teachers" in the assessment area. On the other hand, the review team was told that teachers in Thailand wish to implement good formative assessment, but lack the necessary knowledge.

The review team lacks the information needed to make a final judgement about whether support for assessment is sufficient to maintain and further develop teachers' skills – the quality of the support, its availability and the extent to which it is used. However, general challenges around professional development identified in Chapter 5 suggest that such support is likely to be fragmented, disconnected from the classroom and of uneven quality across the country.

One study of how teachers are implementing portfolio assessment corroborates the view that there are gaps in Thailand's support for teachers' assessment (Tangdhanakanond and Wongwanich, 2012). Portfolio assessment was formally introduced after the passage of the NEA, supported by training sessions and a master teacher dissemination strategy. However initial studies found that teachers had not changed their assessment methods and a later study found that although teachers have positive views of portfolio assessment, they lacked the knowledge and skills needed to successfully implement it in each of its stages. This study concludes that education reform may have concentrated more on updating teaching methods than on providing teachers with a sound assessment toolkit).

Box 4.2. Hong Kong, China: Developing in-service teacher training to facilitate assessment for learning

In 1999 Hong Kong, China conducted a reform of its entire education system using a "whole-system implementation" approach. The overarching goal was to improve student learning; a significant component of the strategy consisted of changes to student assessment. These included the introduction of school-based assessment, and initiatives to help teachers identify how their students were learning and how to change their pedagogy where necessary. All this was coupled with the development of instruction and learning resources for teachers to help them implement assessment changes; these resources included practical examples that could help teachers' approaches in the classroom. New teacher professional development strategies and in-school support were also developed, enabling teachers to undertake professional development through a continuing professional development framework.

Source: Jensen et al. (2012), *Catching Up: Learning from the Best School Systems in East Asia*, http://grattan.edu.au/wp-content/uploads/2014/04/129_report_learning_from_the_best_main.pdf.

The team also heard concerns about how effectively schools and ESAs are making use of assessment data. For instance, in a discussion of the Grade 3 (P3) assessment with central education authorities, the review team inquired whether technical analysis of the assessment's results used item response theory (IRT; see Box 4.3). Despite its potential usefulness, the team was told that it is not used because local ESAs would have difficulty interpreting it. Later, during the team's visit to one ESA, it was reported that no effort has yet been made to perform a differential analysis comparing the results of different subgroups of students – although such analysis would be useful given that the ESA serves a large number of minority students. It was unclear whether this shortfall is linked more to a shortage of staff time or to gaps in technical expertise; it is likely to be a combination of both.

> **Box 4.3. Item response theory**
>
> Item response theory (IRT) is based on the assumption that the probability of a correct response to an item is based on both item and person parameters. IRT makes very clear that the reliability of a testing instrument is not the same for students at all levels of ability, and this in turn enables the determination of the optimal range for which the test is adequately calibrated. The use of IRT leads to a weighted score for the student which is a function of the pattern of responses and the different parameters associated with the items which have been correctly answered. This model puts items and students on the same scale: it determines the ability necessary to respond correctly to an item, and at the same time determines the probability of responding to an item if the ability level is known. These parameters are not norm-referenced as in classical testing theory, but rather are independent of the specific items and/or group of students being tested. This major advantage gives great flexibility to testing, because different students from the same population can be tested with calibrated items from an item bank, and all results are comparable and in the same scale (Hambleton, Swaminathan and Rogers, 1991).

Agencies supporting assessment

Central support is a key component of any effective student assessment system: it provides economies of scale and scope that help manage the cost and complexity of high-quality assessment. NIETS holds real promise as a provider of such support, especially as it brings under a single roof a range of national experts and system functions.

The single most important mission of NIETS is to oversee the production and administration of national standardised tests. The tests are prepared under the direction of NIETS by test development teams. The test items themselves are written by teachers and university instructors across Thailand (chosen in accordance with a variety of criteria including knowledge and teaching experience in the curricular area), and are then reviewed by several committees and groups of specialists.

Test writers do not need experience in test item construction but NIETS does provide workshops in four regions of the country to support the teachers who are selected. The IPST also co-ordinates the preparation of some questions in its area of expertise, providing support to the teachers and instructors who write them. The review team have no evidence that NIETS works closely with authorities responsible for the curriculum and its implementation – and have heard concerns expressed that it does not do this.

Based on its findings, the review team has significant concerns about the capacity of NIETS to adequately meet the needs of student assessment (test construction, test analysis) at the national level:

- On several occasions, the review team asked NIETS to provide technical information about the procedures lying behind its formulation and analysis of national assessments. NIETS proved unable to supply answers to this inquiry, and instead referred the team to high-level statements and recent test data. This suggests, at best, serious time constraints on the work of its technical specialists. But given staffing and resource issues, the lack of response likely reveals gaps in NIETS's technical analytic capacity.

- NIETS employs only five psychometric experts, too few to undertake the many highly demanding tasks linked to multiple assessment programmes in a large and diverse country.

- Key tasks for psychometric experts include guiding test developers, designing tests with an appropriate structure to enable long-term scale maintenance, and generating reliable and valid scores based on modern test theory. NIETS does not appear to have enough high-level technical expertise needed for complex procedures such as test design and exam architecture, form construction, item calibration, equating, and scoring models.

- Involving teachers in the design of standardised assessments can be good practice – enabling a country to build a cadre of experienced test developers, and allowing these individuals to enhance their own teaching practice and provide leadership to their schools in the area of assessment (OECD, 2013a). However, without adequate resources to carefully oversee this involvement, it can compromise the overall quality of an assessment programme. Some experts interviewed in Thailand expressed concern about teachers' involvement in preparing test questions, suggesting that this lowered the quality of tests and had at times undermined public confidence in the national assessment programme.

The review team lacks sufficient information to assess the capacity of other centralised assessment support functions, such as those at OBEC. Discussions with the Educational Standards division of OBEC did reveal a good level of technical literacy.

Policy makers, stakeholders and the public at large

Beyond the resources available at NIETS, Thailand appears to have limited capacity for the central analysis of national and school assessments. For instance, discussions with OBEC revealed that the datasets generated by the Grade 3 (P3) assessment and held by OBEC represent a very significant information resource. However, staffing limitations make it difficult to exploit this data to inform government policy.

Good capacity for central analysis can help ensure that reform processes are self-correcting and self-reinforcing. External agencies such as the World Bank, or arm's-length agencies like the Quality Learning Foundation, appear to be filling the gaps in analytical capacity within the government – but dependence on external capacity, in particular, represents a risk for Thailand as it could prevent the development of capacity among ministerial staff, and expose policy work to the vagaries of external decisions. Moreover, external actors may not always fully understand the potential and the limitations of the data they are accessing.

The overall results of NIETS assessments – in particular, of the O-NET exam – receive wide attention in Thailand. They appear to be considered as broadly indicative of the performance of the education system, and to carry the weight of authority. Whatever their own view of O-NET may be, both senior researchers outside government and senior decision makers are basing policy analysis upon national assessments. But, for reasons that will be further explored in the next section of this chapter, reliance on O-NET may be misplaced: the test appears to face technical difficulties that make interpretation of its results – in particular, interpretation over time – problematic.

Recommendations

The review team recommends that Thailand:

- **Strengthen teacher training and support in the area of assessment.**

Teachers need to be familiar with the development, use and interpretation of assessments for both formative and summative assessments. Good practice allows teachers to plan assessments that are tied to the curricular standards and to the objectives of the class, to appropriately involve students in formative assessments, and to make proper diagnostic use of the assessments to improve student learning and final learning outcomes. At the summative level, teachers should have a good understanding of the psychometric concepts behind national assessments, and therefore be able to better interpret the results in order to improve teaching practices and student learning.

It is critical that Thailand build teachers' professional capacity. Enhanced collaboration among teachers can be a particularly powerful capacity-building process in assessment. Professional development activities are also critical, as are supporting tools such as scoring guides, external benchmarks and innovative assessment tools. Thailand must ensure that teachers have the resources and competencies they need in areas such as employing a wide variety of assessments, making judgments against educational standards, and taking into account cultural and linguistic aspects of student learning.

This aligns with the recommendations in Chapter 5 that Thailand should strengthen teacher preparation and establish a nationwide strategy for professional development in areas key to the country's education reform.

- **Implement policies and programmes to develop measurement and psychometric expertise.**

This is an absolutely necessary precondition of any quality assessment programme that operates in alignment with recognised professional standards. NIETS needs sufficient professionals familiar with current measurement theory and practice to implement and maintain Thailand's many national testing programmes. While this is a long-term issue, it must be addressed early on, given the lag time between the entry of students into advanced programmes and their graduation. It will require an ongoing effort, focused not just on building, but also replenishing the ranks of psychometric and assessment experts.

Developing NIETS will not on its own address the concerns identified above: the technical capacity of other central agencies that support assessment should also be reinforced. Development of capacity at NIETS, the education commissions and elsewhere will require an ongoing commitment of resources.

Because Thailand lacks the number of academics it needs to establish a local programme in this field, it may be advisable to send several cohorts of students abroad to obtain doctoral degrees in educational measurement at foreign universities with good reputations in this field. Upon their return to Thailand, these professionals would gradually enrich the base of local expertise and over time, training could be shifted towards Thai universities. The costs of this initiative would be minimal compared to the benefits and quality gains in the longer term. In the meantime, local and foreign experts (including current and former officials from assessment agencies in other countries) could be employed as a stop gap to raise Thai assessment practice to international standards.

- **Strengthen the capacity of policy makers in central and local government to use data and research generated by student assessments to inform decision making.**

In most circumstances it is advisable to leave the actual manipulation of data and the performance of any necessary research in the hands of technical experts and social scientists. Nevertheless, it is necessary to develop a cadre of ministry personnel who are informed enough to understand the issues raised by experts working with assessment data. In other words, government officials should know enough to know where to go for the information that will allow them to implement the proper programmes and understand the outputs of the educational system. This enables better use of the information, encouraging officials to make informed decisions based on the latest educational and technical knowledge. Formal and informal educational programming, as well as structured exchanges (such as seminars) linking policy makers with domestic and international researchers, can contribute to building this kind of expertise.

Box 4.4. Building national capacity for assessment: the example of Cito in the Netherlands

Based in the Netherlands, Cito is a testing and assessment company that measures learning performance and performance and enables its partnering organisations to build up testing and monitoring expertise. Cito began in 1968 as a national institute for educational measurement. As it achieved international recognition, it became a private organisation (1999) and expanded its work to include various committees and consultative bodies. Cito draws on the latest developments in information and communication technology (ICT) and psychometric research to objectively map the knowledge, skills and competencies of participants. It is responsible for the creation of the tests at the end of primary school, which are administered annually to approximately 160 000 primary school pupils, as well as (in conjunction with the Ministry for Science, Culture and Education) the national final examinations for secondary education, taken by over 200 000 students a year. Cito also provides a monitoring and evaluation system for pupils, and offers support to Municipal Education Providers, helping teachers and students in naturalisation programmes by providing tools and assistance from the point of intake to successful completion. It also offers testing and training for students in teacher-training colleges as well as other types of training.

Source: Cito (n.d.) Cito website, www.cito.nl.

Policy Issue 2: National assessments need to offer greater validity and comparability of results

Standardised national test data plays a critical role in Thailand's education system. The data provide a picture of student achievement used for improvement and accountability purposes and, in the case of O-NET and the GAT and PAT, the tests act as a gatekeeper by helping determine whether, for instance, individual students can pursue higher studies. However, several factors have led the review team to suspect that NIETS standardised tests may not currently be able to play their important role. As discussed in the previous section, NIETS suffers a clear capacity shortfall – something the organisation itself stresses in some of its publications (e.g. NIETS, 2013, 2015b).

What is perhaps most telling is the large annual variation in O-NET scores, seen in Figures 4.1-4.3, suggesting that assessments vary in difficulty from year to year. As already noted, NIETS was unable to produce adequate documentation to allow the review team to fully assess the reasons behind this variation, but it is highly unusual and suggestive of significant underlying technical gaps – something that has also been suggested in the past in the media (e.g. Kaewmala, 2012a).

A high-quality assessment programme must take into consideration several important technical factors. They can be summarised into three major areas, each of which implies technical requirements that are tied to the validity and reliability of the testing, and to the correct interpretation of results:

1. **The quality of the tests,** including their design, internal architecture, item quality, the pre-testing of items and the construction of final forms. It is critical to ensure that results are comparable across forms of the test and over time. This also includes the work needed to maintain the quality of a test.

2. **The linking of the test with the curriculum content and standards**, including issues about whether the content of the exam covers things which all students had the opportunity to learn (see Chapter 3), and the provision of accommodations for students with physical or cognitive special needs. Accommodations for language and cultural differences also fall under this category.

3. **The proper use and interpretation of the test scores**, and the impact of this on the test takers and stakeholders who use the information derived from them. As detailed below, one of the main characteristics of the test is its degree of validity, which means the

extent to which it measures what it is supposed to measure. The way in which a test is used and its results are interpreted determine its appropriateness. For instance, a university admissions test should have data that demonstrate it is appropriate for predicting performance in the educational setting concerned. Tests that serve several purposes at once risk being invalid in each specific case.

National assessments need to take into account complex psychometric issues. There are many publications dealing with this matter, one of the most influential being the *Standards for Educational and Psychological Testing* (AERA, APA and NCME, 2014). These standards provide a concise and clear summary of all the aspects and requirements which must be considered if tests and testing programmes are to generate results with the required reliability and validity, and have a positive influence on the educational process. The OECD/UNESCO team observed no mention of these standards during their visits to ONESQA or NIETS.

It should be noted that the *Standards* call for using multiple measures and/or sources of information to support high-stakes decisions, as these allow more valid inferences to be made which better inform the decision processes. Given the high stakes associated with Thailand's national tests – for individuals, schools, the country's education system and ultimately Thailand's economic and social progress – it is critical that O-NET and similar tests be of consistently high quality. Inaccurate scores can unfairly affect the lives of individual students and can have similar effects on teachers and schools. They can also hinder the effectiveness of public policy. For instance, if it is not possible to meaningfully compare scores year on year, then some policy proposals – such as one that was reported to the team that would require a fixed annual incremental improvement in O-NET scores at each school – would be substantially flawed. Such failure entails risks for the education system, and for the development of the country as a whole.

Validity

Validity is the central concept and most important consideration in evaluating the quality of an assessment programme in terms of the use and interpretation of its results (Linn, 2000). In simple terms, "validity" means that a test must measure, beyond reasonable doubt, what it purports to measure. Validity is based on a complex set of observations and studies that address multiple aspects of how a test is used. Validation of a test confirms that the results are reliable, meaning that they are accurate and consistent.

In a seminal paper, Samuel Messick (1989) provided what is now the standard technical definition of validity: "Validity is an integrated evaluative judgment of the degree to which empirical evidence and theoretical rationales support the adequacy and appropriateness of inferences and actions based on test scores or other modes of assessment". This definition incorporates a number of elements:

- **criterion validity**, or the correlation of a test with a certain criterion, such as another test which purportedly measures the same ability or skill
- **content validity**, or the accuracy with which a test measures what it is intended to measure
- **predictive validity**, or a test's potential to predict another outcomes based on the scores obtained
- **construct validity**, or the appropriateness of the theoretical concept underlying what is being measured; this requires a series of steps and research presenting evidence that the test measures a given construct by, for example, triangulating results with other related research
- **consequential impact**, or the consequences that test results have, not just for the student, but for all stakeholders (e.g. schools, the educational system or policy makers).

When developing an assessment programme, concerns about validity mean that several factors need to be kept in mind: 1) the test's purpose and supporting evidence; 2) the test's content coverage and its cognitive level; 3) the specification of performance standards; 4) the format of the items and other test characteristics; 5) the dimensionality of the test; and 6) construct equivalence and relevance.

Purpose and supporting evidence

There is really no such thing as a "valid test": validity only applies to a specific use of a test and a particular interpretation of its results. Therefore, both of these elements have to be clearly stated, and they need to be based on supporting evidence. Tests need to be designed with their specific purpose in mind.

A test can be validated to fulfil various possible functions. For instance, an assessment might seek to determine how well students meet the expectations of certain content or curriculum standards; to provide information to a variety of stakeholders (teachers, parents, educational authorities, students) about the level of performance attained by students (individually or as a group or cohort); to enable high-stakes decisions, such as those regarding completion of a school cycle or admission to further education; or to monitor school or system performance. For each one of these possible functions, sufficient evidence has to be collected and analysed to demonstrate that the test and test scores are justified for that purpose. Only then can the use of the test and its resulting scores be valid for that specific application.

In Thailand, the review team did not find evidence that the necessary steps have been taken to ensure that national assessments are valid in their use and application. For instance, the team found no evidence of predictive validity analysis for the O-NET test. Without this, using the test to select students for higher education (aside from any quality issues regarding the assessments) would not represent a valid use of the test as the results that do not necessarily predict higher achievement or completion rates in the chosen field. Similarly, using O-NET results to model future policy directions is prone to error if the assessment's results cannot be shown to have predictive validity. Similarly, OVET reported that there has been no attempt to link standardised assessment scores in the V-NET to student labour market outcomes. Such linkages could provide key information about test validity, especially in the vocational sector.

Content coverage and cognitive level

To justify the use of a test for a particular purpose and interpretation of its scores requires a detailed examination of the curricular requirements for a given test, and a logical analysis of the actual processes needed to answer each item. Moreover, the blueprint for a test has to specify how the content standards – what the teachers are supposed to teach and the students are supposed to learn – will be examined through items or questions.

One senior researcher in Thailand observed that "market" evidence (the existence of a large-scale private tutoring industry in Thailand to supplement school instruction) suggests a mismatch between O-NET tests and the curriculum as it is implemented, if not necessarily with the "intended curriculum"(see Chapter 3). Other researchers and school administrators suggested that NIETS officials and officials responsible for the curriculum do not work as closely together as they should and that the practice of employing university instructors to write questions, when these individuals are not fully familiar with the elementary and secondary curriculum, can lead to problems of limited validity.

The year 2012 saw a spate of commentary in the Thai press about certain questions linked to the "health study and physical education" component of the curriculum. At least two questions were publicly reported by students. General confusion ensued over what the correct answer to one of them was, as the question appeared to rely on a fine level of value judgment (Kaewmala, 2012b; Thai Financial Post, 2012). While this debate points to gaps in the rigour of the preparation underlying particular questions, it may also be indicative of overreach in what the O-NET is attempting to assess. It also highlights the risks of security breaches affecting the exam.

No evidence was presented to the team of any formal process to link the assessment to the curriculum, how blueprint specifications are established, how the assessment architecture derives from the blueprint, or how the item requirements determined for each specified content area of the curriculum, such as the item specifications and number of items solicited from item writers (see Annex 4.A1 for the questions posed to NIETS).

The specification of performance standards

As described in Chapter 3, content standards alone do not specify "how well" a student needs to do to be considered at a certain level of performance. Classification of student results needs to be based on appropriately justified criteria expressed in terms of various levels of performance. This means that the development of performance standards needs to be a careful process, well-grounded both theoretically and empirically. In addition, the probability of misclassification has to be determined and minimised, both within the characteristics of the test and in the process of development of the performance standards. This is especially the case for high-stakes tests such as the O-NET or the GAT and PAT whose results can have a significant negative impact on the lives of students.

Students and teachers should always receive carefully designed information about the content and the characteristics of the test to be administered. They also need a detailed explanation of the criteria to be used in the scoring and in assigning their level of performance. In addition, students must have a fair opportunity to learn the material they will be tested on. Teachers need to be capable of teaching the full range of the content included on the test, and to assess the full range of expected performance levels. Students should receive assessments of known psychometric characteristics (including the exam's difficulty and its ability to discriminate between performance levels), and assessment must maintain a constant scale across multiple forms and sessions of administration.

In Thailand, the absence of common student performance standards in the national curriculum suggests that assessment and test preparation differ considerably across the education system (see Chapter 3). The absence of common standards also complicates the development of the NET tests. For example, there are weaknesses in the rationale for the cutscores – used for the classification of students – and the borders for decision making based on the scores in national tests, and in the protocols for making the decisions based on the data available. Cutscores need to be based on adequate standard-setting processes and on the empirical data obtained from the analysis. Such classifications would then have the required validity for their use in the interpretation of results, and in the description of student performances.

Because tests always have a degree of error, high-stakes decisions (such as promotion to the next school level or admission to university) should never be made based on a single test. Such decisions should take into account not only various assessments, but also various other sources of information to reach a decision about a certain student. Fairness and equity also require that adequate and appropriate accommodations be made for students who have disabilities or language deficiencies. These need to be sufficient to compensate for students' performance challenges, while respecting the validity of the construct being measured and the reliability of the test implementation.

There is evidence of issues around the range of adequate reliability for each assessment (taking into account the ability level of the students), as well as the level of discrimination and difficulty of the items for students at different ability levels. For instance, Thailand has sizable linguistic and ethnic minorities who may perform less well than other students on a standardised exam written by teachers who are most familiar with Thai urban students. This may affect student performance in non-valid ways if not carefully controlled for. For example, an administrator in a border-area school reported that language on the Grade 6 (P6) exam was "too difficult" – and that this was a subject of considerable discussion in his area. An administrator in a second border-area school reported that the delay in minority students' reading skills was a key factor in their poorer performance in O-NET assessments. The review team could not identify any procedure in place to correct for this.

A significant issue in Thailand, as in many other countries, is the existence of private tutoring which risks operating as a "shadow education" system. (Dang and Halsey Rogers, 2008) The number of private tutoring schools in Bangkok increased by roughly 125% between 1985 and 2004, and by 325% nationwide over the same period. The average monthly tutoring expenditures among households who were already investing in tutoring rose substantially after the introduction of the GAT and PAT in 2010. (Uruyos and Dheera-aumpon, 2010; Poovudhikul, 2013). Private tutoring does typically boost student performance, but tends to favour those who can best afford it. In Thailand, for instance, the size of investment in private tutoring is highly correlated with a family's socio-economic status (Dang and Halsey Rogers, 2008; Poovudhikul, 2013). This can introduce a source of non-construct related variance into the assessment results of students – i.e. variation in the score that comes from sources which do not make up part of what the assessment is intended to measure – negatively affecting equity, undermining the meaningfulness of assessment results, and leading to inefficient choices in the allocation of education opportunity.

The format of items and other test characteristics

The type of item format to be used is a technical issue of real importance. The use of a multiple-choice format implies several considerations for item development and the construction of test forms. While multiple-choice tests offer overall lower costs and increased reliability, they require sound planning processes if they are to be of good quality. Care must be taken to include items which require different levels of cognitive processing, to provide clear statements, and to provide appropriate distractors (i.e. the "incorrect" options presented to the student in a multiple-choice item, which together with the "key", or correct response option, constitute the response set for each question or item).

The other alternative is the construction of a constructed-response test (such as essays or short answers), which requires the student to carry out a certain performance (writing an essay, for example). That performance then needs to be evaluated based on a carefully constructed scale (rubric) on which human raters are trained so that they can recognise the actual performance level of the student for a specific item. There is ample evidence that multiple-choice tests, in most circumstances, can tap into the same cognitive level depth of topics and questions as an "essay test", with much more reliable results. For certain skills, such as writing and some high order skills, a performance test cannot be avoided.

One issue is the construction of an adequate test item bank. In order to have a rich number of items that can be calibrated and used in a number of tests over the years, it is necessary to securely save test items which have already been used and statistically calibrated. This allows parallel tests to be constructed (that is, tests with equivalent psychometric properties), which will allow the programme to maintain a constant scale through different forms of tests and years. This in turn requires qualified psychometric and test development staff members to develop and maintain this highly technical process. Effective practice requires in-house training as well as regular updating of procedures and techniques.

The review team was informed that a test bank has been developed for the NIETS assessments, and the IPST has developed its own bank in support of NIETS. The team was unable to determine, however, whether these test banks are adequate. The shortfalls observed in NIETS's psychometric capacity suggest that they may not be.

The review team learned that there were banks of items available from previous tests and online practice testing. In general, preparing learners for the kind of test they will be taking is a positive intervention (OECD, 2013a). However, tools like test banks may, like private tutors, lead to non-construct related variance depending on how past items are made available to students. For example, they need to be available to all students on an equal basis – with the availability of computers in schools a potential confounding factor here.

NIETS was unable to respond to the team's questionnaire (Annex 4.A1), making it impossible for us to assess in any detail issues surrounding test construction in Thailand such as the mix of multiple choice and other kinds of questions. The principles outlined in this section, and in others, should however provide guidance to officials as they work to develop the Thai assessment programme.

The dimensionality of the test

In simple terms, dimensionality means that each test should attempt to measure only one main area (Box 4.5). Tests should not try to combine topics that are independent of each other (e.g. religion and economics), unless the test measures a higher-order concept that both share, in which case it no longer specifically measures the constituent topics. It is therefore important to use empirical methods to assess the dimensionality of the assessments: this is particularly important to maintain scale is when tracking system and student performance across several years. Good assessment of dimensionality is also important when reporting sub-scores and when assessing different populations or subgroups. The review team has no evidence that anyone has undertaken the necessary analysis to determine the dimensionality of Thailand's national assessments.

Box 4.5. Dimensionality: Technical considerations

The violation of dimensionality assumptions can have serious consequences when calculating differential item functioning (DIF) for the items of a test to observe their performance in different subgroups and to detect bias; and also when calculating the discriminant validity of sub-scores (that is, the extent to which the test can discriminate between students who have different levels of knowledge on the ability or content being measured). Dimensionality can be checked in many different ways, including through factor analytic methods (both exploratory and confirmatory). In addition, conditional item associations (that is, the relationship among items which is distinct from the relationship that stems from sharing the same content area) need to be considered, after controlling for ability in the observed results.

Source: Phelps (2000), "Trends in large-scale testing outside the United States".

Construct equivalency and construct relevance

Many countries are implementing competency-based assessments, something that Thailand may wish to consider. In particular, this review recommends Thailand moving towards combining the assessment of students' knowledge of a topic with assessment of their ability to use that knowledge in specific problems or situations presented to them. These assessments are by their very nature complex and usually involve a variety of test items such as multiple-choice and constructed response questions. It then becomes a central concern to establish whether these different types of items measure the same cognitive behaviour. They can in fact do so if they are purposely written to achieve this goal.

For instance, the rating process in constructed-response items has to be carefully analysed. Raters need to be systematically trained in specially designed programmes, the criteria used to establish levels of performance need to be critically considered, ratings need to be adjusted and calibrated, and all sources of irrelevant variance (such as raters' biases or severity/leniency) must be minimised. Domain difficulty (the intrinsic "difficulty" of the content area compared to other areas), item/task difficulty (the difficulty of the question or task, meaning the amount of knowledge of the content necessary to answer it correctly), and the structure of the rating scale all also need to be considered (Engelhard, 1997).

Linking and equating between tests

Linking and equating are methods to make different tests comparable. For two tests to be linked, a relationship must be established between the scores in one test and the scores in the other. There are a number of ways to link tests, and these depend not only on the similarities and differences between tests, but also on the different ways in which the links will be used.

Equating is the most stringent way of linking (Box 4.6). It can be carried out only in large-scale testing programmes that use large representative samples of examinees, sound technical procedures and data collection practices, and appropriate statistical methods to link tests built to the same specifications. Under these conditions, equating adjusts for unintended differences in difficulty that occur when different sets of similar test questions are used.

Equating is very important for large-scale national assessment programmes because it ensures scores are comparable, and thus allows all examinees to be treated fairly irrespective of the form of the test they received. Without equating, results from two tests cannot be compared, as each test would be on a different scale even if the scores "look alike". Only a solid equating design, planned to last for many years, can give an assessment system the constant scale which means that a score obtained in a given year in a particular examination is the same as a similar score obtained in a different year, informing policy makers on the progress of education outcomes (Kolen and Brennan, 2004; Dorans, Pommerich and Holland, 2007). Equating also enables comparisons across various testing conditions (e.g. rural vs. urban, or gender or regional comparisons) when the test forms have been properly distributed amongst test takers. This enables informed observations about the performance of education outcomes over time, both for different regions, and for the country as a whole.

Maintaining an accurate scale is one of the most difficult tasks in an assessment programme, but it is an extremely valuable asset that a programme needs to secure (Petersen, Kolen and Hoover, 1989). A good example of a testing programme that is correctly equated over time, with a complex design that facilitates test development and distribution, is the SABER programme developed in Colombia by the national educational assessment centre – the Instituto Colombiano para el Fomento de la Educación Superior – for the Colombian Ministry of Education.

Box 4.6. Technical note on equating

The equating of two tests in the horizontal scaling context is fairly standard using an item response theory (IRT) test characteristic curve approach, assuming the suggested two- or three-parameter IRT model. If it can be assumed that the content dimensionality assumption in vertical scaling is met, then various methods can be adopted to accomplish the task of linking across several grades. Construction of the interim scale is typically done by means of the same IRT models used for year-to-year equating: two-parameter-logistic model for dichotomous constructed response (CR) items, and graded-response or two-parameter-partial-credit model for polytomous CR items.

In order to achieve the common metric for all grades spanned within a vertical scale, or in a horizontal equating between tests at the same level (same grade, for example), there are several methods to transform the score values. The Stocking-Lord transformation method and the fixed common item parameters method are typically used to achieve common scores. Based on recent research evidence, the Stocking-Lord method seems to capture educational growth more accurately than the fixed common item parameters method, but research is still going on in this area and should be carefully monitored (Embretson and Reise, 2000; Hambleton, Swaminathan and Rogers, 1991).

The OECD/UNESCO team did not find any evidence that Thailand is using equating procedures in its national assessments, nor that any technical procedures to achieve this have been discussed. The variability of scores and comments from stakeholders about the "varying difficulty" of the O-NET from year to year, suggest that equating procedures may not be fully in place. If equating procedures are not being used, and if as a consequence no resulting equating designs exist, this lessens the interpretability of results across years, test forms, and test takers. Accurate comparisons cannot be made, as it would not be possible to distinguish between differences that stem from different levels of ability of the test takers, and those that stem from different levels of difficulty of the test forms administered.

Without specific information on the design and structure of the national assessments, it is a concern for this review that, if the number of common items between forms is not sufficient (i.e. the same items present in different forms of a test, and used to equate these forms), this could preclude the possibility of being able to equate forms (Kolen and Brennan, 2004). Similarly, if the reliability of forms of an assessment in the same year or across years is significantly different, this could also preclude the possibility of proper equating.

As things stand, the effects of regional differences and the effects of differences across forms of tests may be confounded as potential sources of variance in assessment results. In other words, forms of different difficulty might be administered in different regions, making it hard to interpret observed differences: it would not be possible to determine if the different results stem from forms which have different difficulty levels, from true differences in ability level of the students, or from a combination of both. This problem could also exist if forms have not been distributed correctly (for example with a spiral design that gives all regions the same number of forms in a stratified random way) or if the forms have not been made comparable by equating. Comparisons between regions, genders, types of school or other variables, could be affected by this problem.

As for the psychometric characteristics of the exams, if they are constructed without correct pilot testing (pre-testing) of the items to obtain stable parameters, it is not possible to know the real difficulty level of the questions, nor their discrimination or comparability across cohorts. This would mean that the various forms used could have significant differences.

Recommendations

The review team recommends that Thailand:

- **Conduct validity studies for all NIETS assessment instruments, with particular focus on the O-NET, the GAT and the PAT.**

Thailand's national assessment programmes must meet international standards of good practice in educational assessment. At primary and secondary levels, assessments need to meet those high standards – not only to ensure proper feedback for students, teachers, schools and regional authorities, but also to provide policy makers and stakeholders with accurate information. Such high-quality assessments will generate much of the information needed to develop sound education policies and support systems.

In order for there to be a transparent and fair university admissions system, which provides opportunities to those students most likely to succeed and to achieve high levels of professional attainment, decisions must be data-driven. They must be based on solid evidence of the validity of the criteria used to admit students to the various programmes. Moreover, these students should be accepted based on comparable criteria and assessment results, which will maximise positive results for the country and satisfy fairness and equity concerns. Studies should be carried out using available admissions data (assessment results, as well as data on performance at the university).

Tests like O-NET face a particular challenge in that they serve so many different purposes at the same time. Thailand may wish to consider developing a broader variety of instruments for its standardised assessment regime, each more closely linked to a defined purpose, and thus more likely to be valid for that specific purpose.

- **Follow a solid approach to equating all forms of assessment in the same year, as well as to equating over time.**

Thailand needs to ensure that it has implemented international best practices in equating. This will help maintain a constant scale of the measure, giving Thailand stable results over time, which will provide a more reliable basis for policy interventions and institutional improvement.

- **Implement the item response theory (IRT) methodology for test development, test data analysis and item bank calibration, together with a rigorous policy that supports the comparability of results for each of the assessment programmes.**

In line with current modern psychometric theory, Thailand should fully implement an IRT methodology to track item quality, developing the appropriate criteria for item inclusion in a test form.[2] Classical theory values will also have to be considered, as well as a good distractor analysis. Using a 2- or 3-parameter unidimensional IRT model (Hambleton, Swaminathan and Rogers, 1991) would present significant advantages for item parameter estimation in pre-testing, and for equivalent form construction in operational administrations – and would also be invaluable for assessment architecture design for a solid equating programme. In addition, this approach would provide more accurate scoring models and allow easy rescaling to the desired reporting scale (thus avoiding reporting theta values that the public at large would have trouble understanding).

Efforts to implement these recommendations – i.e. working towards establishing a world-class assessment programme – will inevitably need to be staged over a period of time. The review team regrets that the lack of information made available to it on the technical aspects of Thailand's current national assessment system make it impossible to describe in more detail the reform path forward.

Policy Issue 3: Thailand does not have the right mix of assessment instruments to measure the full range of skills students need

The mix of skills and knowledge that youth require to succeed in modern societies and economies continues to broaden. Assessment systems need to reflect this. It was of course never sufficient to simply teach students "facts" and have students reproduce these facts in assessments. But it is increasingly apparent to educators and policy makers across the globe that students will require a full set of skills – ranging from foundation skills, to domain-dependent technical skills, to domain-independent skills (e.g. 21st century competencies or "transversal" skills), to broad social and emotional skills – if they are to prosper and contribute to a strong economy and a good society. Well-developed assessment systems incorporate systematically valid tests, which induce "in the education system curricular changes that foster the development of the cognitive skills that the [tests were] designed to measure" (Frederickson and Collins, 1990; cited in Braun et al., 2006). Such assessments can help ensure that students acquire a full set of skills – not just by checking progress at various moments, but by informing curricular choices, shaping how teachers teach and moulding how students learn (see Chapter 5).

With this in mind, the challenge facing any education system is to move beyond the traditional modes of assessment, which have often tended to focus on the reproduction of discrete knowledge, and shift towards a broad mix of assessments that measure – and thus value – the application of knowledge and the development of a broad set of skills. In practical terms, this means that educators and policy makers need to carefully identify and explicitly state what skills students need to develop, and to act on that specification. It also means that, given the diversity of skills students require, no single assessment instrument or approach can possibly suffice. This recognition is at the root of recent policy recommendations around building a diversified assessment system, i.e. one that makes good use of both formative assessments as pedagogical tools and summative assessments. Such a system must use a wide variety of assessment tools to assess a wide variety of skills (OECD 2013a, UNESCO 2012a). The challenge then is one of balance and economy: it is easy to diversify assessment in ways that lead to excessive complexity and poor co-ordination.

Effective use of assessment in the classroom

Formative assessments are above all a key pedagogical instrument in a teacher's toolbox. They are typically not rigorous measurement instruments, and in general it is unwise to attempt to treat them as such. What they do provide are ways for teachers to continually gauge student progress, and to adapt instruction to the evolving needs of learners. Formative evaluation comes in many forms including student portfolios, reflection sheets, self- and peer-assessment, requests for immediate feedback after a lesson, and requests for early drafts that help students structure their work. Whatever shape it takes, good formative assessment provides timely feedback to students, helps them feel safe to take risks, diagnoses learning needs and allows teachers to differentiate teaching accordingly, and engages students in their own learning process (OECD, 2013a).

The increased policy attention paid to formative assessment strategies in recent years stems in part from a growing body of evidence regarding their positive outcomes. A review of the research on classroom-based formative assessment found that the achievement gains associated with formative assessment were among the highest ever reported for any educational intervention (Black and William, 1998). The review also found that formative assessment has particularly strong effect on lower achieving students, and therefore helps reduce inequality in student outcomes while improving overall achievement. Additional research has found that self-assessment training on student performance – for teachers and for students – leads to positive effects in external evaluations (McDonald and Boud, 2003).

The benefits of formative assessment policies depend on effective implementation, though. Formative assessment should take place in an environment conducive to the improvement of classroom practice, addressing potential logistical obstacles such as overly large groups of students or excessive curriculum requirements. Since overemphasis on "results" (teaching overly driven by preparation for summative tests) often leads to an underdeveloped formative assessment approach, one of the most crucial considerations in designing an assessment framework is to effectively link it to everyday classroom practice.

As already highlighted in Policy Issue 1, building teachers' capacity can increase the usefulness of assessment results and translate into better education outcomes. Part of building capacity involves improving teachers' formative assessment skills – both through high-quality initial teacher education, and ongoing professional development. Ideally teachers should be able to move beyond superficial approaches to formative assessment (sometimes characterised as "summative assessment done more often") and develop the skills required to provide students with detailed, timely and specific feedback on their performance. Shifting attention away from a teacher-centred approach and towards one that focuses on students themselves requires teachers to adapt their techniques to meet diverse learning needs and help students build their own assessment skills to inform their future learning. For instance, teachers need to be skilled at ensuring that students can play an active role in the process through self- and peer-assessment. Collaboration amongst teachers at the school, local, regional and even national levels can be an effective way of further developing such capacities (see Chapter 5).

Effective summative assessment – assessment that validly and reliably measures what a student has achieved, and provides a sound base for further learning – is a similarly complex skill. It may be one that many teachers may instinctively feel more comfortable with, in particular if they have come up through an educational system with a strong emphasis on summative assessment. But the kind of "pre-understanding" that teachers bring to a classroom – and that education systems themselves can embody – requires examination and critique. Such reflection is at the heart of any good teacher training system (see Chapter 5). One key way that systems can strengthen teachers' capacity for effective summative assessment is by providing tools and guidelines such as scoring guides, scoring criteria and external benchmarks. Teachers also need to be skilled – and supported by the broader design of the school system – at reporting the results of assessments to students and parents in ways that ensure their constructive use. Finally, good-quality summative and formative assessment both require teachers to have access to – and skill in using – the tools provided by ICT (see Chapter 6).

As noted above, it was beyond the scope of the present review to examine the actual classroom practice of Thailand's teachers; something which could very usefully be the subject of its own study. The observations under Policy Issue 1 in this chapter, combined with those on the relationship between the curriculum and assessment in Chapter 3 and those on teacher preparation and continuing professional development in Chapter 5, suggest that Thailand would do well to re-examine the measures it has in place to train teachers in assessment techniques and to integrate assessment with broad curricular goals. In this regard it is particularly critical (as Chapter 3 also argues) that assessment be linked to students' acquisition of key competencies, e.g. the so-called "21st century competencies".

National assessments and the curriculum

The review team was able to identify some of the effects that national assessments (principally those developed by NIETS) appear to be having on the broader Thai assessment system. The tests focus on the reproduction of factual knowledge via a multiple-choice format. Some experts expressed concern that the national tests play too much of a role in what goes on in the classroom – and that because of their focus, they have what is sometimes called a "backwash" effect on teachers and students. This means that they end up restricting the kinds of skills that students develop, such as critical thinking skills: the existence of national standardised tests end up dictating the curriculum, rather than supporting it – and can run counter to the intended curriculum that was carefully conceptualised in 2008.

Some stakeholders indicated that preparation for national assessments can become an end in itself, taking up time that could be better spent on other activities. For instance, the review team heard that exam preparation ate into time set aside for the local curriculum that was an important part of the 2008 reforms, and that aimed to broaden students' skills sets. Other stakeholders pointed to an "excess of testing" that saps students' learning and enthusiasm for learning.

On the one hand, Thailand's NIETS tests are quite ambitious, covering a wide range of curricular subjects (perhaps too wide a range, given NIETS's finite resources and the time available). On the other hand, as stakeholders and experts suggested, they do not appear to be well adapted to testing transversal skills such as critical thinking, or determining how well students are able to apply knowledge to concrete tasks. Their focus on mastery of some parts of the curriculum's content, while important, is not sufficient.

These concerns are not unique to Thailand. Any country that relies heavily on centralised tests – as many Asian nations do – will have to contend with the risk that assessments (in particular those with gatekeeping functions) will set up incentives that are not, from a larger perspective, ideal (UNESCO, 2012a; OECD, 2013a). These risks can, however, be mitigated through careful design and deployment.

There are two potentially mutually reinforcing ways to address the challenge of building a national assessment system that drives the right kinds of learning: broadening and refining national-level testing and/or enhancing and co-ordinating local-level testing, potentially in conjunction with national assessments, to more systematically capture the variety of skills that students need to acquire. For the first option, some international tests such as PISA are a sound reference, showing how testing can help assess key competencies that learners need to acquire, for example. For the second option, Thailand could follow the example of a number of countries, and strengthen the system of school-based assessment (SBA) so that a greater degree of nationally comparable data can be derived from them (Box 4.7).

Implementing SBA requires a strong commitment to building capacity both within the education system itself, and among teachers. The keys to successful SBA – as a complement to standardised national assessments – include: a sound system for moderating results to ensure they are comparable, a clear statement of the relationship between the tasks and processes in the SBA system and those in the public examination system, appropriate techniques and methodologies for implementing SBA in classrooms and schools (through models, examples and samples), professional development for teachers, and clarity on how students' final results will be determined using data from both SBA and examinations (Brown, 2011; OECD, 2013a, UNESCO 2012b). The review team heard concerns about the lack of consistency of assessment across areas of the country, suggesting significant work would need to be done if Thailand was to implement reliable SBA nationally. Significant and sustained investment and effort would be needed.

Whichever option Thailand chooses, as discussed in Chapter 3, its assessment system would benefit from a better specification of performance standards that cover the broad range of skills that students need to acquire and make those skills tangible to teachers and students. While the 2008 curriculum outlines the competencies desired in a broad variety of areas and on a wide range of levels, it does not mention performance standards or their link to the educational objectives. This in turn means that there are no broadly shared reference points that would allow students, parents, teachers, administrators and policy makers to identify how good individual and collective performance is. The problems that this gap leads to are seen in the annual production and dissemination of NIETS scores. Reporting focuses on the percentage of questions students correctly answered across curricular areas; the values (with an average almost invariably below 50%, and thus theoretically "failing") are reported without the context and tangible reference points that would help various stakeholders make good use of them. Indeed, it was reported to the team that teacher are often unclear about how to use NIETS results – in particular, how to interpret the standardised scores of weaker students, and how to intervene to address issues that these may point to.

> **Box 4.7. School-based assessment: Lessons from New Zealand**
>
> In New Zealand, SBA is widely used at the upper secondary level, and teacher support materials are readily available. The 2007 curriculum explicitly mentions good assessment practice and its benefits for students and teachers. SBA is meant to improve students' learning and the quality of programmes, provide feedback to parents and students, award qualifications at upper secondary school level, and monitor overall national educational standards. A reform in 2004 of the National Certificate of Educational Achievement introduced a standard-/criterion-based assessment system which has become part of the national curriculum and qualifications framework. The New Zealand Qualifications Authority provides feedback to principals on how effectively their school manages subject assessment and advises schools on improvement measures. Schools must report back on the measures taken to improve their internal systems, and sanctions are applied to schools which show no improvement. These sanctions can include loss of accreditation for the subjects that are of concern.
>
> *Source*: UNESCO (2012a), "Student learning assessment", http://unesdoc.unesco.org/images/0021/002178/217816E.pdf.

Effective use of international assessments

Comparative international assessments such as the TIMSS and PISA can make a valuable contribution to the national assessment system mix. They provide a broader context in which to interpret national performance, giving countries information that allows them to identify areas of relative strength and weakness, and to monitor the pace of progress in education outcomes both internally and in relation to other countries. They can allow countries to monitor the progress of various student subgroups or regions which are not differentiated in national assessments. And they can help validate national assessment data.

International assessments also serve an important purpose by revealing what is possible in education, and by helping countries identify potentially relevant best practices elsewhere. They can help countries set appropriate policy targets, and provide support to a broader education reform agenda (Schleicher, 2009). And they may contribute to improving the quality of national evaluation systems, increasing their scope and acting as a best-practice model or guide for the formation and adaptation of national or federal assessment policies (OECD, 2012).

As noted above, Thailand has actively participated in international educational assessment programmes such as PISA and TIMSS over the last decades. These have resulted in a number of data sets on the performance of children aged 10 to 15, providing a good insight into the performance of various cohorts and the evolution of the country's performance as a whole. Thailand specifically can derive further benefits from using these tests, including the gathering of important data to drive policy, outlined below.

Benchmarking in test design

Although international tests have their own particular requirements and characteristics given their international scope, for many technical matters they can be used as a model for a high-quality large-scale assessment programme, both to enhance existing practices and to identify new ones. Comparing international to national student tests provides not just additional information on student performance, but also on the national assessments themselves, for example in areas such as data validation, coherence and cost effectiveness. In some countries, PISA plays an important role in guiding technical and methodological developments. For example, France uses the PISA methodology to establish competence scales for national assessments on large samples, while Chile has used PISA methodologies to improve procedures, manuals, item construction, statistical analysis and record keeping.

Expansion of coverage

International tests can provide guidance to Thailand on how to expand its suite of current national tests to cover a broader range of critical competencies. For instance, the experience of international tests in effective sampling can be valuable to individual countries. At the moment, all national-level assessments in Thailand are census-type instruments: in theory, every student is assessed. This has the advantage of providing rich data that can be used (if analytical capacity is sufficient) to explore issues affecting the outcomes of relatively small subsets of students. However, because of the time and resource requirements of census-type tests (as mentioned above, well over 2 million students in Thailand take them annually), their ability to cover all relevant skills and knowledge is severely constricted (OECD, 2013a). Sample-based tests could enable Thailand to assess a range of outcomes such as practical literacy and numeracy, problem solving, and ICT competencies in a comparatively cost- and time-effective manner.

Capacity building

International tests also provide capacity-development opportunities for officials and teachers as well as the entire assessment system. Capacity development for local officials and teachers can take the form of access to networks of experts on item development or on equating procedures. More broadly, participation in international assessments can improve assessment capacity at the national level by supporting better organisational structures and effective use of human resources, helping set clear policy objectives, and strengthening public support. International assessments can also improve the technical quality of national assessments. For instance, PISA contributes to capacity building by providing National Project Manager's manuals as well as through ongoing technical support, including trainings and tailored consultations.

Supplementary, complementary and corroborating information

International exams can provide tools to make valid comparisons amongst groups of test takers in Thailand where national exams (such as O-NET) still lack the technical qualities needed to allow reliable comparison. Relevant comparisons might include differences in scores linked to gender, region, ethnicity, language and urban/rural geography. For instance, many countries use PISA data to compare and validate data from their own national and subnational assessments (e.g. Spain), or to monitor the performance of specific student groups or subregions (e.g. Canada) (OECD, 2012).

Furthermore, many countries extend or adapt their assessment practices to enable comparisons between the outcomes of national assessments with those of tests like PISA, and to increase the overlap between the two. For instance, countries have linked performance indexes in order to produce an internationally benchmarked index of school and state performance (Brazil), linked cohorts (Canada), linked national/province assessment with PISA (Chile, Mexico), matched national assessment achievement levels to PISA or TIMSS reporting scales (United States), and embedded PISA items in state assessments to set performance standards (United States) (OECD, 2012).

The potential to drive policy reform

The appropriate use of the results from international assessments can generate diverse, useful and promising changes in the education systems of many countries, leading to improvements in quality and enhanced inclusion. For instance, PISA provides a rich evidence base that combines performance data with other system indicators, enabling governments to understand the factors correlated with performance.

For a country like Thailand, which has been included since 2000, PISA also provides very valuable trend data. To exploit its potential, Thailand would require national research on PISA data to better understand the factors that underlie performance differentials, and the challenges that demand policy responses. For instance in response to merely average performance levels on PISA, England has stressed the importance of teacher qualifications and school autonomy. In addition, the government required the national examinations regulator to conduct research on the comparability of English examinations with international tests, to ensure that they meet international standards (Baird et al., 2011).

International assessments can also guide curriculum developments – for instance to include PISA-style competencies in local content and performance standards. Such curriculum reforms have been conducted in Korea (revision of science curriculum standards), Mexico (revision of the curriculum at the lower secondary level) and Norway (revision of subject curricula to include basic skills in reading and mathematics). In all, 18 countries or economies have reported setting PISA-based national or subnational performance targets and indicators. Thailand could consider this as part of the review and reform of curriculum recommended in Chapter 3.

Recommendations

The review team recommends that Thailand:

- **Examine its overall framework for assessment and evaluation, to ensure that its various components are well balanced, and that they work together effectively to support student learning.**

Such an exercise would need to be based on clear objectives for students, and on clear goals for the system. It should not be a stand-alone exercise, but should be part of, and take its direction from, the curriculum review process recommended in Chapter 3. This would entail a multi-year effort.

In the immediate term, Thailand can take concrete actions to improve the overall performance of its student assessment and evaluation system. A review of system-wide assessment policies and practices, like the one described in *Synergies for Better Learning* (OECD, 2013a), would jump-start reflection on reform. The aims of such a review's would include: taking a holistic look at all of the education system's assessments, including school and student assessments, in order to eliminate duplication and increase co-ordination; aligning assessments with the goals of the education system and students' broader learning outcomes; engaging stakeholders to gather input and build consensus around proposed changes; and improving classroom practice. Such an exercise would be particularly beneficial in light of the country's efforts to increase the effectiveness, efficiency and equity of its education system and improve student performance, and its continuing decentralisation, which places greater demands on schools, principals and teachers. Combined with a review of the curriculum, such an approach could confirm professional learning needs relating to assessment and curriculum, and thus also inform the development of a nationwide strategy for professional development (as recommended in Chapter 5).

- **Broaden its range of student assessments.**

Thailand should work to better support school-based assessment, reducing the weight placed on national-level assessments. To inform policy, Thailand needs to ensure a robust range of school-based (and/or district-based) assessments which cover the specific educational environment and needs of regions and school objectives. These assessments should be properly standardised and follow all the same procedures and standards already mentioned for the nationwide instruments.

Thailand needs to ensure that students are being assessed in the classroom in ways that contribute actively towards their learning. Over-reliance on summative testing – in particular, on high-stakes testing linked to national examinations – needs to give way to a strategy that expressly supports the innovative use of formative assessment techniques.

- **Support the development of assessments that enable sound evaluation of key competencies identified in the curriculum.**

Starting with the analysis of what students need to know and be able to do in situations that are varying and complex, Thailand should steer the curriculum and its assessment towards an additional focus on outcomes (competencies) related to these. Such competencies are complex, and cannot be thought of as a simple sum of lower-level objectives and knowledge. Therefore, they need complex assessments which can address the higher-order thinking skills that need to be acquired in the context of each topic area. Such assessments can range from complex items in multiple-choice or other objective tests, to other kinds of performance assessments in various contexts. They could be developed in conjunction with the curriculum review to, among other things, place greater emphasis on the acquisition of complex competencies for the 21st century, as recommended in Chapter 3.

Competencies in different areas can require different combinations of skills, knowledge and behavioural factors. In all areas, however, the skill sets they require can be analysed as sequential levels of mastery. Assessments therefore need to be able to discriminate accurately between the stages of development of the corresponding competencies, and to determine whether students have achieved mastery in each of them. Such assessments are challenging to prepare, but they will provide invaluable information to educators and to education policy experts. Officials at the national and regional levels as well as teachers will need support to develop the skills that such assessments require.

For these reasons, it is also essential that Thailand move forward with developing common student performance standards, as recommended in Chapter 3.

- **Use international tests as a guide to improve its standardised testing**

International assessments are elaborated and standardised through a rigorous design process, with a focus on validity, reliability and representativeness of the samples used in their administration. Thailand should follow other countries' examples and adapt its national tests to meet international standards, such as those delineated in the *Standards for Educational and Psychological Testing* (AERA, APA and NCME, 2014). The many potential benefits include enhancements to technical and policy capacity, a broadened knowledge base and potential impetus for positive change.

Conclusion

This chapter has analysed Thailand's complex educational assessment system, which encompasses a wide variety of established testing programmes. It has a national testing centre that provides the nucleus for real improvement in assessment, and regulations providing a mandate for a series of quality assurance and quality control processes. Based on the information gathered for this review, it is clear that Thailand has made substantial progress in this area, but there is also evidence that its national assessment programme faces significant challenges. These include technical concerns and a lack of sufficient staff competent in the measurement and psychometric field. These challenges, as well as issues with teacher training and support in the area of assessment, and a traditional emphasis on summative assessment, are hindering policy development and the improvement of student outcomes.

Design flaws in Thailand's standardised student assessments and their architecture, together with an apparent lack of comparability of results over time (and even within each year), raise significant risks if test scores are taken at face value in the design of policies, programmes and interventions across the education system. Of equal concern is the impact technical flaws can have on fairness and equity, as they may misclassify performance levels, affecting students' academic future. For these reasons, improving the design and methodological rigour of the country's student assessments should be Thailand's top priority in reforming the assessment system.

Thailand already has the infrastructure in place to implement a high-quality educational assessment programme. If an institute like NIETS were strengthened both in terms of financial resources and qualified personnel; the national examinations were brought more into line with international professional standards; an enhanced mix of assessments were put in place, guided by common student performance standards; and assessments measuring students', schools' and educators' performance were aligned to meet clear reform objectives, Thailand could make real progress towards developing a world-class assessment system. If all this were coupled with a well-trained teaching profession able to confidently make use of classroom assessments, and interpret and integrate test results into their teaching practice, Thailand would be well on the way to ensuring its education system reliably and efficiently produces the good student outcomes that are a key contributor to economic and social success.

Notes

1. Many countries have recently introduced centralised assessment programmes, including Austria (2012), the Flemish Community of Belgium (2002), the French Community of Belgium (2009), Denmark (2009), Germany (2007), Hungary (2001), Iceland (2009), Ireland (2007), Israel (2002), Italy (2008), Japan (2007), Korea (2001), Luxembourg (2008), Mexico (2006), Norway (2004), Portugal (2001), Spain (2007) and the Slovak Republic (2004) (OECD, 2013).

2. Some suggested values are: discrimination parameter > 0.50; $-2.75 <$ difficulty parameter < 2.75 in the theta scale.

Bibliography

AERA, APA and NCME (2014), *Standards for Educational and Psychological Testing*, American Educational Research Association, Washington, DC.

Angoff, W.H. (1971), "Scales, norms, and equivalent scores", in R.L. Thorndike (ed.), *Educational Measurement*, Second Edition, American Council on Education, Washington, DC, pp. 508-600.

Baird, J.-A. et al. (2011), *Policy Effects of PISA*, Oxford University Centre for Educational Assessment, Oxford.

Bishop, J.H. (2006), "Drinking from the fountain of knowledge: Student incentives to study and learn – Externalities, information problems and peer pressure", in *Handbook of the Economics of Education*, Vol. 2, pp. 910-944.

Bishop, J.H. (1997), "The effect of national standards and curriculum-based exams on achievement", *American Economic Review*, Vol. 87/2, pp.260-264.

Black, P. et al. (2003), *Assessment for Learning: Putting it into Practice*, Open University Press, Maidenhead.

Black, P. and D. William (1998), *Inside the Black Box*, GL Assessment, London.

Braun, H. (2005), *Using Student Progress to Evaluate Teachers: A Primer on Value-Added Models*, Educational Testing Service, Princeton, NJ.

Braun, H., A. Kanjee, E. Bettinger and M. Kremer (2006), *Improving Education through Assessment, Innovation and Evaluation*, American Academy of Arts and Sciences, Cambridge, MA, www.amacad.org/publications/braun.pdf.

Bray, M. (2009), *Confronting the Shadow Education System: What Government Policies for What Private Tutoring?*, International Institute for Educational Planning, Paris.

Breakspear, S. (2012), "The policy impact of PISA: An exploration of the normative effects of international benchmarking in school system performance", *OECD Education Working Papers*, No. 71, OECD Publishing, Paris, http://dx.doi.org/10.1787/5k9fdfqffr28-en.

Brown, G. (2011), "School based assessment methods: Development and implementation", *Journal of Assessment Paradigms*, Vol. 1/1, pp. 30-32, http://libir1.ied.edu.hk/pubdata/ir/link/pub/2011%20Brown%20Develop%20SBA%20Jnl%20Assmnt%20Paradigms.pdf.

Butler, D.L. and P.H. Winne (1995), "Feedback and self-regulated learning: A theoretical synthesis", *Review of Educational Research*, Vol. 65/3, pp. 245-281.

Cito (n.d.) Cito website, www.cito.nl.

Dang, H-A and F. Halsey Rogers (2008), "The growing phenomenon of private tutoring: Does it deepen human capital, widen inequalities, or waste resources?", *World Bank Research Observer*, Vol. 23/2, http://siteresources.worldbank.org/INTPUBSERV/Resources/Dang_private_tutoring.pdf.

Deutsch, J. and J. Silber (2013), "On the determinants of scholastic performance in five Asian countries", *ADB Economics Working Paper Series*, No. 335 (March), Asian Development Bank, Manila, Philippines.

Dorans, N.J., M. Pommerich and P.W. Holland (eds.) (2007), *Linking and Aligning Scores and Scales*, Springer, New York.

Draper, J. (21 February 2014), "PISA Thailand regional breakdown shows inequalities between Bangkok and upper north with the rest of Thailand", the Isaan Record, http://isaanrecord.com/2014/02/21/pisa-thailand-regional-breakdown-shows-inequalities-between-bangkok-and-upper-north-with-the-rest-of-thailand/.

Edwards, C. (2000), "Assessing what we value and valuing what we assess?: Constraints and opportunities for promoting lifelong learning with postgraduate professionals", *Studies in Continuing Education*, Vol. 22/2, pp 201-217.

Embretson, S.E. and S.P. Reise (2000), *Item Response Theory for Psychologists,* Lawrence Erlbaum, Mahwah, NJ.

Engelhard, G. (1997), "Constructing rater and task banks for performance assessments", *Journal of Outcome Measurement*, Vol. 1/1, pp. 19-33.

Eurydice (2009), *National Testing of Pupils in Europe: Objectives, Organisation and Use of Results*, Education, Audiovisual and Culture Executive Agency, Brussels.

Frederickson, J.R. and A. Collins (1990), "A systems approach to educational testing", *Technical Report*, No. 2, Center for Technology in Education, New York, http://files.eric.ed.gov/fulltext/ED325484.pdf.

Government of Thailand (2010), "Ministerial Regulations Governing the Systems, Criteria and Procedure for Internal Quality Assurance of Educational Institutions B.E. 2553", *Government Gazette*, Vol. 127/23, pp. 22-35.

Government of Thailand (2003), "Administrative Organization of the Ministry of Education Act of B.E. 2546", *Government Gazette*, Vol. 120/62, pp. 1-30.

Haladyna, T.M. and R.K. Hess (1999), "An evaluation of conjunctive and compensatory standard-setting strategies for test decisions", *Educational Assessment*, Vol. 6/2, pp. 129-153.

Hambleton, R.K., H. Swaminathan and H.J. Rogers (1991), *Fundamentals of Item Response Theory*, Sage, Newbury Park, CA.

Hanna, G.S. and P.A. Dettmer (2004), Assessment for Effective Teaching: Using Context-Adaptive Planning, Pearson A&B, Boston, MA.

Hanushek, E.A. and L. Wößmann (2007), *Education Quality and Economic Growth*, World Bank, Washington, DC.

Jensen, B., A. Hunter, J. Sonnemann and T. Burns (2012), *Catching Up: Learning from the Best School Systems in East Asia*, Grattan Institute, Carlton, Australia, http://grattan.edu.au/wp-content/uploads/2014/04/129_report_learning_from_the_best_main.pdf.

Kaewmala (27 February 2012a), "Thai education failures – Part 2: Test scores, standards and accountability", *Asian Correspondent*, http://asiancorrespondent.com/76877/thai-education-part-2-test-scores-standards-and-accountability/ (accessed 24 April 2015).

Kaewmala (23 February 2012b), "Thai education failures – Part 1: Ridiculous O-NET questions", *Asian Correspondent*, http://asiancorrespondent.com/76664/thai-education-part-1-ridiculous-o-net-questions/ (accessed 24 April 2015).

Kellaghan, T. and V. Greaney (2001), "The globalisation of assessment in the 20th century", *Assessment in Education*, Vol. 8/1, pp. 87-102.

Kolen, M.J. and R.L. Brennan (2004), *Test Equating, Scaling, and Linking: Methods and Practices*, Second Edition, Springer-Verlag, New York.

Linn, R.I. (2000), "Assessment and accountability", *Educational Researcher*, Vol. 29/2, pp. 4-16.

Lounkaew, K. (2011), "Explaining urban-rural differences in literacy, mathematics and science: Evidence from PISA 2009", paper presented at the conference ANU-DBU Economics of Education Policy: Access and Equity at Dhurakij Pundit University, Bangkok, Thailand, 14-16 June 2011.

Luedemann, E. (2011), "Intended and unintended short-run effects of the introduction of central exit exams: Evidence from Germany", in E. Luedemann, *Schooling and the Formation of Cognitive and Non-cognitive Outcomes*, Chapter 4, ifo Beiträge zur Wirtschaftsforschung 39, ifo Institut, Munich.

McDonald, B. and D. Boud (2003), "The Impact of self-assessment on achievement: the effects of self-assessment training on performance in external examinations", *Assessment in Education*, Vol. 10/2, pp. 209-220.

Messick, S. (1995), "Standards of validity and the validity of standards in performance assessment", *Educational Measurement: Issues and Practice*, Vol. 14/4, pp. 5-8.

Messick, S. (1989), "Validity", in R.I. Linn (ed.), *Educational Measurement*, Third Edition, Macmillllan, New York, pp. 13-103.

Ministry of Education (2013), "Eight Educational Policies", Mr Chaturon Chaisang, Minister of Education of Thailand, Bangkok.

Ministry of Education (4 July 2012), "Ministry of Education's announcement on implementation of vocational education standards for internal quality assurance of educational institutions", Ministry of Education of Thailand, Bangkok.

Mislevy, R.J. (1992), "Linking Educational Assessments: Concepts, Issues, Methods, and Prospects", Educational Testing Service, Princeton, NJ.

Nakornthap, A. (2008), "Quality assurance and quality issues in Thai education: Toward research-driven strategies for improving quality", *The International Journal of Quality Assurance and Accreditation*, Vol. 1/2.

National Research Council (2001), *Knowing What Students Know: The Science and Design of Educational Assessment*, National Academy Press, Washington, DC.

Newton, P. (2007), "Clarifying the purposes of educational assessment", *Assessment in Education*, Vol. 14/2, pp. 149-170.

NIETS (2015a), "O-NET (Ordinary National Educational Test)", National Institute of Educational Testing Service website, www.niets.or.th/en/catalog/view/2211 (accessed 10 January 2016).

NIETS (2015b), "Country report on National Educational Testing and Assessment: Thailand", Powerpoint presentation to the OECD/UNESCO Review Team, 19 February 2015.

NIETS (2013), "Country report on National Educational Testing and Assessment: Thailand", NIETS International Symposium on National Educational Testing and Assessment in ASEAN: Share & Learn, Bangkok, 3 September 2013.

NIETS (2009), *The National Institute of Educational Testing Service (Public Organization) – Thailand,* National Institute of Educational Testing Service, Bangkok, www.niets.or.th/upload-files/uploadfile/5/5113f2fc40d9b7ccbf26972226c1a536.pdf.

OECD (2015), *Education Policy Outlook 2015: Making Reforms Happen*, OECD Publishing, Paris, http://dx.doi.org/10.1787/9789264225442-en.

OECD (2014), *PISA 2012 Results: What Students Know and Can Do (Volume I, Revised Edition, February 2014): Student Performance in Mathematics, Reading and Science*, PISA, OECD Publishing, Paris, http://dx.doi.org/10.1787/9789264208780-en.

OECD (2013a), *Synergies for Better Learning: An International Perspective on Evaluation and Assessment*, OECD Reviews of Evaluation and Assessment in Education, OECD Publishing, Paris, http://dx.doi.org/10.1787/9789264190658-en.

OECD (2013b), *PISA 2012 Results: What Makes a School Successful (Volume IV): Resources, Policies and Practices,* PISA, OECD Publishing, Paris, http://dx.doi.org/10.1787/9789264201156-en.

OECD (2013c), *Trends Shaping Education 2013*, OECD Publishing, Paris http://dx.doi.org/10.1787/trends_edu-2013-en.

OECD (2013d), *Teachers for the 21st Century: Using Evaluation to Improve Teaching*, International Summit on the Teaching Profession, OECD Publishing, Paris, http://dx.doi.org/10.1787/9789264193864-en.

OECD (2013e), *Southeast Asian Economic Outlook 2013: With Perspectives on China and India*, OECD Publishing, Paris, http://dx.doi.org/10.1787/saeo-2013-en.

OECD (2012), *Education at a Glance 2012: OECD Indicators*, OECD Publishing, Paris, http://dx.doi.org/10.1787/eag-2012-en.

OECD (2010), *PISA 2009 Results: Learning Trends: Changes in Student Performance Since 2000 (Volume V)*, PISA, OECD Publishing, Paris, http://dx.doi.org/10.1787/9789264091580-en.

OECD (2009), *Creative Effective Teaching and Learning Environments: First Results from TALIS*, TALIS, OECD Publishing, Paris, http://dx.doi.org/10.1787/9789264068780-en.

Office of the National Education Council (2004), *National Education Standards*, Office of the National Education Council, Ministry of Education of Thailand, Bangkok.

Office of the Higher Education Commission (2015), *Seminar on Teacher Production and Reform and Teacher Development in the Future: Problems and Solutions*, Bureau of Policy and Planning, Office of the Higher Education Commission, Bangkok.

Office of the National Education Commission (2003), *National Education Act B.E. 2542 (1999) and Amendments (Second National Education Act B.E. 2545 (2002))*, Office of the National Education Commission, Office of the Prime Minister, Bangkok.

ONESQA (2015), *Quality Assurance in Thailand,* Office for National Education Standards and Quality Assessment, Bangkok.

Petersen, N.S., M.J. Kolen and H.D. Hoover (1989), "Scaling, norming, and equating", in R.L. Linn (ed.), *Educational Measurement*, Third Edition, Macmillan, Washington, DC, pp. 221-262.

Phelps, R.P. (2000), "Trends in large-scale testing outside the United States", *Educational Measurement: Issues and Practice*, Vol. 19/1, pp. 11-21.

Poovudhikul, V. (2013), "The effects of the Thai college admissions system on private tutoring expenditure, income and achievement disparities", Honors Thesis, Department of Economics, Stanford University, https://economics.stanford.edu/sites/default/files/publications/venussapoovudhikulhonors_thesis-may2013.pdf.

Redick, T.S. and R.W. Engle (2006), "Working memory capacity and attention network test performance", *Applied Cognitive Psychology*, Vol. 20/5, pp. 713-721.

Sadler, D.R. (1998), "Formative assessment: Revisiting the territory", *Assessment in Education*, Vol.5/1, pp. 77-84.

Schleicher, A. (2009), "International assessments of student learning outcomes", in L.M. Pinkus (ed.), *Meaningful Measurement: The Role of Assessments in Improving High School Education in the Twenty-First Century*, Alliance for Excellent Education, Washington, DC.

Segers, M., F. Dochy and E. Cascallar (2003), "The era of assessment engineering: Changing perspectives on teaching and learning and the role of new modes of assessment", in M. Segers, F. Dochy and E. Cascallar (eds.), *Optimising New Modes of Assessment: In Search of Qualities and Standards*, Kluwer, Dordrecht, Netherlands.

Shipstsead, Z., D.R.B. Lindsey, R. Marshall and R.W. Engle (2014), "The mechanisms of working memory capacity: Primary memory, secondary memory, and attention control", *Journal of Memory and Language*, Vol. 72, pp. 116-141.

Skorupski, W.P., M.G. Jodoin, L.A. Keller and H. Swaminathan (2003), "An evaluation of equating procedures for capturing growth", Paper presented at the meeting of the National Council on Measurement in Education, Chicago, IL, April 2003.

Smuthkochorn, S. (2012), "External quality assurance in Thailand", Presentation from S. Smuthkochorn, Advisor to Director of ONESQA, http://asean-qa.de/media/asean-qa.de/Workshop_BKK/1_Day/External_Quality_Assurance_in_Thailand-Sutassi_Smuthkochorn.pdf (accessed December 2015).

Stocking, M.L. and F.M. Lord (1983), "Developing a common metric in item response theory", *Applied Psychological Measurement*, Vol.7/2, pp. 201-210.

Tangdhanakanond, K. and S. Wongwanich (2012), "Teacher attitude and needs assessment concerning the use of student portfolio assessment in Thailand's educational reform process", *International Journal of Psychology: A Biopsychosocial Approach*, Vol.10, pp. 71-88.

TDRI (2012), "Revamping Thai education system: Quality for all", paper presented at the TDRI Year-End Conference 2012, Thailand Development Research Institute, February.

Thai Financial Post (24 February 2012), "NIETS says the controversial O-net exams contain required standards", *Thai Financial Post*, http://thaifinancialpost.com/2012/02/24/niets-says-the-controversial-o-net-exams-contain-required-standards/ (accessed 24 April 2015).

UNESCO (2012a), "Student learning assessment", *Asia-Pacific Education System Review Series*, No. 5, United Nations Educational, Scientific and Cultural Organization, Bangkok, http://unesdoc.unesco.org/images/0021/002178/217816E.pdf.

UNESCO (2012b), *Malaysia Education Policy Review*, United Nations Educational, Scientific and Cultural Organization, Paris.

Uruyos, M. and S. Dheera-aumpon (2010), "Entrance examination, private tutoring and economic growth", Conference paper, Chulalongkorn University, https://editorialexpress.com/cgi-bin/conference/download.cgi?db_name=SERC2007&paper_id=132.

World Bank (2015), *Thailand: Wanted, A Quality Education for All*, World Bank, Bangkok.

World Bank (2014), *Education Statistics* (database), http://knoema.com/WBEdStats2014Apr/education-statistics-world-bank-april-2014?country=1000320-thailand&action=download.

Annex 4.A1

The information request made by the OECD/UNESCO team to the National Institute of Educational Testing Service

Please provide information on the following items:

A. National education testing

1. O-NET

    1. Grade 6
    2. Grade 9
    3. Grade 12

    - Learning material groups for each exam

    For each of the above exams (6, 9, 12) the following information is needed:

    - Additional secondary analyses of the data (such as: interaction with socio-economic level, background variables, etc.)
    - Process of design of each test:
        – How is the blueprint developed?
        – Which are the criteria used to select specific curriculum elements to test in each administration?
    - Architecture of the exam
        – Which are the design specifications for each exam in terms of percentages of weight assigned to each curricular area for each administration?
    - Item development process
        – How many item developers participate in the development of each exam?
        – How much training do they receive in item construction?

- Item review and selection criteria
  - Which are the item-review steps?
- Pilot testing
  - Is there any pilot-testing (pre-testing) of items before their use in operational administrations?
  - Which are the statistical criteria use to accept an item as part of the scorable set to determine the score of students?
- Form construction
  - Which is the process followed for form construction for each operational administration of each exam?
- Form equivalency
  - How are forms determined to be equivalent?
  - Which statistical analyses are carried out to guarantee such equivalency?
- Equating process
  - How are scores equated across forms of the same year?
  - Are the same forms used across all regions? (spiralled administration?)
  - How are these regional results reported in the same scale?
  - How are scores equated across different years of administration to make results comparable?
- Scoring methods
  - Which scoring method is used for each of the exams?
  - Is IRT scoring also used?
    - Please provide the Test Information Function for each of the exam.
    - Please provide all the item parameter values for each exam.

- Criteria for item analysis
  - Please specify the criteria for items to be accepted as part of the score.
- Score reporting
  - How are scores reported:
    - To individual students.
    - Schools – Regional authorities – Ministry.
  - How are cut-points determined?
  - Which is the error of measurement at each cut-point?

Please provide similar information on the following examination programmes:

1. V-NET
2. N-NET
3. I-NET
4. B-Net

B. Higher Education admissions

1. General Aptitude Test (GAT)

2. Professional and Academic Aptitude Test (PAT)

- Additional secondary analyses of the data (such as: interaction with socioeconomic level, background variables, etc.)
- Process of design of each test:
  A. How is the blueprint developed?
  B. Which are the criteria used to select specific elements to test in each administration?
- Architecture of the exam
  A. How are the weights for each element of the blueprint determined, and which are those weights?

- Item development process
    A. How many item developers participate in the development of each exam?
    B. How much training do they receive in item construction?
- Item review and selection criteria
    A. Which are the item-review steps?
- Pilot testing
    A. Is there any pilot-testing (pre-testing) of items before their use in operational adminstrations?
    B. Which are the statistical criteria use to accept an item as part of the scorable set to determine the score of students?
- Form construction
    A. Which is the process followed for form construction for each operational administration of each exam?
- Form equivalency
    A. How are forms determined to be equivalent?
    B. Which statistical analyses are carried out to guarantee such equivalency?
- Equating process
    A. How are scores equated across forms of the same year?
    B. Are the same forms used across all regions? (spiralled administration?)
    C. How are these regional results reported in the same scale?
    D. How are scores equated across different years of administration to make results comparable?
    E. Please provide results of the equating for each exam.
- Scoring methods
    A. Which scoring method is used for each of the exams?
    B. Is IRT scoring also used?

Chapter 5

Thailand's teachers and school leaders

The quality of teachers and school leaders are the most important school-related factors in student outcome. This chapter reviews Thailand's teacher and principal preparation, licensing, assessment and continuing development policies and the structures and organisations that support them. It identifies five policy issues that may be preventing the development of a high-quality education profession: 1) inadequate teacher preparation programmes; 2) a lack of a strategic approach to teachers' professional development; 3) administrative burdens keeping teachers away from the classroom; 4) no strategic framework to support the development of school leaders; and 5) a fragmented approach to data management and teacher deployment making it harder to tackle teacher shortages.

It recommends as a top priority the development of a holistic strategy to build capacity among teachers and school leaders to support Thailand's education reform goals. This should be developed in consultation with teachers, school leaders and their associations. Teacher funding and deployment should better reflect local needs to ensure all students are taught by highly qualified and high-quality teachers.

Introduction

Teachers are crucial to learning and key partners in education reform. Research has found that the quality of teachers and their teaching are the most important school-related factors in student outcomes (Darling-Hammond, 2000; OECD, 2005). Teachers are also at the front line of any education reform movement, ideally providing input when policies are being developed, and tasked with understanding and implementing the new vision (OECD, 2005; Jensen et al., 2012). As a representative of Thailand's Office of the Basic Education Commission (OBEC) said to the review team, "teachers are the heart of the matter".

School leaders also play an essential role in improving school and student performance (Pont et al., 2008; Schleicher, 2012). That role goes far beyond administration; school leaders shape the culture of their schools and have the power to continuously improve teaching and learning. They are also responsible for reaching out to stakeholders and other schools to build support for education in their local communities.

Thailand's recent education reforms have placed increased importance, and responsibility, on teachers and school leaders as agents of school change. The national curriculum first implemented in 2001 and revised in 2008 changed expectations of teachers from top-down lecturers in a culture of rote learning to facilitators who are mindful of each student's unique aptitudes and abilities. As with their counterparts worldwide, Thai teachers are expected to teach 21st century skills, such as analytical thinking, creativity, problem solving and teamwork, and encourage learning outside of the classroom. They need to continuously evaluate students' performance using diverse assessment techniques, and provide remedial support to struggling learners (OBEC, 2013a). They must be knowledgeable about and use information and communication technology (ICT) to enhance learning, and be inclusive of students with special needs and from different backgrounds. They are expected to prepare students for active participation in the Association of Southeast Asian Nations (ASEAN) community and the competitive global marketplace, while also promoting Thai values and culture.

The country's current education reforms focus on quality, equity, effectiveness and efficiency. Teachers and school leaders are instrumental to achieving these overarching goals, and they will have a good chance of success if Thailand makes efforts to strengthen teacher preparation, support continuing teacher development, enable teachers to focus on the classroom, enhance school leadership and more efficiently manage its school workforce. This chapter explores the policy issues and options facing

Thailand as it seeks to effect such reforms. It begins with an overview of the current teaching workforce and the policies and institutions that have shaped its development.

Thailand's teaching workforce

Most (78%) of Thailand's almost 700 000 teachers belong to the country's public service, and 62% are employed by the Ministry of Education. However, as with other aspects of the Thai education system, the employment of teachers is administratively complex, with many different employers, including private schools, other ministries (such as the Ministry of Interior), and the autonomous Bangkok Metropolitan Authority. In addition, police officers work as teachers in Thailand's 196 Border Patrol Schools, located in the higher-risk regions of the country (Table 5.1). A small but increasing percentage – 5.4% of the basic education teaching workforce as of November 2014 – are hired on contract rather than as permanent civil servants (OBEC, 2015a).

Table 5.1. Teachers' employers, 2013/14 school year

Employer	Number
Office of the Basic Education Commission	397 733
Office of the Higher Education Commission Demonstration Schools	3 099
Office of the Vocational Education Commission	25 685
Private Education Promotion Commission (private schools) General Education Vocational Education	136 114 15 452
Mahidol Wittayanusorn School* (Supervised by Ministry of Education)	138
Ministry of Tourism and Sports	576
Ministry of Culture	1 040
Ministry of Interior	84 577
Bangkok Metropolitan Administration	16 397
Ministry of Social Development and Human Security	54
Royal Thai Police	1 628
Total	682 493

Note: This table excludes higher education teachers and soldiers and nurses who teach special subjects.
* An autonomous public organisation that provides education to gifted science and mathematics students.
Source: OEC (2015a), *Thailand Education Statistics, Academic Year 2013-2014.*

The Thai teaching population is ageing. In 2013, the Office of the Teacher Civil Service and Educational Personnel Commission (OTEPC) estimated that 68.2% of the country's basic education teachers and 61.8% of vocational education teachers would retire within the next 15 years (OEC, 2015b). As of 2012, approximately 56% of teachers in Thailand were women: 60% in primary education and 51% in secondary education (UIS, 2015). By comparison, 67% of teachers were women – 74% in primary and 60% in secondary – on average across other East Asian and Pacific countries (Indonesia, Korea, Malaysia and New Zealand) (UIS, 2015). Thai teachers are highly educated (Atagi, 2011). In the 2012 Programme for International Student Assessment (PISA) study, Thai principals reported that 99.2% of teachers in their secondary schools had a qualification equivalent to ISCED 5A (a bachelor's or master's degree) compared to the OECD average of 84.4% (OECD, 2013a). A study comparing the People's Republic of China, Hong Kong–China, Japan, Korea, Singapore, Thailand and the United States found a higher share of Thai primary teachers with bachelor's degrees and secondary teachers with master's degrees than in the other Asian jurisdictions (Ingersoll, 2007).

Evidence suggests that Thailand has a general oversupply of teachers but shortages in specific subjects (mathematics, science, foreign languages, Thai, arts and vocational education; see Table 5.3) and in certain regions of the country (Atagi, 2011; OEC, 2014). Recent research from the World Bank confirms that the teacher shortage is most acute among small schools in the poorer regions of the country, including the northern provinces of Mae Hong Son, Tak and Amnat Charoen, where schools have, on average, less than one teacher per classroom (Lathapipat, 2015). However, it is difficult to assess Thailand's teaching needs due to the multitude of institutions involved in the management of the workforce and a lack of consistent data.

There may also be a shortage of school leaders. In the 2013/14 school year, OBEC reported a shortage of 825 educational administrators in schools (OHEC, 2015). The OTEPC has predicted that 66% of basic education administrators will retire between 2013 and 2027 (OBEC, 2015a). As of November 2014, there were 39 168 school principals and deputy directors in the basic education system (OBEC, 2015a).[1]

Assessing teacher personnel shortages in Thailand is challenging due to the difficulty of measuring the country's student-teacher ratio, which is set and most often reported at the national level, despite the great variety in school size across the country. The Office of the Teacher Civil Service and Educational Personnel Commission (OTEPC) established the standard ratio of 25:1 across primary and secondary education (OEC, 2014). In 2012, the average student-teacher ratio in Thailand was 16:1 in primary schools and 20:1 in secondary schools (UIS, 2015). Research indicates there is little variation across socio-economically advantaged and disadvantaged schools (21.1:1 compared with 19.8:1), although significantly more across rural (15.2:1) and urban (21.5:1) schools (OECD, 2013a). A low student-teacher ratio is not necessarily a positive phenomenon in rural areas, as schools may still be understaffed, requiring teachers to teach multiple grades and bear a heavy workload (Jones, 2014). This is a particular problem for Thailand's many small schools in poor regions, where low ratios often mask challenging classroom environments for which teachers are poorly prepared (Jones, 2014; Lathapipat, 2015).

Teacher and school leader reform

Thailand's 1999 National Education Act introduced changes to the teaching profession, raising standards and supporting the country's shift towards a more learner-centred education system. The Teachers and Educational Personnel Act enacted many of these reforms in 2004. The Act also established or revised the responsibilities of a range of organisations tasked with overseeing the country's teaching profession, including:

- The Teachers' Council of Thailand (TCT), responsible for establishing standards for the teaching profession, licensing teachers according to those standards, accrediting teacher pre-service education programmes and setting out requirements for and delivering in-service education.

- The Committee for Promotion of the Benefits and Welfare of Teachers and Educational Personnel, responsible for policies to support teachers' financial well-being.

- The OTEPC, responsible for policies relating to teachers' deployment, promotion, compensation and workload.

In 2005, the government also established the National Institute for the Development of Teachers, Faculty staff and Educational Personnel (NIDTEP) to oversee the in-service training of education personnel, replacing other organisations such as the Institute for the Development of Educational Administrators. With a view to improving teaching quality, Thailand extended the length of its teacher pre-service education programme from four to five years in 2002. It has also introduced scholarship programmes to attract high-achieving students to the profession and address subject-specific and region-specific teacher shortages. One such programme is the recent New Breed of Teachers Project (2010-15) described later in this chapter.

The licensing system, first implemented in 2005, requires individuals to obtain a licence from the TCT and renew it every five years in order to work as a teacher in the country. Before this system was put in place, anyone with a four-year bachelor's degree in any discipline could complete 24 credits of study in education or take an exam to become a teacher (Atagi, 2011). In order to obtain a teaching licence, individuals must:

1. be at least 20 years old
2. have an education degree or equivalent or other educational qualification accredited by the Teachers' Council of Thailand
3. have completed at least one year of practical training in a school
4. not have any of the following characteristics: improper behaviour or immorality, incompetence or quasi-incompetence, and prior imprisonment which may bring dishonour upon the profession (Government of Thailand, 2003).

Since the advent of Thailand's Second Decade of Education Reform in 2009, the government has consistently called for reforms to further improve the training, development and utilisation of educational personnel. Proposals that are still part of the government's reform agenda include calls to:

- attract a sufficient number of high-quality candidates to the profession, including individuals qualified in fields other than education
- upgrade human resources (HR) management and deployment practices
- support teachers' continual self-development and improve their performance evaluation
- reduce teachers' administrative workload to allow them to focus more on teaching (OEC, 2009; OBEC, 2015b).

The current government has also placed particular emphasis on supporting students' school-to-work transitions through more vocational education and better preparation in Thai and English, recently announcing plans to evaluate the skills of the country's English-language teachers. This has important implications for the teaching workforce, as vocational education, Thai and English are all areas where the country is experiencing a shortage of teachers.

Thailand's teacher education organisations

Thailand's education system has a high degree of institutional complexity, with many organisations involved in different aspects of the teaching profession (Figure 5.1).

Figure 5.1. Teacher-related institutions in Thailand

Policy development	Teacher preparation policy and accreditation	Teacher employment exam, salary, career progression and workload
Ministry of Education Offices Office of the Education Council (OEC) Office of the Basic Education Commission (OBEC) Office of the Vocational Education Commission (OVEC) Office of the Private Education Commission (OPEC) Office of Non-Formal and Informal Education (ONIE) National Institute for Development of Teachers, Faculty Staff and Educational Personnel (NIDTEP) Office of the Teacher Civil Service and Educational Personnel Commission (OTEPC) **Other organisations** Teachers' Council of Thailand (TCT) Office of the Welfare Promotion Commission for Teachers and Educational Personnel Institute for the Promotion of Teaching Science and Technology (IPST)	Teachers' Council of Thailand (TCT) Office of the Higher Education Commission (OHEC) **University accreditation** Office for National Education Standards and Quality Assessment (ONESQA) **Pre-service providers** 143 providers	Office of the Teacher Civil Service and Educational Personnel Commission (OTEPC)
		Teacher certification and standards Teachers' Council of Thailand (TCT)
	Teacher profissional development (PD) policy National Institute for the Development of Teachers, Faculty, Staff and Educational Personnel (NIDTEP) **PD providers:** NIDTEP, TCT, OBEC, OVEC, OPEC, universities, Institute for the Promotion of Teaching and Learning	**School assessments** ONESQA and OBEC
		Teachers' associations

Source: OEC (2014), "Country background report – Thailand", internal report provided to the OECD, Office of the Education Council (OEC), Bangkok.

Policy Issue 1: Teacher preparation is inadequate to support the country's education reforms

Teacher preparation is important as the first building block in a teacher's ongoing learning and development. The types of qualifications (e.g. bachelor's degree), the duration of initial training and pre-service programme content can all influence the extent to which initial teacher education prepares teachers for their role (OECD, 2014a). Well-designed teacher preparation can also be a powerful vehicle for education reform, preparing the next generation of teachers to implement new curriculum and innovative teaching methods (Darling-Hammond and Lieberman, 2012; Jensen et al., 2012).

Pre-service providers and programme structure

As of 2009/10, 103 institutions in Thailand were offering accredited pre-service programmes leading to a bachelor's degree or graduate degree (Table 5.2). While there are benefits to having higher education institutions in different, even remote, regions of the country (see the example of Lao People's Democratic Republic in Box 5.13 below), the large number of pre-service programme providers raises concerns about quality assurance. Rajabhat universities, the country's historical teachers' colleges, make up just under 40% of the pre-service institutions, and their standards vary significantly (Atagi, 2011). The Office of the Higher Education Commission (OHEC) ranked the Rajabhats as only "fairly good" or "needing improvement" in 2006 (Atagi, 2011). A research report calls them "substandard" and states that the government universities are more prestigious (Tongliemnak, 2010).

Thailand has a five-year concurrent pre-service programme leading to a bachelor of education degree (Atagi, 2011). An alternative certificate programme consists of one year of practice teaching and a certain number of credits in pedagogical courses specified by the TCT, followed by an exam. This seems to be a common route into the profession for prospective vocational teachers. In 2010, Thailand introduced a one-year New Breed of Teachers scholarship programme for students who already had a degree as a temporary measure to address shortage areas. Stakeholders indicated that the country is considering moving towards consecutive secondary preparation and concurrent elementary preparation. There are benefits and drawbacks to both the concurrent and consecutive programme model. Concurrent programmes offer a more integrated learning experience because subject matter and pedagogical training occur at the same time, while consecutive programmes offer the ability to enter the teaching profession more quickly (Musset, 2010). Across OECD countries, primary teacher preparation is typically concurrent (in 22 out of 36 OECD countries) and secondary preparation is more commonly consecutive (16 countries) (OECD, 2014a). The research literature offers different opinions about the optimal structure of pre-service programmes, but there is consensus that the quality of teacher preparation is even more important than the structure.

Table 5.2. **Number of institutions offering accredited pre-service programmes, 2009/10**

Institution	Number*
Rajabhat universities	40
Private universities	20
State universities	12
Private colleges	10
State-supervised universities	9
Rajamangala universities of technology	6
Buddhist universities	2
Private institutes	2
Physical Education Institute	1
Bunditpatanasilpa Institute	1
Total	**103**

*These include different campuses of the same institution.

Source: OEC (2015c), "Teacher education institutions", information provided to the review team.

Entry requirements

High-performing education systems tend to recruit their student teachers from the top third of graduating cohorts entering tertiary education (Barber and Mourshed, 2007). OECD countries tend to select students based on secondary grade point average, followed by interviews and competitive exams, and finally, standardised tests (OECD, 2014a). Half of OECD countries limit the number of pre-service programme places available to student teachers (OECD, 2014a).

In Thailand, pre-service programme providers select candidates for admission. OHEC recommends that providers use applicants' scores from the Ordinary National Educational Test (O-NET), General Aptitude Test (GAT) and Professional and Academic Aptitude Test (PAT) for admission, and faculties may use their own criteria (such as a university exam). There are significant concerns about the quality of Thailand's national assessments, including these ones (Chapter 4).

Thailand does not have minimum requirements for admission into pre-service education programmes, suggesting that intake may vary significantly across institutions. The country's two open universities (or open-admission universities), where "any person wishing to enrol can apply without having to take an entrance examination" (Tongliemnak, 2010), produce approximately 25% of the pre-service programme graduates in the country (Vanichseni and Associates, 2012). This has implications for both the quantity and quality of graduates moving into the teaching profession. In general, failure to control entry into pre-service programmes can lead to an oversupply of low-qualified teachers, whereas greater selectivity can make the teaching profession more attractive to high performers (Hobson et al., 2010). Top-performing school systems tend to select candidates admission with "a high overall level of literacy and numeracy, strong interpersonal and communications skills, a willingness to learn, and the motivation to teach" (Barber and Mourshed, 2007). Adopting high minimum standards for admission would put Thailand in a stronger position to ensure an appropriate supply of high-quality teachers.

Pre-service programme content and delivery

It is common in OECD countries for a government body or independent authority to establish a framework for pre-service programme content (OECD, 2014a). Typically, programmes consist of three content areas: 1) foundation courses (learning and development, multicultural education); 2) pedagogical courses (classroom management, teaching methods); and 3) subject matter courses, combined with a practicum component, linking the theory learned in the courses to the practice of teaching (Boyd et al., 2007). Teachers who complete programmes that include "content, pedagogy and practical components for the subjects they teach feel better prepared for their work than their colleagues whose formal education did not contain these elements" (OECD, 2014b).

Research recommends the following for the design and delivery of pre-service programme content:

- Programme providers and schools should share a common vision of good teaching – or standards – to promote coherence across the education system.
- Programme providers should collaborate internally, with other faculties and with schools and other key stakeholders to ensure programme content is up to date and coherent.
- Programme providers should ensure courses are delivered by faculty who are highly qualified and up to date on current and innovative teaching methods (e.g. by offering sabbaticals to academic staff and having practising teachers deliver some courses).

- The practicum should be lengthy and interwoven with coursework, offering a range of teaching experiences and highly skilled, well-trained supervising teachers.
- Both preparation in subject matter and pedagogy should be treated as equally important.
- Programmes should provide sufficient preparation in learner-centred teaching methods, student assessment techniques, inclusive education and ICT to foster "learning without limit" and the acquisition of 21st century skills.
- Theory and practice should be integrated through reflective practice (e.g. by having student teachers examine case studies, develop portfolios, or conduct research on issues identified during the practicum)[2] (Darling-Hammond, 2006; Levine, 2006).

Do Thailand's pre-service programmes reflect these features?

The established standards for Thailand's pre-service programmes are the Standards of Knowledge in the TCT's Regulation on Professional Standards and Ethics. These standards require individuals seeking a teacher's licence to have knowledge of typical foundation and pedagogical topics like curriculum development, educational measurement and evaluation, and classroom management. The standards are used for licensing and pre-service accreditation and they provide the basis for pre-service courses. Less clear is whether the standards (and the TCT's professional and ethical standards) are used as tools to create coherence as part of the country's education reform or for collaboration between pre-service programme providers and schools.

There are indications that the practicum component could be designed better to encourage greater reflection on teaching practice and closer connections with schools. In Thailand, the practicum requirements are simply a checklist ("practised" or "not practised") rather than a thorough assessment of student teachers, and there are no selection requirements for the valuable role of supervising teachers (Vanichseni and Associates, 2012). The entire year-long practicum is conducted at the end of the programme rather than being interwoven with coursework. Stakeholders reported that more back-and-forth between practice teaching and coursework over the final year and a half of the programme would be preferable.

Thailand's pre-service programmes appear to cover the three broad content areas typical of teacher preparation courses (foundation, pedagogy and subject matter), but discussions with stakeholders in Thailand, as well as some research, indicate that gaps remain in topics important to supporting the country's education reform. Most notably, programmes are not specifically required to prepare student teachers in the basic education curriculum, the linchpin of the country's learner-centred education reform, or impart an understanding of the theory of learning underpinning the curriculum and the reform (see Chapter 3).

Stakeholders also stated that programmes need to provide better preparation in pedagogy, assessment (see Chapter 4) and teaching students with special needs. This is particularly important as training in the use of diagnostic and formative assessment tools to identify weak learners and provide targeted support is essential preparation for inclusive and learner-centred classrooms.

Box 5.1. Teacher preparation in Singapore

Singapore's teacher preparation system features strong course content, delivery, practice teaching and collaborative relationships. Although Singapore's higher education system differs from Thailand's in that it is highly centralised with only one teacher pre-service education institution, the National Institute of Education (NIE), a number of its practices are relevant.

Key features of teacher preparation in Singapore include:

- A four-year pre-service programme that includes high subject content knowledge (equivalent to a specialist degree) and pedagogical knowledge and skills with very few electives. Courses prepare student teachers to use problem-based, inquiry learning and learner-centred teaching methods.

- A 20-week practicum, spread throughout the duration of the four-year programme. This uses a "school partnership" model whereby student teachers are placed in the classrooms of selected teachers and supervised by a lecturer from the NIE and a senior teacher in the school.

- Faculty are rewarded for their teaching effectiveness and school-based research; feedback on the latter is gathered from schools, the Ministry of Education and parents to determine its impact on school practice and education policy.

- Most importantly, an "Enhanced Partnership Model" connects the NIE, the Ministry of Education and schools, which provides a strong link between theory and practice, as well as in-service and pre-service education. The partnership involves secondments, regular strategy sessions and constant feedback and evaluation of the pre-service programme.

Sources: Lay Choo and Darling-Hammond (2011), "Creating effective teachers and leaders in Singapore", in Darling-Hammond and Rothman (2011) (eds.), *Teacher and Leader Effectiveness in High-Performing Education System*, http://pasisahlberg.com/wp-content/uploads/2012/12/Teacher-Leader-Effectiveness-Report-2011.pdf; Jensen et al. (2012), *Catching Up: Learning from the Best School Systems in East Asia*, http://grattan.edu.au/wp-content/uploads/2014/04/129_report_learning_from_the_best_main.pdf.

The accreditation process

Pre-service accreditation, either by a government agency or an independent body, is common in OECD countries as a quality assurance measure and a means of ensuring that teacher preparation delivers what the education system needs (OECD, 2014a).

Thailand has internal and external pre-service accreditation processes, but the three different external assessments may not work optimally together.

1. The ONESQA assesses a sample of all higher education institutions every year.

2. The TCT, in co-operation with OHEC, assesses pre-service programmes once every five years when the programme curriculum is updated. This process includes a document review and interviews with students and professors.

3. OHEC assesses each programme's material against the standards in the Thai Qualifications Framework once it has been reviewed by the TCT. Generally, if the TCT approves a programme, it will be approved by OHEC.

It was reported that the accreditation process is complicated and onerous because the different accreditors do not work together and the accreditation requirements overlap rather than complement each other. In some instances the accreditation results also appear to be inconsistent; some programmes are only "partially accredited" (Vanichseni and Associates, 2012).

Stakeholders' comments indicate a mismatch between how pre-service programmes are preparing teachers and the needs of the education system, which also suggests a problem with the accreditation process. The basic education system in Thailand, like many worldwide, is based on a model of specialist knowledge at the secondary level and generalist knowledge at the primary level. However, it was reported that some programmes prepare generalist secondary teachers, while others prepare specialist teachers without regard for the primary/secondary divide. A certain amount of variety among pre-service programmes is expected and encouraged in a decentralised higher education system, but if programmes are not preparing teachers for the country's education system, this is a real concern.

> **Box 5.2. Pre-service programme accreditation in Korea**
>
> Korea has a large pre-service education system with multiple providers (43 teachers' colleges, 55 university faculties of education, 160 university teacher education courses and 136 graduates schools of education) and a comprehensive accreditation process, recently overhauled to address concerns about quality assurance and a teacher oversupply. Accreditations are now conducted by the Korean Educational Development Institute (KEDI) every five years and include the following elements:
>
> - a self-evaluation by the institution, based on KEDI criteria, followed by expert team visits
>
> - a detailed assessment focused on three areas: management and environment (e.g. facilities, resources), the programme (e.g. curriculum, faculty, connections with schools) and outcomes (e.g. graduate satisfaction and rates of employment)
>
> - published results that can lead to financial rewards if satisfactory or a reduction in the number of student spaces if unsatisfactory.
>
> While it is too soon to determine the long-term impact of the new accreditation process, changes are already apparent, with some providers introducing new curricula and hiring new faculty, and an increased flow of information between institutions, schools, the government and student teachers.
>
> *Source*: Jensen, et al. (2012), *Catching Up: Learning from the Best School Systems in East Asia*, http://grattan.edu.au/wp-content/uploads/2014/04/129_report_learning_from_the_best_main.pdf.

Recommendations

The review team recommends that Thailand:

- **Establish minimum criteria for entry into teacher preparation in consultation with pre-service programme providers.**

As described in Chapter 4, the review team has concerns about the validity, fairness and reliability of the national standardised tests that are currently used to inform entry to higher education, including pre-service programmes. It recommended validity studies and other changes to ensure these tests meet international standards of good practice.

At the same time, Thailand should review the admission practices and criteria used in high-performing education systems around the world to select the methods most likely to identify the best candidates, and work with pre-service programme providers to introduce them. These methods could include interviews designed to measure attributes like interpersonal skills and a strong motivation to teach, which are difficult to assess with standardised tests. Pre-service programme providers without admission requirements would need to adopt them.

An accurate understanding of the country's future teaching needs will assist Thailand and its higher education institutions to decide how high to set the bar for entry into pre-service education programmes (see also Policy Issue 5, below).

- **Strengthen teacher preparation in areas key to learning goals.**

Thailand would benefit from reviewing the content of its pre-service education programmes in consultation with key stakeholders, to determine how they could provide better preparation in pedagogy, as well as key areas like assessment, ICT and 21st century skills.

As described in Chapter 3, teachers are not receiving sufficient preparation in the philosophy underpinning the current standards-based curriculum, nor how to implement it successfully (for example developing lesson plans, selecting resources and using appropriate teaching and assessment strategies). Preparation in the curriculum, both in its current form and as it evolves over time, should be a pre-service programme requirement. Programmes should prepare primary teachers to be generalists and secondary teachers to be specialists to match the expectations of the curriculum. In short, student teachers should be prepared in the basic education curriculum subjects they will be expected to teach.

Given the importance of the practicum and the benefits to student teachers of interweaving theory and practice, the practical teaching component should be restructured so that it does not take place exclusively in the final year of the programme. To support the practicum, Thailand should establish common expectations for learners, guidance for supervising teachers and standards for student teacher evaluations which should relate to the performance appraisal assistant teachers (i.e. teachers in the first two years of their teaching career) will receive when they start work, albeit less stringent. The practicum should be delivered as a partnership between providers and schools; Thailand should adopt formal partnership relationships, borrowing elements from Singapore's "Enhanced Partnership Model".

- **Streamline and strengthen the pre-service accreditation process.**

The accreditation requirements should be streamlined and, at the same time, made more thorough. Thailand might consider adopting aspects of the Korean accreditation process (Box 5.2) and closing down low-rated pre-service programme providers. One organisation should have primary responsibility for accreditation.

The accreditation process should include a review of the relevant faculty to ensure they are up to date on the basic education curriculum, the theory behind it, and innovative teaching methods to support it.

Many of the above recommendations are also relevant to the alternative certificate programme.

Policy Issue 2: Thailand lacks a holistic strategy for professional development

Induction and sustained teacher professional development

There is a correlation between sustained teacher professional development (PD) and improvements in student achievement (OECD, 2014a). PD is also a more cost-effective way of improving student outcomes than reducing class size or increasing student learning time (Musset, 2010). Research recommends that the stages of initial teacher education and professional development be interconnected to create a continuum of teacher learning and development (OECD, 2005, 2014b). High-performing education systems around the world tend to invest the most in teachers' initial and ongoing learning and ensure that teachers' professional development begins with induction (Barber and Mourshed, 2007; UNESCO, 2014). Formal induction for beginning teachers is mandatory in 18 out of the 33 OECD countries with available data (OECD, 2014a). If well designed, this type of PD can improve retention, effectiveness and job satisfaction among new teachers (OECD, 2005).

In a promising move, Thailand introduced an induction programme for new teachers in 2013. Assistant teachers are evaluated by their principal, a senior teacher and a member of the school board every three months throughout their first two years on the job. It was reported that evaluators receive a manual to support their work and that assistant teachers receive on-the-job training in the form of written material on how to perform their duties in the school. If assistant teachers do not pass the induction, they are required to quit their teaching position within five days. However, no data on delivery or completion rates are being collected, so the pass rate of assistant teachers is not known.

What Thailand's induction programme seems to lack is mentoring, a key component of most induction programmes. Nor does it have any bearing on teacher certification. This is contrary to international practice; most countries with mandatory induction programmes require the successful completion of the programme for full teacher certification (OECD, 2005). Thailand should also ensure that the programme is available to assistant teachers working on temporary contracts.

Providers, planning and funding

Internationally, having a range of professional development providers is recognised as a good thing as long as PD meets quality standards (OECD, 2005). In Thailand, the NIDTEP oversees the professional development of teachers, but its capacity to co-ordinate and guarantee quality across the multiplicity of providers of PD appears limited (Atagi, 2011). There is conflicting information about whether a professional development accreditation process is being implemented. Given the high number of PD providers and programmes, it seems likely that, if an accreditation process exists, it may not be thorough.

There is encouraging evidence that school leaders and teachers work together to plan for participation in professional development and that schools sometimes work together to provide it. Teachers identify training they would like to take, sometimes using annual self-assessment reports (SARs) or individual development plans, and depending on the cost, may have to ask their principal for permission to participate in it. OBEC recently provided vouchers worth THB 3 000 (Thai baht, just under USD 100) to each teacher to participate in the professional development of their choice. Principals make decisions about the training needs of staff in their schools, based in part on information teachers provide in their SARs. Education Service Areas (ESAs) survey schools and review teachers' qualifications to determine the region's training needs, and invite schools to participate in the PD they deem important. The Ministry of Education sets professional development priorities and provides training, often using the "train the trainer" model, on national policies such as inclusive education (OBEC, 2013b). Thailand does not currently use student assessments such as PISA or national standardised tests to identify schools' or teachers' professional development needs as some countries do (see, for example, UNESCO, 2014). In order to do so, Thailand would first need to ensure that its assessment data are accurate and reliable (see Chapter 4).

Participation, delivery and content

Out of 33 OECD and partner countries, three-quarters require teachers to participate in professional development. Eight countries require it for promotion or salary increases and in Japan it is required for licence renewal (OECD, 2014a). Requirements for annual PD participation range from a minimum of 8 hours per year in Luxembourg to 150 hours per year in

Iceland (OECD, 2014a). In Thailand, the TCT requires teachers to participate in at least 20 hours of professional development per year in order to maintain their teaching licence, a requirement that may also be necessary for promotion. It was also reported that, by regulation, teachers are entitled to leave their classroom to participate in 50 hours of training per year. Actual rates of participation in professional development in Thailand appear to be high. A 2007 Teacher Watch survey found that 92.6% of Thai teachers attended training programmes three times a year (Atagi, 2011). More recent PISA data confirms this trend (OECD, 2010a). The major issues with professional development in Thailand seem to be its delivery outside of the school and its relevance. The 2007 Teacher Watch survey found that 42% of teachers could not fulfil their teaching assignments due to the need to attend training, suggesting that a large proportion of professional development takes place off-site and is not embedded in the classroom (Atagi, 2011). There are encouraging signs that Thailand has recently made efforts to provide more training in school, for example introducing a coaching and mentoring programme for teachers in 60 different ESAs. However, the review team's discussions with stakeholders and recent research conducted by the Quality Learning Foundation (see next section) verify that professional development is still taking teachers away from their schools. According to stakeholders, the commonest professional development teachers take is on English language, ASEAN language and culture, ICT, 21st century skills, and the 30% of the basic education curriculum that is supposed to be developed locally. However, the review team also heard widespread comments that training on ICT and 21st century skills, as well as key issues in the curriculum like assessment, was lacking. This could indicate inefficiency in the way the PD is delivered or ineffectiveness in the training.

Thailand has introduced a lighthouse-type model of professional development through a nationwide Institute for the Promotion of Teaching Science and Technology (IPST) programme whereby exemplary schools disseminate effective practices for teaching science, technology, engineering and mathematics (STEM) to neighbouring schools. The initiative currently reaches around 100 institutions. The Thai government and other education organisations, such as the Quality Learning Foundation, have also introduced awards to acknowledge exemplary teachers and encourage them to serve as role models to develop other education personnel (QLF, 2015). Although these discrete initiatives have their value, Thailand would benefit more from developing a structured capacity-building plan for the entire education system.

Processes to support continued professional development and high-quality teaching

> **Box 5.3. Moving towards a framework for good teaching: The example of Chile**
>
> Chile's Framework for Good Teaching is organised into four areas: 1) preparation for teaching; 2) creation of an adequate learning environment; 3) teaching for the learning of all students; and 4) professional development. The standards are expressed in 20 criteria and 70 descriptors, and are used to certify new teachers, select and promote teachers, appraise teachers' performance and provide them with support, identify excellent teachers, and accredit professional development programmes. Research recommends the development of standards that:
>
> - are understandable and aligned with good teacher performance and student learning standards
> - relate to all of the domains of teacher performance, with indicators of good practice
> - express different levels of competency for each domain
> - relate to teachers in diverse contexts across different school;
> - define the goals and outcomes of good teacher performance without prescribing specific practices
> - are dynamic and updated periodically in consultation with teachers.
>
> *Source*: OECD (2010b), "Teacher career paths: Consolidating a quality profession", http://dx.doi.org/10.1787/9789264087040-5-en.

According to research, standards describing what teachers should know and be able to do should be used to align all of the elements of the teaching profession relating to teachers' knowledge and skills (see Box 5.3 for an example). These include pre-service education, continuing professional development, certification, performance appraisal and career progression (Darling-Hammond and Lieberman, 2012; CEPPE, 2013). These standards – or profiles – should be based on objectives for student learning, informed by evidence and input from teachers and different stakeholders, and appropriate to teachers at different stages of their careers (OECD, 2005). They should describe teacher competencies, as well as "strong subject matter knowledge, pedagogical skills, the capacity to work effectively with a wide range of students and colleagues, contribution to the school and the wider profession, and the teacher's capacity to continue developing" (OECD, 2005). The importance of involving teachers in the development of these standards cannot be stressed enough, considering that the profession needs to feel ownership of the standards in order for them to be viewed as valid and meaningful (OECD, 2010b). Research also advises that standards be accompanied by assessment mechanisms to determine whether they have been achieved (Kleinhenz and Ingvarson, 2007; CEPPE, 2013).

A strength of the Thai education system is that it has developed standards for teachers: the TCT's standards of knowledge, performance and conduct (TCT, 2005). They include some key knowledge areas, skills and practices recommended in the research on this subject, although their wording is sometimes vague (e.g. "make decisions to practice various activities, taking into account consequences on learners"). However, it is unclear whether the TCT provides a full description of each of the standards or any related competencies. In addition, the standards may be out of step with the expectations in the evolving curriculum (see Chapter 3). These are things that the TCT should address in its announced plans to upgrade teacher standards over the next three years. The Southeast Asian Ministers of Education Organization Regional Center for Educational Innovation and Technology (SEAMEO INNOTECH) recently developed 11 suggested teaching competency standards for the Southeast Asian region for use in capacity building and training (SEAMEO INNOTECH, 2010). These competency standards may provide useful guidance to the government in its reforms.

Thailand does not use its standards to align all relevant aspects of the teaching profession. They are a part of the processes to accredit pre-service programmes and license teachers, but teachers' performance is not actually evaluated against the standards as part of the licensing process. Other areas – continuing professional development, performance appraisal and career progression – fall under the mandates of different organisations with their own assessment criteria. Below is an overview of Thailand's recertification, performance appraisal and career progression processes. They are all largely paper-based and focus on compliance.

Certification and recertification

The TCT issues initial teaching licences to individuals who graduate from the country's pre-service programmes, relying on the programmes to address the standards of knowledge necessary for certification. Teachers are recertified every five years, with the current process relying solely on teachers self-reporting that they are continually developing their practice and meeting the TCT's standards, which is not a reliable quality assurance measure. The OECD has previously recommended that Thailand's licensing system involve a more "stringent, demanding evaluation of applicants' qualifications" (OECD, 2014c). More troubling are concerns stakeholders in

Thailand raised about the TCT's standards being ignored and bribery leading to licence renewal. The lack of a fair and transparent licensing process raises serious doubts about the status and legitimacy of the teaching profession as a whole. Claims of bribery should be investigated as a priority.

As well as establishing an efficient, transparent and fair process, research recommends the use of authentic and performance-based methods of assessing knowledge and capabilities for licence renewal, including interviews, thorough examinations of work portfolios and psychometric tests (OECD, 2010b). A well-designed, standards-based performance appraisal system can also provide an authentic form of evaluation as it offers the best opportunity to assess actual teaching practice with ongoing improvement as a major goal.

Performance appraisal

Key components of an effective appraisal system include:

- the teaching standards and competencies to be assessed, including those related to equity
- the designated sources of information for the appraisal (countries commonly use classroom observations, teacher interviews, portfolios, tests and some measure of student performance)
- evaluators who are knowledgeable about teachers' work (e.g. experienced teachers), impartial and trained to conduct the evaluations
- mechanisms like school-based professional development to foster improvement, given the formative nature of performance appraisal (OECD, 2010b).

Most OECD countries implement a formal teacher evaluation process, conducted by the principal or other senior school staff, which commonly involves classroom observations, interviews and a review of documentation such as lesson plans, pupil performance data and teacher self-evaluations (Schleicher, 2012). The frequency of classroom observations ranges from three to six times per year in England to once every four years in Chile, but where evaluation is implemented, it almost always involves a formal annual meeting between the principal and the teacher (Schleicher, 2012). Self-assessments of teaching practice are important, but on their own, they do not provide assurances of high-quality teaching or effective formative development like that offered by a standardised performance appraisal system. The most effective evaluation systems link to and provide opportunities for continuing professional development and reward effective teaching (Santiago and Benavides, 2009, in OECD, 2010b). See Box 5.4 for an example from Canada.

In Thailand, ONESQA school assessment requirements mandate that teachers' lesson plans, classroom management, performance, evaluation forms and tests be assessed at least once per academic term and that assessment results be applied to individual teachers' professional development (ONESQA, 2013). However, there is no formalised growth-oriented performance appraisal process, and ONESQA does not provide schools with material to support teacher appraisal, standards against which teachers are assessed, or training for principals on how to provide constructive feedback. Stakeholder groups and working teachers reported to the review team that the ONESQA school assessments and other school-based appraisal processes, which vary across the country, do not provide useful feedback on teaching practice or support professional development. In many regions, schools rely on teachers to assess their own practice.

Box 5.4. Performance appraisal in Ontario, Canada

Ontario has a standards-based teacher performance appraisal system with two components: one designed for new teachers and one for experienced teachers. Both components were designed based on extensive consultations with stakeholders as part of a Working Table on Teacher Development. For both, principals appraise teachers using guidelines and templates provided by the Ministry of Education. Teachers' performance is appraised against competency statements that describe the skills, knowledge and attitudes required to reflect the Ontario College of Teachers' Standards of Practice for the Teaching Profession in five domains: 1) commitment to students and student learning; 2) professional knowledge; 3) professional practice; 4) leadership in learning communities; and 5) ongoing professional learning. Each of the competency statements is accompanied by information about the possible ways the competency may be demonstrated in practice.

All performance appraisals include classroom observation, appraisal meetings to discuss performance, a summative report, feedback, a rating and a process for providing additional support. Multiple unsatisfactory ratings lead to termination of employment and a review conducted by the Ontario College of Teachers, which may result in limitations being placed on a teacher's certificate or its revocation. New teachers are appraised twice in their first 12 months of employment as part of the province's New Teacher Induction Program. Appraisals are specifically designed to assess beginning teachers' competencies. Two satisfactory ratings lead to full teacher certification. Experienced teachers are appraised by their principals every five years. An important element of this system is the Annual Learning Plan experienced teachers complete in consultation with their principal to identify strategies for professional development.

Sources: Ontario Ministry of Education (2010), *Teacher Performance Appraisal: Technical Requirements Manual*, www.edu.gov.on.ca/eng/teacher/pdfs/TPA_Manual_English_september2010l.pdf; Ontario Ministry of Education (2012), *Teacher performance appraisal system*, www.edu.gov.on.ca/eng/teacher/appraise.html.

Career progression

A career progression structure which rewards improvements in teaching quality and increases teacher retention requires teaching standards and performance assessment. In Thailand, teachers have an established career path and career advancement process overseen by the OTEPC. They start as assistant teachers for the first two years of their teaching career, then become teachers. After teaching for a specified number of years, they can progress to professional teacher, senior professional teacher, expert teacher and finally senior expert teacher (see Policy Issue 4 for the progression to school leadership). It is commendable that Thailand has developed a career path that allows diversity within the classroom teacher role. However, it is not clear whether there are articulated responsibilities that distinguish each level or whether assessments for promotion relate to the TCT's standards, both of which are important to ensure quality.

The career advancement process requires teachers to submit an application to their local ESA and the OTEPC describing how they meet certain criteria for "academic standing" in order to be promoted. In a separate process, teachers also apply to their principal for incremental (0.5-2%) semi-annual salary increases. The current weighting system for promotion and salary assessments favours factors other than high-quality teaching:

For promotion, the weighting is:

- 9.9% for students' learning outcomes, including standard test results (3.3%) and grade-point average (6.6%)
- 33.3% for teaching skills
- 56.6% for other factors such as ethics and research.

For salary, the weighting is:

- nil for students' learning outcomes
- 30% for teaching skills
- 70% for other factors such as ethics and research (TDRI, 2015).

A common criticism of these assessments is that they focus teachers' attention away from students' learning onto action research. The concept of the "teacher as researcher" is frequently associated with the successful education systems in Finland and Shanghai, and some research has recommended it as a professional development model (Schleicher, 2012). However, such research is generally conducted collaboratively and used to improve teaching and learning at the group or school level. In Thailand, it seems to be a requirement that is performed in isolation, for the purposes of documentation only, with no expectation that results will be disseminated and analysed to build other teachers' capacity.

To focus the process more on high-quality teaching, Thailand appears to be moving towards using student performance results to assess teachers for promotion, and a pilot project is currently in place to test this model (OEC, 2014). Research indicates that this should be done with caution (UNESCO, 2014). Using student performance results as the sole or main measure of a teacher's (or principal's) performance is inadvisable because, among other things, it reduces a complex web of factors influencing student achievement to the performance of a particular teacher (CEPPE, 2013). It can also have important negative implications for equity by discouraging teachers from working in schools with low-achieving students (OECD, 2014c; UNESCO, 2014). In Thailand it would be particularly inadvisable to use student performance results in this way, given concerns about the validity of student assessments (see Chapter 4). If assessments were improved to meet high standards, student performance data could be used as one of several different sources of evidence in a standardised teacher performance appraisal system. The results of teacher performance appraisals could be one factor considered for the purposes of promotion (Box 5.5).

Box 5.5. Pathways to teacher promotion

Several jurisdictions (e.g. Australia, England and Wales, and Ireland) have developed competency-based career paths for teachers that associate higher-level teaching positions with additional responsibilities to improve teaching quality in the school.

In Shanghai, teachers are expected to improve student learning and develop other teachers in order to be promoted. Mentoring is an explicit component of a teacher's job description and a requirement for promotion. Research is also a requirement for promotion, but rather than being an isolated pursuit, it is conducted collaboratively as part of a "teaching and research group". These groups are allotted time to meet on a regular basis, conduct classroom observations, share constructive feedback and apply teaching and pedagogical theory in their teaching practice.

Source: Jensen et al. (2012), *Catching Up: Learning from the Best School Systems in East Asia*, http://grattan.edu.au/wp-content/uploads/2014/04/129_report_learning_from_the_best_main.pdf; Schleicher (2012), *Preparing Teachers and Developing School Leaders for the 21st Century: Lessons from Around the World*, http://dx.doi.org/10.1787/9789264174559-en.

Recommendations

The review team recommends that Thailand:

- **Establish a nationwide strategy for professional development to support the country's education reform.**

An existing agency should take responsibility for co-ordinating the development of this strategy and work closely with relevant government bodies and in consultation with stakeholders. To promote alignment across the system, the same agency should probably also be responsible for pre-service education requirements. This could involve consolidating organisations like the TCT and NIDTEP into one agency.

The strategy should develop a catalogue of professional development opportunities based on the skills needed to deliver the basic education curriculum, work towards system-wide education reform goals, and the needs identified by teachers and schools. A gap analysis could be used to gather information for the last of these. Based on this information, the strategy could set funding priorities for the development, accreditation and delivery of this training. The strategy should focus not only on the content of the training but also on delivery methods, prioritising school-based, job-embedded learning opportunities whenever possible (e.g. mentoring, classroom observations and staff discussions, or joint planning focused on different aspects of the curriculum or the development of particular skills). The training should be evaluated on an ongoing basis to ensure it is meeting the strategy's goals.

Related to this, Thailand should ensure that teachers are provided with relevant professional development at each stage of their careers, aligned with national standards (see below). The country has taken a major step in this direction by introducing an induction programme but this should be enhanced to include mentoring as a key component, aligned with professional standards, and made available to assistant teachers working on temporary contracts. The programme's effectiveness should also be evaluated.

- **Update and amend the standards for teaching and establish an authentic process to assess whether teachers are meeting those standards.**

Thailand already has standards for the teaching profession, but they could be amended, in consultation with teachers and stakeholders, to apply to and align more aspects of the profession, including pre-service education, continuing professional development, certification, performance appraisal and career progression, and to ensure they reflect the objectives for student learning in the basic education curriculum (see Chapter 3).

To support teacher quality, a well-designed performance appraisal system should be implemented, assessing performance against standards. This system should be designed to ensure teachers' ongoing professional development to support student learning. Valuable components would include: criteria to evaluate good performance based the on standards, classroom observation, meaningful feedback, a learning plan, professional development support, and a process for removing unsuccessful teachers.

Every education system has quality assurance checks and balances. The performance appraisal system could be the most stringent teaching-related quality assurance measure in Thailand's system and its results could be used as a key factor when making decisions about certification and promotion. Performance appraisals as part of the induction programme should be tailored to the competencies of assistant teachers, and their successful completion should be a requirement for full teacher certification. As a priority, Thailand should investigate and put an end to any bribery that may be occurring in the certification process.

Policy Issue 3: Administrative burdens, particularly in rural schools, keep teachers away from the classroom

Teaching hours and administrative duties

The OECD study *Teachers Matter: Attracting, Developing and Retaining Effective Teachers, Education and Training Policy* (OECD, 2005) found that "teachers are highly motivated by the intrinsic benefits of teaching – working with children and young people, helping them to develop, and making a contribution to society – and that system structures and school workplaces need to ensure that teachers are able to focus on these tasks". Teaching hours and non-teaching duties may affect the attractiveness of the teaching profession (OECD, 2014a). They can also affect teaching quality. In OECD countries, teachers spend an average of 19 hours per week teaching, 3 hours doing administrative work and 2 hours participating in school management activities (OECD, 2014b). Required non-teaching tasks tend to revolve around preparing lessons, teamwork, engaging in dialogue with colleagues and communicating with parents. See Box 5.6 for an example of how non-teaching workload can be reduced to improve conditions.

In Thailand, the OTEPC requires primary and secondary teachers to have a workload of 30 hours per week, of which:

- teaching should constitute 18 hours
- work related to teaching, such as lesson planning, media preparation and evaluation, should constitute 10 hours

- other work assigned by the administrator, such as meetings, should constitute 2 hours (OTEPC, n.d.).

Although the number of teaching hours per week is in line with the OECD average, evidence suggests that teachers in Thailand are working more than the required hours set by the OTEPC and that their administrative tasks are encroaching on their teaching time.

Thai teachers are expected to provide support with the management of the school (e.g. fundraising, overseeing delivery of O-NET assessments, cleaning school grounds in preparation for school assessments), and some take on administrative positions, such as heading a curriculum area (OEC, 2014). Depending on the school, teachers may also have supervisory responsibilities, which require them to check the number of students at the beginning and end of the day, look after students during the lunch break, and supervise meditation. Teachers also appear to be assigned tasks specific to their role as civil servants. For example, it was reported that, because schools are considered government buildings, on a rotating basis, one teacher at each school is required to supervise the school grounds on the weekend. The review team's discussions with stakeholders in Thailand confirmed that the main task that draws teachers' attention away from the classroom is paperwork associated with the different school assessment procedures.

Teachers seem to have little power to refuse tasks assigned to them. According to a 2007 Teacher Watch survey, Thai teachers at the basic education level were teaching "up to four subjects, 22 hours a week" (Jo-Kim, 2010). Teacher Watch also reported that 46% of teachers were spending 20% of their time on administration, and 36% of teachers missed one lesson per week to attend meetings, training and other school-related activities (Atagi, 2011). Since the Teacher Watch survey was conducted eight years ago, the problem may have become worse. In 2014, the Quality Learning Foundation conducted a survey of 427 winners of its Good Teacher Awards and found that:

- Teachers spent 3 or more hours on duties outside the classroom on 84 of the 200 days in the school year.
- The top three activities occupying teachers' time were assessments by external agencies (e.g. ONESQA), academic competitions between students at different schools and training.
- More than 90% of teachers felt that more school autonomy over academic, financial and personnel management would support teachers in improving classroom instruction (QLF, 2014).

Thailand has collected data in preparation for full participation in the OECD study *TALIS 2013 Results: An International Perspective on Teaching and Learning,* and analysis of the results should yield useful information about teachers' working conditions.

Box 5.6. Improving the school working and learning environment: The example of England

In 2003, England implemented a programme entitled Raising Standards and Tackling Workload – A National Agreement in response to research indicating that the country's teachers were spending two-thirds of their time on non-teaching activities and that workload was contributing to teacher retirements and attrition. The programme included measures to improve the working and learning environment of schools, such as:

- reducing working hours in teacher contracts and adding guaranteed planning, preparation and assessment time

- reducing paperwork requirements

- adding support staff to conduct administrative work and support teachers and students, and recognising their importance by providing them with training and development opportunities.

The results were positive. After it was implemented, over 97% of teachers surveyed reported that teaching and learning had improved and approximately 50% reported that workload had decreased.

Source: Schleicher (2012), *Preparing Teachers and Developing School Leaders for the 21st Century: Lessons from Around the World*, http://dx.doi.org/10.1787/9789264174559-en.

Social dialogue

In many countries, teachers have unions to advocate on their behalf and participate in the development of policies that affect them. This kind of consensus-building social dialogue between the government, unions and other major stakeholder groups is crucial to ensuring reforms are successful and equitable (Vere, 2007; UNESCO, 2014). A Thai National Teachers Union was established in 1999 to support teachers and educational personnel with negotiations regarding their salary, benefits, employment and licences.

There is also a Federation of Northern Teachers, Federation of Southern Teachers and Teachers Confederation of Thailand (OEC, 2014). The national union has submitted proposals for education reform to the government, including calls to bring teachers back to the classroom and reduce their non-teaching activities. It would like to be more involved in developing reforms, but it was reported that the government does not support its role. This is a concern. Teachers' voices, articulated by their representative associations, need to be heard to ensure that teachers' rights are respected and reforms affecting teachers are effective.

Challenges in small rural schools

Teachers and school leaders in small schools in rural areas serving disadvantaged students face particular workload challenges. This is especially problematic in Thailand given the high number of such schools and the recent PISA results pointing to inequities in the education system. As stated the UNESCO report, *Learning to Live Together Through Education*:

> [A] principal at a small Northeast Thai rural school…
> ….reaffirmed that there was a shortage of teachers and he had to teach as well as serve as principal. Sometimes classes had to be combined with mixed aged students. Funding from the sub-district office was not the full allotment and led to a shortage of supplies that he and the teachers would cover with out of pocket money. He also mentioned that, in addition to teaching and administrative duties, he and the other teachers had to fulfil all other functions too, such as: janitorial work, grounds-keeping, cooking and preparing food, record-keeping, driver for special occasions and emergencies, and taking care of students who were temporarily abandoned. (Jones, 2014)

Such challenges seem to be widespread. The review team spoke to rural school staff in a disadvantaged area. They stated that teachers sometimes have to home-school particularly vulnerable students, and that to compensate for a teacher shortage, they contribute a portion of their salary to pay for local professionals (e.g. a physicist) to share their hands-on knowledge with students. The staff at this school seemed to be doing a remarkable job under the circumstances, but their experience raises troubling concerns about equity. To better support staff in small, rural schools, Thailand should adopt practices outlined in Box 5.7 below.

Box 5.7. Attracting, supporting and retaining teachers and school leaders in disadvantaged schools

The OECD recommends that countries consider the following policy options to attract, support and retain high-quality teachers and school leaders in disadvantaged schools:

Teachers

- Align pre-service and in-service teacher education with the needs of disadvantaged schools (e.g. by providing practicum opportunities in disadvantaged schools, and offering pre-service and in-service education on diagnosing student problems).

- Provide mentoring. For new teachers, this can increase retention and teaching effectiveness.

- Improve working conditions. Significant factors that improve teacher retention in these schools include support from principals, a collaborative work environment, adequate resources, enough teaching staff to alleviate workloads, and the time and facilities to meet to jointly plan instruction.

- Provide financial incentives to attract and retain teachers. The incentives need to be "large enough to make a difference" and their effectiveness is dependent on teachers' remuneration rates in relation to other professions.

School leaders

- Develop and strengthen training to prepare school leaders to address the particular challenges associated with disadvantaged schools (e.g. preparation on improving student behaviour and engagement, improving the school environment, and nurturing a culture of care and achievement).

- Provide coaching and mentoring by experienced school leaders and opportunities to build school networks.

- Attract and retain school leaders by offering good working conditions, remuneration that is commensurate with their responsibilities, and performance-related rewards and incentives based on clear and accurate assessment criteria.

- Provide systemic support by giving schools the opportunity to develop their own action plans for improvement; providing additional, temporary funding to low-performing schools to use towards training or extra resources; rewarding disadvantaged schools that improve and sharing their successful strategies with other schools; and restructuring consistently low-performing schools.

Source: OECD (2012), *Equity and Quality in Education: Supporting Disadvantaged Students and Schools*, http://dx.doi.org/10.1787/9789264130852-en.

Recommendations

The review team recommends that policy makers:

- **Make efforts to reduce the workload that is taking teachers' attention away from the classroom.**

In consultation with stakeholders, Thailand should review teachers' workload and use the results to reduce the tasks that are not related to teaching and learning, including reducing documentation required by the ONESQA and OBEC school assessments, and adjusting the assessment procedures for licence renewal and promotion. Thailand should draft clear guidelines for teachers' responsibilities and expectations for workload, and should consider whether any regulated civil service tasks should be removed from teachers' responsibility.

Thailand should hire support staff to relieve the administrative burden on teachers and school leaders. Implementing this recommendation would require a financial investment.

- **Reduce inequities by supporting rural schools in their efforts to improve students' learning outcomes.**

The workload challenges faced by schools in rural areas of Thailand are intrinsically linked to the undersupply of teachers in those areas. In addition to hiring support staff to help all schools, Thailand should implement measures to attract, retain and support teachers and school leaders in rural schools, both financial and non-financial. Other particularly effective measures would be adequately funding rural schools and providing targeted in-service professional development (e.g. mentoring, collaborative networks within and across schools) to help teachers and school leaders address their specific challenges.

- **Conduct ongoing dialogue with teachers' associations to ensure teachers' voices are heard.**

Teachers, individually and as represented by their associations, should be viewed as partners in Thailand's education reform. They must be involved in the education policy-development process if reforms are to be developed and implemented successfully. The associations' role is an important one, helping to ensure that the rights of teachers as professionals are respected and that policy reforms address the needs of the teaching profession and the realities of the classroom.

Policy Issue 4: Thailand is not making effective use of the school leaders' role to improve teaching and learning in an increasingly decentralised system.

School leadership

Few of Thailand's proposed reforms seem to relate specifically to school leaders, which may reflect the less-defined nature of their role. As part of the Second Decade of Education Reform (2009-18), the government proposed further decentralisation of the education system, and to support this, the creation of a leadership development plan to set out qualifications required for the school leadership role, and the recruitment process, career path and incentives. This plan does not seem to have been implemented yet and it is not known whether it is a part of the current reform.

After teaching, school leadership is the most important factor affecting student learning that is open to policy influence. Some countries have developed comprehensive leadership frameworks, including standards relevant to principals across different school contexts (e.g. elementary, secondary or vocational), to inform recruitment procedures, specify the expectations of the role, guide professional development and serve as criteria for assessment (see Box 5.8; CEPPE, 2013). They are also intended to make school leadership more attractive at a time when increasing demands are being placed on the role. Remuneration is another key factor in the attractiveness of the role. The review team received no information about current salaries for Thai principals but it is known that the country is experiencing a shortage of school leaders.

The TCT has developed standards of knowledge and performance for school leaders. They cover both school leaders (Educational Institution Administrators) and the educational administrators who work in ESAs, though their roles are very different. They are based closely on the standards of performance for teachers, again, despite differences in their roles. Seemingly as a result of this, the standards do not sufficiently reflect some of the major instructional and school management functions of the role. As with the teacher standards, some of these standards are also vaguely worded (e.g. "seek and use information for development") (TCT, 2005). It is not clear whether the TCT describes them more explicitly elsewhere.

Like teachers, principals are required to maintain their licences and to self report every five years that they have met the standards of performance and other requirements set out by the TCT. The unreliability of a licensing system based on self-reporting has already been covered. Thailand does not seem to use the standards to inform the recruitment, in-service professional development or assessment of school leaders. The country would benefit from enhancing them and developing other elements of a leadership framework.

> **Box 5.8. Standards for school leadership**
>
> In the face of increasingly demanding responsibilities, some countries have made efforts to broadly define the role of the school leader by developing standards. For example, England has the National Standards of Excellence for Headteachers, which were revised in 2015 following a review process. The standards are organised into four domains, with six standards per domain:
>
> - qualities and knowledge
> - pupils and staff
> - systems and process
> - the self-improving school system.
>
> They are used to shape headteachers' practice and professional development, including training to prepare for the role, and inform their recruitment, appointment and performance appraisals.
>
> *Source*: UK Department for Education (2015), *National Standards of Excellence for Headteachers*, www.gov.uk/government/uploads/system/uploads/attachment_data/file/396247/National_Standards_of_Excellence_for_Headteachers.pdf.

Selection and preparation

In many countries, teachers decide whether to train to pursue school leadership rather than being recruited for the role. This self-selection is common but often inefficient; it does not ensure the best candidates for the role nor does it address the leadership needs of the particular region or school (Pont et al., 2008; Schleicher, 2012). Countries or leadership programmes that do use selection criteria – for example, the New Leaders organisation in the United States – may select trainees based on their instructional knowledge, success with student learning, leadership ability and inclusive outlook (Schleicher, 2012). Succession planning, proactively identifying teachers with leadership potential, can improve the quantity and quality of candidates (Pont et al., 2008). Box 5.9 covers Singapore's succession planning system.

Approximately half of the 22 countries that participated in the OECD study, *Improving School Leadership* (Pont et al., 2008), offered pre-service development programmes to future school leaders, and most of them required them to complete the programme before taking on the role. Training can be a way to align the efforts of future school leaders with the priorities of the education system, as well as preparing them for the expanded responsibilities that now characterise the role (Schleicher, 2012).

In Thailand, the TCT sets out the requirements for a teacher to become a school leader. They include:

- a bachelor's degree in educational administration or equivalent, which includes knowledge in 10 areas (administering academic, personnel and student activities; administrative, financial, procurement, building and IT management; education policy and planning, etc.)
- at least five years of experience as a teacher
- at least two years of experience as a teacher in an administrative position (TCT, 2005).

Thai teachers who want to become principals take an exam to participate in a mandatory, month-long pre-service training programme offered by NIDTEP and accredited by the TCT. Critics have questioned this emphasis on selection through examination, stating that "[s]chool principal integrity has been compromised by those undergoing tutorial preparation] towards "principal examination" not unlike student tutorials in shadow schools" (Vanichseni and Associates, 2012). If the contents of the programme are based on the TCT's standards of knowledge, they would be heavily weighted towards the administrative rather than the instructional management aspects of the role. A programme with more content on leading teaching and learning in schools, with a focus on school leaders' key role as reformers, would put new school leaders in a better position to support the country's education reforms.

Box 5.9. Succession planning in Singapore

One country that has established succession planning and training for its principals is Singapore, where teachers are assessed for their leadership potential and are given opportunities to develop their leadership skills on an ongoing basis. Education leadership positions (e.g. head of department) are built into the teacher career path to smooth the way for progression towards leadership roles. Candidates are selected to participate in leadership training based on their performance in interviews and leadership simulation exercises. The country's National Institute for Education, which is also responsible for teacher pre-service education, provides a four-month Management and Leadership in School programme to selected candidates, who are paid while they participate in the training. Once in the role, new school leaders are mentored by more experienced principals.

Source: Schleicher (2012), *Preparing Teachers and Developing School Leaders for the 21st Century: Lessons from Around the World*, http://dx.doi.org/10.1787/9789264174559-en.

Responsibilities and appraisal

A focus on supporting, evaluating and developing teacher quality is recognised internationally as being at the core of effective school leadership. This includes co-ordinating the curriculum, monitoring and evaluating teaching practice, promoting teachers' professional development and supporting a collaborative work culture (Schleicher, 2012). School leaders are also generally responsible for goal setting, assessment and accountability; strategic financial and HR management; and collaborating with other schools (Pont et al., 2008). Primary and secondary school principals tend to have their own distinct responsibilities and challenges reflecting their different contexts. For example, elementary principals are more likely to have a teaching workload and have more opportunities to spend time in the classroom to monitor instruction; by contrast, secondary principals tend to influence instruction more indirectly through department heads (Pont et al., 2008) Studies in OECD countries have found that school leaders are increasingly affected by demands on their time, with administrative duties taking up 34% of their time and competing with education leadership as their top priority (Pont et al., 2008; Schleicher, 2012).

Internationally, greater autonomy is associated with an expansion of the role of the principal to encompass more responsibilities. Results from recent PISA studies indicate that Thailand's lower secondary school principals have a significant amount of autonomy over curriculum and assessment, such as deciding which courses to offer, and some resource allocation responsibilities such as allocating budgets within the school (OECD, 2010a). Thai principals also reported that they often performed duties supporting teaching and learning in their schools at around the same rate as the OECD average (OECD, 2013c). For example, the percentage of students in Thai schools whose principal reported that, once a month to once a week or more than once a week, they worked with teachers to solve classroom problems and promoted teaching practices based on recent educational research was 81.5% and 39.4% respectively (compared to an OECD average of 75.4% and 42.2%) (OECD, 2013c).

Despite this, stakeholders in Thailand told the review team that the country's principals, in general, still focus more on administrative duties than on teaching and learning. As with teachers, Thai principals' workload was reported to be heavy, often taking them out of the school, and that the documentation required for the ONESQA school assessments is particularly onerous. The principal's role is even more challenging in small schools where school leaders must perform the same duties as their counterparts in larger schools but with fewer resources and staff, and frequent staff shortages (OBEC, 2013c).

All of this points to the need for more support for school leaders to help them manage their responsibilities and a less onerous school assessment process. Many OECD countries use performance appraisal of school leaders to identify their need for improvement and to ensure that they are provided with the appropriate support and development opportunities (Pont et al., 2008). Common practices include assessment based on predetermined goals, a review of information about the school and student performance data, and feedback from parents, teachers and students. In Thailand, ONESQA school assessments include an evaluation of the academic administration of the school (e.g. leadership in curriculum design), budgetary control, human resource management (e.g. recruitment and assignment of teachers) and general administration (e.g. using data to inform policy development) (ONESQA, 2013). Other than these school assessments, which reportedly do not provide useful feedback on performance, school leaders' performance does not seem to be appraised.

Continuing development and support

OECD research recommends that school leaders be given specific training to respond to the broadened responsibilities of their role (Pont et al., 2008). This training could take the form of formal induction programmes, periodic in-service offerings to help them update their skills, and collaborative activities like coaching and peer learning (Pont et al., 2008). Social networks are a particularly powerful way for school leaders to learn (Elmore, 2008).

In Thailand, school leaders are required to participate in the same kinds of professional development activities as teachers in order to maintain their licences (TCT, 2009). The country previously had an Institute for the Development of Educational Administrators, but that was replaced by NIDTEP, which does not focus exclusively on school leaders.

Some leadership training programmes for teachers and principals have recently been developed, but it is not clear how much and what kinds of professional development are specifically targeted on school leaders. The SEAMEO INNOTECH provides school leadership training to principals in the region based around a competency framework that defines skills and attributes school leaders need. This training framework is promising, but the review team has no information about participation rates among Thai principals.

Although some recent research indicates that Thai school leaders have great strengths in certain areas such as communication skills, team building and critical thinking (Prasertcharoensuk and Promprakone, 2014), a 2010 study conducted by OBEC found that 42.6% of Thailand's school administrators had low competency and 41.1% had a medium level of competency in education administration (Vanichseni and Associates., 2012). The review team's discussions with stakeholders also revealed concerns about school leaders' competencies and a lack of support for principals once they are in the role.

As a first step towards better supporting school leaders, Thailand could develop a professional development strategy (see the previous section) that addresses both teachers' and principals' development needs to improve student learning within the country's reform context.

Recommendation

The review team recommends that Thailand:

- **Develop a framework, including standards, to improve and support school leadership in the country.**

This leadership framework should be established in consultation with school leaders and relevant stakeholders. The Ministry of Education should create a new office to take responsibility for the development and implementation of this and other policies related to school leaders. In developing the framework, policy makers should keep in mind the different needs and responsibilities of principals in primary and secondary schools and other school contexts. Thailand should amend its standards for school leaders to make them more specific to the role of the principal, and use them as the basis to develop succession planning procedures, pre-service training, professional development and performance appraisal. The standards would also help to orient school leaders' work towards teaching and learning in the school.

Pre-service training should not only encompass the administrative responsibilities of the role but also the responsibilities related to improving teaching and learning, with an emphasis on the expectations in the school curriculum (see Box 5.10 for an example of how Hong Kong, China uses school leader development to support reform). In-service training should include mentoring and opportunities to collaborate within and across schools. Thailand should develop a new performance appraisal system based on the standards, to support school leaders in setting and achieving goals and continuing to develop.

> **Box 5.10. Measures to improve school leadership in Hong Kong, China**
>
> Hong Kong, China has made efforts to improve school leaders in a way that takes into account their important role in the jurisdiction's system-wide education reform. It implemented a new development programme for aspiring, new and experienced principals that focuses on their ability to implement reform. As part of a "Certificate for Principalship" process, aspiring principals are required to conduct an analysis of their professional learning needs and complete a course designed to develop skills as reformers in six key areas of responsibility:
>
> - strategic direction and policy environment
> - learning, teaching and curriculum
> - teachers' professional growth and development
> - staff and resource management
> - quality assurance and accountability
> - external communication.
>
> The Education Bureau provides an induction programme and other structured support for new principals. Experienced principals are provided with support programmes based on their identified needs.
>
> *Source*: Jensen et al. (2012), *Catching Up: Learning from the Best School Systems in East Asia*, http://grattan.edu.au/wp-content/uploads/2014/04/129_report_learning_from_the_best_main.pdf.

Other recommendations in this chapter are particularly relevant to school leaders, and their support and development. These include:

- developing a strategic, system-wide professional development strategy, designed to provide relevant PD to school leaders as well as teachers
- reducing workloads by making the school assessment processes less onerous, hiring support staff and adopting measures to support harder-to-staff schools
- involving schools in the teacher hiring process (see Policy Issue 5) and introducing a new teacher performance appraisal process.

This last would have significant implications for school leaders' responsibilities. School leaders would need to be supported and trained to implement these particular changes.

Policy Issue 5: Thailand's procedures for teacher deployment fail to meet local and national school workforce needs

Teacher supply and demand

It is not uncommon for countries to experience an over- or undersupply of teachers and to be concerned about an unfair distribution of teachers. There is a clear link between the quantity and quality of teachers, as a shortage of teachers is likely to increase out-of-field teaching and subject-matter knowledge is one aspect of teaching that has been shown to improve student learning (Jensen et al., 2012; UNESCO, 2014).

Teachers are more likely to work in regions that pay a higher starting salary and have favourable school facilities, class sizes and socio-economic characteristics. For this reason, schools in disadvantaged areas tend to have difficulty finding qualified teachers and may need more resources to attract and retain skilled teachers (OECD, 2005). Effective management of the teaching workforce is thus particularly important to ensure teacher quality and address any inequities in the education system.

In Thailand, pre-service education programmes are graduating more teachers than there are new positions available. In 2014, 104 576 individuals took the employment exam to obtain a teaching position, and out of the 23 073 who passed the exam, only 5 634 became employed as teachers (OBEC, 2015c).

At the same time, OBEC reported that, in the 2013/14 school year, 10 548 schools (roughly one-third of the country's basic education schools) were experiencing a shortage of teachers, mainly at the secondary level, and/or school leaders (Table 5.3).

Table 5.3. Number of teachers needed by subject in schools experiencing a shortage, 2013/14 school year

Subject	Number of teachers needed
Science	6 173
Mathematics	6 031
Foreign language	5 809
Thai	4 764
Arts	4 493
Vocational and technology	3 420
Social, religious and culture	3 105
Early childhood	2 884
Health and physical education	2 707
Computing	2 594
Special education	1 700
Primary	1 351
Psychology and counsellor	1 233
Education administrator	825
Librarian	607
Total	**47 696**

Source: OHEC (2015), "Seminar on teacher production and reform and teacher development in the future: problems and solutions".

Results from the PISA 2012 study show that Thailand's teacher shortage in certain subjects has worsened over the past decade across all school types (socio-economically advantaged and disadvantaged, rural and urban), in contrast to the OECD average (Table 5.4).

Table 5.4. **Schools hindered by a lack of qualified teachers, 2002 and 2013**

Percentage of students in schools whose principal reported that the school's capacity is hindered to some extent or a lot by lack of qualified teachers

School type	Socio-economically disadvantaged		Socio-economically advantaged		Rural		Urban	
Year	2003	2012	2003	2012	2003	2012	2003	2012
Qualified mathematics teachers (%)								
OECD average	25.7	19.8	17.1	13.5	22.4	16.6	20.4	13.4
Thailand	46.7	47.8	30.7	47	49.9	65.3	21	45.1
Qualified language-of-assessment teachers (%)								
OECD average	19.1	10.3	12.5	6.5	16.4	8.5	13.6	6.8
Thailand	41.6	48.4	10.2	37.9	43.8	52.6	11	38.1
Qualified science teachers (%)								
OECD average	26.1	19.1	16.1	12.3	19.2	12.8	20.1	13.7
Thailand	38.5	50.1	29.3	44.9	42.7	56.8	17.6	43.9

Source: OECD (2013c), *PISA 2012 Results: What Makes Schools Successful (Volume IV): Resources, Policies and Practices*, http://dx.doi.org/10.1787/9789264201156-en.

The Office of the Education Council has classified Thailand's current shortages as "a crisis in education" primarily caused by a 2000-05 civil service downsizing policy which led to 59 384 basic education teachers and 3 146 higher education teachers retiring early (OEC, 2015b). Since then, not enough funding has been made available to hire new teachers to replace them. Between 2013 and 2027, the OEC expects the teacher shortage to become more severe as a large number of the country's ageing teachers begin to retire (OEC, 2015b).

Despite the OEC's current data and projections, there is disagreement over the extent of the teacher shortage. An important factor behind these diverging views is the lack of a co-ordinated education data system in Thailand. Different education organisations collect their own data, making it difficult to reliably monitor and predict the demand for teachers and manage supply and deployment effectively. Better data management systems would enable the government to manage payroll costs more efficiently and the labour market more effectively. Box 5.11 has examples of systems to forecast future teacher supply and demand.

> **Box 5.11. Models for forecasting teacher supply and demand**
>
> Forecasting teacher supply and demand requires an understanding of the complex relationships that exist between different data variables. One example of a forecasting model is the UK Department for Education's Teacher Supply Model, which the government uses to calculate the number of teacher preparation places required to meet future demand. The model uses projections of pupil numbers and the predicted number of teachers needed to implement new government policy initiatives.
>
> An example of a model that is based more on local needs is the Netherlands Ministry of Education, Culture and Science's MIRROR forecasting model, which is intended to identify teacher demand at the regional and sub-regional levels. Developed in 2002, the model uses central and local data on the age distribution of teachers, the number of recent graduates from initial teacher education, the employment status of teachers, teacher qualifications, rates of teacher transfers between schools and the projected supply behaviour of individuals, among other variables, to monitor teacher supply and demand, and to assess the effects of different scenarios on teacher recruitment. It provides regions and school boards with information about the labour market in their immediate area, enabling the identification of subject areas and regions at risk of experiencing teacher shortages.
>
> *Source:* OECD (2005), *Teachers Matter: Attracting, Developing and Retaining Effective Teachers*, http://dx.doi.org/10.1787/9789264018044-en; UK Department for Education (2014), *Teacher Supply Model: A Technical Description*, www.gov.uk/government/publications/teacher-supply-model-a-technical-description.

General and targeted measures to manage supply

Countries tend to use a combination of general and targeted measures to manage the supply of teachers. General measures are intended to make the teaching profession as attractive as possible by making the salary, benefits and working conditions of teachers more appealing (see Box 5.12 for examples), whereas targeted measures include incentives to increase the number of teachers for certain areas or subjects (Schleicher, 2012). The Thai government is currently considering reforms to improve teachers' quality of life (general measures) and to increase opportunities for qualified individuals to become teachers in shortage areas by adjusting the recruitment and preparation systems (targeted measures).

General measures

Historically, teaching has been a relatively high-status profession in Thailand. However, although teachers are still respected, their prestige has declined over the years. Research and discussions with stakeholders point to a low salary compared to other professions; the amount of teacher debt, given that teachers are still expected to maintain a certain standard of living, including car and home ownership; and heavy workload as factors that are making the teaching profession less attractive in Thailand (Atagi, 2011; Jones, 2014).

Teachers' salaries are the largest single cost in formal education systems and they have a direct impact on the attractiveness of the teaching profession relative to comparable professions (OECD, 2005, 2014a). In OECD countries, on average, primary teachers earn 85% and secondary teachers earn 92% of a tertiary-educated, 25-64 year-old full-time, full-year worker. Teachers' salaries tend to increase with the level of education they teach, and top salaries are generally 61% higher than starting salaries (OECD, 2014a).

Thailand's current teacher salary scheme was first implemented in 2004 and significantly increased teacher compensation at the time (Atagi, 2011). In 2014, the government introduced changes to the salary scale to pay teachers more for higher-level qualifications such as longer bachelor's degree programmes, master's or doctoral degrees (OEC, 2014). The scale makes no distinction between primary and secondary teachers. As public-sector workers, Thai teachers also receive benefits such as coverage of medical expenses, educational fees for children and housing costs.

As of 2011, the monthly salary ranges for teachers in Thailand were:

- assistant teacher: THB 8 340 - 17 690
- teacher: THB 12 530 - 31 190
- professional teacher: THB 16 190 - 37 830
- senior professional teacher: THB 19 860 - 53 080
- expert teacher: THB 24 400 - 62 760
- senior expert teacher: THB 29 980 - 69 810 (OTEP, 2011).

The absence of any significant pay differential between primary and secondary teachers, as well as the higher earning potential of those trained in specialised subjects such as mathematics and science, may be contributing to the shortage of teachers in the upper levels of the basic education system. Recent research found that, in Thailand, teaching was the lowest-paying job compared to public sector workers and five mathematics and science professions (engineers, medical doctors, scientists, accountants and nurses) (Tongliemnak, 2010).

In addition, Thailand's salary range is wide, with a senior expert teacher at the top end of the scale making 8 times more than a beginning assistant teacher. This suggests positive opportunities for career progression but also the possibility that starting salaries are too low to be competitive with other professions. Thailand will need to closely monitor its teacher remuneration in the future to determine whether the 2014 salary increase has had any impact on the profession and its ability to attract high-quality teachers. Additional allowances for mathematics and science teachers and improvements to teachers' welfare could also help offset lower salaries.

The amount of teacher debt in the country also affects the attractiveness of the teaching profession. In 2008, 140 000 Thai teachers sought help from a Teachers Indebtedness Problem-Solving Fund (Pongwat, 2012). Approximately 200 000 of the 1 million licensed teachers in the country are reportedly in debt, a problem associated with both low pay and the social pressures teachers face to maintain a certain style of living. Research indicates that the majority of teachers experiencing debt are women and that this debt has a negative impact on their teaching performance, causing stress and requiring them to take on second jobs (OTEP, 2011).

Thailand has taken some measures to address the teacher debt problem. For example, the Office of the Welfare Promotion Commission for Teachers and Educational Personnel (OTEP) provides teachers with hostels, healthcare, insurance and scholarships; works to improve teachers' quality of life and problems with debt, in part through free training on financial planning; and offers legal consultancy. However, more needs to be done, as the current government has acknowledged by making the alleviation of teacher debt a priority in its education reform. Teachers need additional help with financial management, as well as information and support for career progression.

Box 5.12. Increasing the attractiveness of the teaching profession

Countries have implemented a range of different policies to increase the attractiveness of the teaching profession in order to encourage an appropriate supply of high-quality teachers. Singapore closely monitors its labour market to ensure teachers' starting salaries are competitive. Switzerland, which offers relatively high salaries to its teachers, found that it needed to increase teachers' salaries considerably to have an impact on the supply of teachers, whereas in the United Kingdom, a small increase had a larger impact because the teacher salary was relatively low.

Countries can survey their teachers to find out why they joined (or left) the teaching profession and use this information to develop recruitment strategies. France and Australia did this in 2000 and 2002 respectively, and found that intrinsic factors, like desire to work with children, to teach and to make a difference, were the strongest motivators, followed by extrinsic factors like job security and working conditions.

Research recommends that countries consider the following policy priorities to improve the attractiveness of the teaching profession:

- improving the status of the profession (e.g. by building stronger links between schools and the community, and promoting positive teaching role models)
- improving teachers' salary competitiveness (e.g. by increasing the starting salary, offering financial incentives to teachers in short supply, and opting to fund higher salaries rather than reduce the student-teacher ratio)
- improving employment conditions (e.g. by providing a work-life balance or sabbaticals)
- expanding the pool of candidates (e.g. by introducing a starting salary that rewards prior experience in other careers)
- introducing reward mechanisms (e.g. by providing financial and non-financial incentives to teachers to work in harder-to-staff schools or regions)
- improving entrance to the profession (e.g. by ensuring that deployment procedures are well-designed, providing induction programmes).

Source: OECD (2005), *Teachers Matter: Attracting, Developing and Retaining Effective Teachers*, http://dx.doi.org/10.1787/9789264018044-en; Schleicher (2012), *Preparing Teachers and Developing School Leaders for the 21st Century: Lessons from Around the World*, http://dx.doi.org/10.1787/9789264174559-en.

Targeted measures

The experience of OECD countries suggests that both financial and non-financial incentives can be effective at increasing the supply of teachers for particular subjects and regions (Box 5.13).

Financial incentives can include salary allowances, tuition-fee waivers, scholarships and forgivable loans, whereas non-financial incentives usually include measures to make teachers' working conditions more favourable, like less class time, smaller class sizes or faster career progression (Schleicher, 2012; OECD, 2014b). Incentives can be an important way to address inequities by attracting teachers to disadvantaged areas (OECD, 2005, 2013b).

Thailand has traditionally used scholarship programmes to try to increase the supply of high-quality teachers in shortage subjects and rural areas of the country. The largest programme, and a flagship of Thailand's recent education reform, is the country's New Breed of Teachers Project, a THB 4 234 million (USD 150 million) programme to produce 30 000 high-quality teachers, including teachers in shortage subjects, between 2010 and 2015.

The project consists of a five-year programme for new students and a one-year programmes for students who already had a bachelor's degree in a shortage subject area. Scholarship recipients are guaranteed employment if they commit to working as teachers, and, once employed, receive a large bonus of THB 15 000 (USD 413) per month. Previous scholarship programmes introduced over the past 15 years were weakened by budget cuts or did not attract or produce as many teachers as hoped, with some graduates opting to pursue other careers (Atagi, 2011; Pongwat, 2012).

The government provides hardship pay and accelerated promotion opportunities to teachers in the southernmost part of the country (Atagi, 2011; OTEPC, n.d.). Some teachers in rural areas also receive free or subsidised housing (Tongliemnak, 2010). The review team lacks information about incentive amounts and the scale of their implementation, although there are indications that they are not offered to hardship areas outside of the southern provinces, such as the north and northeast. There is little evidence of the impact of these financial incentives and scholarship programmes.

Box 5.13. Attracting teachers to poor and remote areas

UNESCO cautions that there is no simple solution to the problem of an unequal allocation of teachers, which affects education systems in countries across the income spectrum. To address this problem, jurisdictions commonly create overarching deployment plans to place high-quality teachers in harder-to-staff schools, provide opportunities for rural students to become teachers in their home regions and offer financial and non-financial incentives to teachers like housing, monetary benefits, accelerated promotions and subsidised loans.

Indonesia established a remote area allowance for teachers working in remote schools for at least two years, but as of 2007/08, it had not been widely implemented. In 2011, the country issued guidelines to districts to redeploy teachers more equally across schools; teacher transfers had not been common up to that point. In response, some districts recruited new teachers on the condition that they could be transferred, and merged smaller schools unimpeded by geographic obstacles.

The Free Teacher Education Programme of the People's Republic of China offers free tuition and 10 years of job security to high-performing students who study to become teachers and commit to at least 2 years of teaching in a rural area. In 2007, most of these students came from regions with lower socio-economic status.

In Lao People's Democratic Republic, financial incentives were unsuccessful in attracting teachers to remote schools, so the country adopted a localised approach by training individuals to become teachers within their own remote, rural home districts.

In Korea, to attract teachers to regions with lower socio-economic status, the government offers incentives like additional salary, smaller class sizes, less instructional time, credit towards future promotion to administrative positions and the ability to choose the next school where they will work. Students in these regions are more likely to be taught by high-quality maths teachers (with full certification, a specialist maths education and three or more years of experience) than students in regions with higher socio-economic status.

Source: Gannicott (2009), *Secondary Teacher Policy Research in Asia: Teacher Numbers, Teacher Quality: Lessons from Secondary Education in Asia*, http://unesdoc.unesco.org/images/0018/001888/188852e.pdf; UNESCO (2014), *EFA Global Monitoring Report – Teaching and Learning: Achieving Quality for All*, http://unesdoc.unesco.org/images/0022/002256/225660e.pdf.

Deployment procedures

OECD research indicates that an effective teacher labour market is transparent, accountable and efficient, providing teachers with timely information about the positions available, ensuring that school leaders play an important role in the hiring process to create a good match between teacher and school, and providing disadvantaged schools with more resources to recruit high-quality teachers; all of this should be overseen by a central authority that manages the equitable distribution of teachers and forecasts supply and demand (OECD, 2005; Schleicher, 2012). In order to attract the best candidates to the teaching profession, countries need well organised recruitment procedures to facilitate initial entry into the job market. In 2012, the World Bank recommended that Thailand give schools more authority over teacher recruitment to strengthen the relationship between teachers and their schools and to create more accountability.

The recruitment of teachers in Thailand is determined on a national, rather than a school-by-school basis, using a funding formula that may be inequitable to Thailand's large number of small schools. Each year, ESAs provide data on schools' personnel needs to OBEC, which calculates the nation-wide demand for basic education teachers using a set formula. The OBEC funding formula for the country's small schools (defined by the Thai government as those with fewer than 120 students) only allows 1 teacher per 20 students, which means that individual teachers in these schools are likely to have to teach multiple grades and subjects (Lathapipat, 2015).

The allocation of new teachers is overseen by the OTEPC and implemented by staff in each ESA, based on the results of a competitive employment exam. The teacher with the highest result on the employment exam gets the first choice of the positions available, and then each is allowed to make their selection in descending order. The names of the specific schools seeking teachers are withheld from candidates. Once teachers have made their choice, they must also pass a selection test, which is similar to the employment exam (OBEC, 2015c). Staff in the ESA may also interview candidates. Thai schools generally play no role in this process.

OBEC data indicate that Thailand is attracting enough individuals to the teaching profession, even in shortage subject areas, but a large percentage are not making it past the steps in the recruitment process to find teaching positions (Table 5.5). In 2014, the overall pass rate on this exam was only 22% (OBEC, 2015c). It is worth investigating whether the low pass rate is due to the exam measuring the wrong things or whether the pre-service education programmes are inadequately preparing new graduates. Given the concerns raised about Thailand's other national standardised assessments in

Chapter 4, it is possible that the employment exam does not meet acceptable standards of validity, fairness and reliability. It is also worth asking why so few teachers who pass the exam find employment in high-demand subject areas (albeit with the caveat that these data do not include positions filled by scholarship recipients who are not required to take the exam). The likely reasons are the lack of funding for the teaching positions needed and the centralised deployment procedures, which do not take into account school's actual needs.

Table 5.5. Employment exam results and jobs for shortage subjects, 2014

Subject	Number of teachers needed	Number of exam applicants	Number who passed the exam	Number who obtained a job
Science*	6 173	17 233	4 323	750
Maths	6 031	9 001	1 907	980
Foreign languages**	5 809	11 581	2 364	921
Thai	4 764	6 762	1 785	838
Arts***	4 493	1 456	247	89
Primary	1 351	3 250	964	213

Note: Exam and employment data are for the following subjects:

* Science, general science, biology, physics and chemistry. Excluding the latter three subjects, there were 13 336 exam applicants; of these, 3 309 passed and 469 obtained a job.

** English, Chinese, French, Japanese, Spanish, Korean, Bahasa Melayu and Burmese. For English, there were 10 631 applicants; of these 2 178 passed and 803 obtained a job.

*** Arts, visual arts and fine arts.

Source: OHEC (2015), "Seminar on teacher production and reform and teacher development in the future: problems and solutions"; OBEC (2015c), *Number of People who Applied for Teaching Positions in OBEC Schools, 2010-2014*.

Rather than having a high bar for entry into pre-service education programmes, as discussed above, Thailand may be using the employment exam to determine the suitability of candidates for the teaching profession. This is an inefficient method of teacher recruitment. Research advises countries that use employment exams to supplement them with more authentic methods of assessing candidates' competence and fitness for a position. It is important that, in the long term, these countries improve pre-service education, in lieu of continuing to use employment exams, so that entry to and successful completion of pre-service programmes provide the necessary assurances that teachers are ready to teach (Hobson et al., 2010).

> **Box 5.14. Teacher recruitment policies in OECD countries**
>
> In most OECD countries, the recruitment of teachers falls to the level of government – national, regional or local – that is responsible for employing teachers, but OECD research recommends school involvement in this process. Eight OECD countries have a high level of individual school involvement in teacher recruitment: Belgium (Flemish Community), Denmark, England and Wales, Hungary, Ireland, the Netherlands, the Slovak Republic and Sweden.
>
> To provide both teachers and schools with greater choice in the hiring process, the OECD previously suggested that Mexico allow candidates with the top three results on the country's employment exam to interview for a position at a school and for the school to be able to select which candidate to hire.
>
> Schools need not be solely responsible for the hiring process; they may simply benefit from some involvement that ensures the best candidate is selected for the position available. For example, in some countries, a school principal may serve as a member of a district hiring panel, providing input into staffing decisions relating to his or her school.
>
> *Sources*: OECD (2005), *Teachers Matter: Attracting, Developing and Retaining Effective Teachers*, http://dx.doi.org/10.1787/9789264018044-en; OECD (2010b), "Teacher career paths: Consolidating a quality profession", in OECD, *Improving Schools: Strategies for Action in Mexico*, http://dx.doi.org/10.1787/9789264087040-5-en.

Although the employment exam and initial allocation to a school are based on the subject a teacher studied to teach, it was reported that a teacher's specialisation makes no difference to their assignment once they arrive at the school. Recent research found that 25% of science and maths teachers in Thailand did not have relevant educational training in the subjects they were teaching and that this problem was worse in small, rural schools (Siribanpitak and Boonyananta, 2007; Tongliemnak, 2010). Thailand seems to be taking a much-needed step towards recognising the importance of teachers' training with its plans to revise the teaching licence to identify specialisations. It is essential that this information be taken into account when hiring and assignment decisions are made.

Assistant teachers in Thailand are required to stay in their first school for at least four years before requesting a school transfer (OTEPC, n.d.). Transfers are only made for personal reasons (e.g. wanting to live closer to home), and they are not easily honoured (Pongwat, 2012). Neither the teacher's specialisation nor the needs of the school seem to be taken into account. As a result, some schools may have an adequate number of teachers overall but an undersupply of qualified teachers, while other schools have an oversupply of teaching staff. For example, a 2007 OEC study found that 5 165 basic education schools in Thailand had a surplus of teachers (Atagi, 2011). OBEC has identified the "deployment of teachers both across and within districts ... unrelated to measures of need" as one of the barriers to efficiency in the Thai education system (OBEC, 2013c). Stakeholders told the review team that the government is planning to address the country's deployment issues by requiring teachers to commit to living and working in a particular region for a longer period of time. However, this is likely to hamper efficiency, given that the system is already very rigid, and it may have a negative impact on the attractiveness of the teaching profession.

Recommendations

The review team recommends that Thailand:

- **Develops a co-ordinated data gathering mechanism to support decision making about current and future teacher supply needs.**

A co-ordinated data gathering mechanism would allow Thailand to more effectively manage the teaching workforce. Such a mechanism should be the responsibility of one government department, probably in the Ministry of Education, which would work in collaboration with other relevant government bodies, pre-service programme providers, ESAs and schools to gather reliable data to determine the current supply of and demand for teachers and to forecast future needs. Thailand should use these data to, among other things, work with pre-service programme providers to ensure that an adequate number of teachers are prepared for shortage subject areas and work with ESAs and schools to meet local needs.

Given the OEC's forecast that a large number of the country's teachers will retire within the next 15 years, the government should wait for accurate projections of future demand before making any decisions about reducing the supply of teachers. If possible, the government should fund the filling of more teaching positions, based on accurate data, in order to address the undersupply of teachers in some schools.

- **Review hiring and transfer processes to ensure their fairness, reduce unnecessary rigidities and enable greater responsiveness to local needs.**

The system-wide changeover of staff that will result from projected retirements provides an opportunity to phase in new systems of teacher hiring, transfer and assignment. In the medium term, key steps would include conducting a psychometric analysis of the employment exam to ensure it meets international standards of good practice for standardised assessments (see Chapter 4), and involving schools more in the hiring process. Thailand should also encourage assignment decisions to be made based on a teacher's specialisation to reduce the incidence of out-of-field teaching.

In the medium to long term, Thailand would benefit from changing the formula for funding teaching positions so that it takes into account, and responds to, local data and local needs, and opening up all vacant positions for competition by new or transferring teachers. These competitions and any ensuing appointments would take into account a teacher's specialisation. Accurate and timely information sharing would need to be a key component of this system.

- **Use teacher placement policies as a tool to reduce inequities in the education system by targeting shortage areas.**

In order to make the education system more equitable, Thailand should take steps towards ensuring that all students are taught by highly qualified and high-quality teachers. As a first step, the government should evaluate the impact of its current scholarship and incentive programmes to determine whether they are effectively filling regional and subject shortage areas. Based on this information, Thailand could modify existing policies or introduce new ones to attract teachers to harder-to-staff schools and subjects. For example, depending on the results of the evaluation, Thailand may wish to put more funding towards attracting students from poorer regions of the country to become teachers or to expand accelerated promotion opportunities to teachers in more regions of the country. As a priority, sufficient financial incentives should be provided to all teachers in high-risk regions of the country (e.g. districts in the south).

Conclusions

This chapter has provided an overview of teacher and school leadership policies and practices in Thailand based on information provided by representatives of different branches of the Ministry of Education and major stakeholder organisations, the National Teachers Union, the staff of universities, ESAs and schools, and individual teachers during the review team's site visit. It also offers data, advice and effective practices from national and international research literature, notably OECD and UNESCO publications.

Thailand has made a significant commitment to improving the quality of the teaching profession in the past, recognising the essential role teachers play in student learning. The five main areas where policy reforms are needed to further strengthen the profession are: 1) teacher preparation to support education reform; 2) professional development and practices to promote high-quality teaching (amended standards for the teaching profession, certification, performance appraisal, and career progression); 3) the factors affecting educators' ability to focus on the classroom and to support students in small, rural schools; 4) the role of the school leader to improve teaching and learning; and 5) teacher deployment procedures. Changes to policy in these areas will address inequities across the education system and inefficiencies in human resource allocation, and improve training and support for Thailand's educators to move the country's education reform forward.

Of the recommendations in this chapter, the top priority should be to provide professional development to teachers and school leaders through a holistic capacity-building strategy. This would improve the overall effectiveness of Thailand's educators and support them in making the best use of the basic education curriculum, appropriate assessment strategies, and ICT, as well as drive their efforts to achieve system-wide education reform goals. It would also address another priority for Thailand, which is to ensure that all students, regardless of their background, have the opportunity to succeed. Attracting, retaining and supporting educators in the country's many small rural schools to improve the learning outcomes of those students who are at the greatest risk of falling behind would be crucial to achieving a more equitable education system.

In moving forward with work to strengthen the teaching profession and improve the education system as a whole, it is essential that Thailand consult with teachers, their associations, and school leaders to ensure they feel ownership of the reform efforts. As experts in their field, those most affected by the policy changes, and educators at the front lines of the reform, their contributions to the policy development process are of great importance. Their motivation to achieve reform will be fundamental to its success.

Notes

1. This figure may include deputy principals or deputy directors of Education Service Areas.

2. Theory and practice can also be integrated through a "lab school" or "professional development school" model, but this model has been criticised for its cost and workload and the difficulty in finding schools for placements (Levine, 2006).

Bibliography

Atagi, Rie (2011), *Secondary Teacher Policy Research in Asia: Secondary Teachers in Thailand*, UNESCO Bangkok.

Barber, M. and M. Mourshed (2007), *How the World's Best Performing Schools Come out on Top*, McKinsey & Company, London, http://mckinseyonsociety.com/downloads/reports/Education/Worlds_School_Systems_Final.pdf (accessed 27 January 2015).

Boyd, D., D. Goldhaber, H. Lankford and J. Wyckoff (2007), "The effect of certification and preparation on teacher quality", *The Future of Children*, Vol. 17/1, pp. 45-68, http://futureofchildren.org/futureofchildren/publications/docs/17_01_03.pdf (accessed 3 February 2015).

CEPPE (Centre of Study for Policies and Practices in Education, Chile) (2013), "Learning standards, teaching standards and standards for school principals: A comparative study", *OECD Education Working Papers*, No. 99, OECD Publishing, Paris, http://dx.doi.org/10.1787/5k3tsjqtp90v-en (accessed 18 March 2015).

Lay Choo and Darling-Hammond (2011), "Creating effective teachers and leaders in Singapore", in Darling-Hammond and Rothman (eds.), *Teacher and Leader Effectiveness in High-Performing Education System*, Alliance for Excellent Education, Washington DC; Stanford Center for Opportunity Policy in Education, California, http://pasisahlberg.com/wp-content/uploads/2012/12/Teacher-Leader-Effectiveness-Report-2011.pdf

Darling-Hammond, L. (2006), *Powerful Teacher Education: Lessons from Exemplary Programs*, Jossey-Bass, San Francisco.

Darling-Hammond, L. (2000), "Teacher quality and student achievement: A review of state policy evidence", *Education Policy Analysis Archives*, Vol. 8/1, http://epaa.asu.edu/ojs/article/view/392/515 (accessed 23 January 2015).

Darling-Hammond, L. and A. Lieberman (eds.) (2012), *Teacher Education around the World: Changing Policies and Practices*, Routledge, London and New York.

Elmore, F.R. (2008), "Leadership as the practice of improvement", in OECD, *Improving School Leadership, Volume 2: Case Studies on System Leadership*, OECD Publishing, Paris, http://dx.doi.org/10.1787/9789264039551-4-en.

Gannicott, K. (2009), *Secondary Teacher Policy Research in Asia: Teacher Numbers, Teacher Quality: Lessons from Secondary Education in Asia*, UNESCO Bangkok, http://unesdoc.unesco.org/images/0018/001888/188852e.pdf (accessed 13 July 2015).

Government of Thailand (2003), "The Teachers and Educational Personnel Council Act", B.E. 2546, *Government Gazette*, Vol. 57/10, Bangkok.

Hobson, A.J., P. Ashby, J. McIntyre and A. Malderez (2010), "International approaches to teacher selection and recruitment", *OECD Education Working Papers*, No. 47, OECD Publishing, Paris, http://dx.doi.org/10.1787/5kmbphhh6qmx-en.

Ingersoll, R. (ed.) (2007), "A comparative study of teacher preparation and qualifications in six nations", *CPRE Policy Briefs*, RB-47, Graduate School of Education, University of Pennsylvania, www.cpre.org/images/stories/cpre_pdfs/RB47.pdf, (accessed 14 April 2015).

Jensen, B., A. Hunter, J. Sonnemann and T. Burns (2012), *Catching Up: Learning from the Best School Systems in East Asia*, Grattan Institute, Carlton, Australia, http://grattan.edu.au/wp-content/uploads/2014/04/129_report_learning_from_the_best_main.pdf (accessed 23 January 2015).

Jo-Kim, G. (5 October 2010), "Quality learning for a quality life: Teachers matter", *The Nation*, www.nationmultimedia.com/home/2010/10/05/opinion/Quality-learning-for-a-quality-life-Teachers-matte-30139374.html (accessed 26 February 2015).

Jones, M.E. (2014), *Learning to Live Together Through Education – Country Case Study: Thailand*, UNESCO Bangkok.

Kleinhenz, E. and L. Ingvarson (2007), *Standards for Teaching: Theoretical Underpinnings and Applications*, Australian Council for Educational Research, http://research.acer.edu.au/teaching_standards/1/.

Lathapipat, D. (2015), "Closing the school performance gap through better public resource allocation: The case of Thailand", preliminary draft (March), World Bank Group, Washington, DC.

Lay Choo, T. and L. Darling-Hammond (2011), "Creating effective teachers and leaders in Singapore", in L. Darling-Hammond and R. Rothman (eds.), *Teacher and Leader Effectiveness in High-Performing Education Systems, Alliance for Excellent Education and Stanford Center for Opportunity Policy in Education*, Stanford, CA, pp. 33-42, http://pasisahlberg.com/wp-content/uploads/2012/12/Teacher-Leader-Effectiveness-Report-2011.pdf (accessed 14 February 2015).

Levine, A. (2006), *Educating School Teachers*, The Education Schools Project, Washington, DC.

Musset, P. (2010), "Initial teacher education and continuing training policies in a comparative perspective: Current practices in OECD countries and a literature review on potential effects", *OECD Education Working Papers*, No. 48, OECD Publishing, Paris http://dx.doi.org/10.1787/5kmbphh7s47h-en.

OBEC (2015a), *Teacher Manpower in OBEC Schools 2014*, Office of the Basic Education Commission, Bangkok.

OBEC (2015b), *Basic Education Reform*, Office of the Basic Education Commission, Bangkok.

OBEC (2015c), *Number of People who Applied for Teaching Positions in OBEC Schools*, 2010-2014, Office of the Basic Education Commission, Bangkok.

OBEC (2013a), *Curriculum 2008: Help Students Dream Big*, OBEC Foreign Relations Group, Policy and Planning Bureau, Office of the Basic Education Commission, Bangkok.

OBEC (2013b), *Basic Education in Thailand: Universal Right – Not Charity*, Foreign Relations Group, Policy and Planning Bureau, Office of the Basic Education Commission, Bangkok.

OBEC (2013c), *Efficiency ... More Results... Fewer Resources*, OBEC Foreign Relations Group, Policy and Planning Bureau, Office of the Basic Education Commission, Bangkok.

OEC (2015a), *Thailand Education Statistics, Academic Year 2013-2014*, Prigwan Graphic, Bangkok.

OEC (2015b), "Shortage of teachers", information provided to the review team, Office of the Education Council, Bangkok.

OEC (2015c), "Teacher education institutions", information provided to the review team, Office of the Education Council, Bangkok.

OEC (2014), "Country background report – Thailand", internal report provided to the OECD, Office of the Education Council, Bangkok.

OEC (2009), *Proposals for the Second Decade of Education Reform (2009-2018)*, Education Policy and Planning Bureau, Office of the Education Council, Bangkok.

OECD (2014a), *Education at a Glance 2014: OECD Indicators*, OECD Publishing, Paris, http://dx.doi.org/10.1787/eag-2014-en.

OECD (2014b), *TALIS 2013 Results: An International Perspective on Teaching and Learning*, TALIS, OECD Publishing, Paris, http://dx.doi.org/10.1787/9789264196261-en.

OECD (2014c), "Structural policy country notes: Thailand", in *Economic Outlook for Southeast Asia, China and India 2014: Beyond the Middle-Income Trap*, OECD Publishing, Paris, http://dx.doi.org/10.1787/saeo-2014-en.

OECD (2013a), *PISA 2012 Results: What Makes Schools Successful (Volume IV): Resources*, Policies and Practices, PISA, OECD Publishing, Paris, http://dx.doi.org/10.1787/9789264201156-en.

OECD (2013b), *Education at a Glance 2013: OECD Indicators*, OECD Publishing, Paris, http://dx.doi.org/10.1787/eag-2013-en.

OECD (2012), *Equity and Quality in Education: Supporting Disadvantaged Students and Schools*, OECD Publishing, Paris, http://dx.doi.org/10.1787/9789264130852-en.

OECD (2010a), *PISA 2009 Results: What Makes a School Successful?: Resources, Policies and Practices (Volume IV)*, PISA, OECD Publishing, Paris, http://dx.doi.org/10.1787/9789264091559-en.

OECD (2010b), "Teacher career paths: Consolidating a quality profession", in OECD, *Improving Schools: Strategies for Action in Mexico*, OECD Publishing, Paris, http://dx.doi.org/10.1787/9789264087040-5-en.

OECD (2005), *Teachers Matter: Attracting, Developing and Retaining Effective Teachers*, Education and Training Policy, OECD Publishing, Paris, http://dx.doi.org/10.1787/9789264018044-en.

OHEC (2015), "Seminar on teacher production and reform and teacher development in the future: Problems and solutions", Bureau of Policy and Planning, Office of the Higher Education Commission, Bangkok.

ONESQA (2013), *Manual for Basic Education Institutions: The Third-Round of External Quality Assessment (2011-2015)*, Office for National Education Standards and Quality Assessment, Bangkok, www.onesqa.or.th/upload/download/201506181027441.pdf.

Ontario Ministry of Education (2012), "Teacher performance appraisal system", Ontario Ministry of Education website, www.edu.gov.on.ca/eng/teacher/appraise.html (accessed 17 March 2015).

Ontario Ministry of Education (2010), *Teacher Performance Appraisal: Technical Requirements Manual*, Ontario Ministry of Education, www.edu.gov.on.ca/eng/teacher/pdfs/TPA_Manual_English_september2010l.pdf (accessed 17 March 2015).

OTEP (2011), *A Study on the Economic and Financial Conditions and Needs of the Teacher Civil Service under the Office of the Basic Education Commission*, research summary, Office of the Welfare Promotion Commission for Teachers and Educational Personnel, Bangkok.

OTEPC (n.d.), "Data related to OTEPC's Mission and Duty", Office of the Teacher Civil Service and Educational Personnel Commission, Bangkok.

Pongwat, A. (2012), *A New Breed of Teachers: Thailand's Efforts to Improve the Quality of Her Teachers*, Center for the Study of International Cooperation in Education Hiroshima University, Vol. 4/2, pp. 155-166, http://ir.lib.hiroshima-u.ac.jp/files/public/34475/20141016202510961752/CICEseries_4-2_155.pdf (accessed 5 January 2015).

Pont, B., D. Nusche and H. Moorman (2008), *Improving School Leadership, Volume 1: Policy and Practice*, OECD Publishing, Paris, http://dx.doi.org/10.1787/9789264044715-en.

Prasertcharoensuk, T. and D. Promprakone (2014), "Relationship between administrators' competencies and internal quality assurance", *Procedia – Social and Behavioral Sciences*, Vol. 116, pp. 808-814, www.sciencedirect.com/science/article/pii/S187704281400319X (accessed 16 March 2015).

QLF (2015), *QLF under the Quality Learning Fund Bill*, Quality Learning Foundation, Bangkok.

QLF (2014), *Research on Teacher Workload*, 2014, Quality Learning Foundation, Bangkok.

Santiago, P. and F. Benavides (2009), "Teacher Evaluation: A Conceptual Framework and Examples of Country Practices", analytical paper, OECD, Paris.

Schleicher, A. (ed.) (2012), *Preparing Teachers and Developing School Leaders for the 21st Century: Lessons from Around the World*, International Summit on the Teaching Profession, OECD Publishing, Paris, http://dx.doi.org/10.1787/9789264174559-en.

SEAMEO INNOTECH (2010), *Teaching Competency Standards in Southeast Asian Countries: Eleven Country Audit*, Southeast Asian Ministers of Education Organization Regional Center for Educational Innovation and Technology, Philippines, http://mmpt.pasca.ugm.ac.id/downloads/131218074436TeachingCompetencyStd.pdf (accessed 11 March 2015).

Siribanpitak, P. and S. Boonyananta (2007), "Chapter 7 – Teacher qualification of the teacher force in Thailand", in Ingersoll, R. (ed.) (2007), *A comparative study of teacher preparation and qualifications in six nations*, Consortium for Policy Research in Education (CPRE), www.cpre.org/images/stories/cpre_pdfs/sixnations_final.pdf.

TCT (2009), "Notification of the Teachers' Council of Thailand Board Re: Qualification Requirements for Education Professional License Renewal B.E. 2552", Teachers' Council of Thailand, Bangkok.

TCT (2005), "Regulation of the Teachers' Council of Thailand on Professional Standards and Ethics B.E. 2548", *Government Gazette*, Vol. 122/76D, Bangkok.

TDRI (2015), "Challenges in Thailand's Education Reform", 19 February, Thailand Development Research Institute, Bangkok.

Tongliemnak, P. (2010), "Three essays on teacher labor markets in Thailand", PhD Thesis, Stanford University, *http://purl.stanford.edu/yw658sz0538* (accessed 10 March 2015).

UIS (2015), "Human resources", in *Education Statistics* (dataset), UNESCO Institute for Statistics, http://data.uis.unesco.org (accessed 2 March 2015).

UK Department for Education (2015), *National Standards of Excellence for Headteachers*, Department for Education, London, www.gov.uk/government/uploads/system/uploads/attachment_data/file/396247/National_Standards_of_Excellence_for_Headteachers.pdf, (accessed 18 March 2015).

UK Department for Education (2014), *Teacher Supply Model: A Technical Description,* Department for Education, London, www.gov.uk/government/publications/teacher-supply-model-a-technical-description (accessed 16 March 2015).

UNESCO (2014), *EFA Global Monitoring Report 2013/4 – Teaching and Learning: Achieving Quality for All*, United Nations Educational, Scientific and Cultural Organization, http://unesdoc.unesco.org/images/0022/002256/225660e.pdf (accessed 7 July 2015).

UNESCO-ILO (1966), "Recommendation concerning the Status of Teachers", adopted on 5 October 1966 by the Special Intergovernmental Conference on the Status of Teachers, convened by UNESCO, Paris, in cooperation with the ILO, UNESCO, Paris; International Labour Organisation, Geneva.

Vanichseni, S. and Associates (2012), "Thailand K-12 education system: Progress and failure", Report to the Education Knowledge Group, Pico Thailand CSV Institute, May.

Vere, A. (2007), "Social dialogue in the education sector: An overview", *Working Paper*, No. 256, International Labour Organization, Geneva.

World Bank (2012), "Thailand: Benchmarking Policy Intent in School Autonomy and Accountability", SABER – System Assessment for Benchmarking Education Results, January, http://siteresources.worldbank.org/EDUCATION/Resources/278200-1290520949227/7575842-1339186330807/Thailand_report_for_School_Autonomy_AccountabilityV2.pdf (accessed 19 January 2015).

Chapter 6

Thailand's information and communication technology in education

Good information and communication technology (ICT) skills are essential for effective participation in today's world. This chapter outlines Thailand's ICT education policies and explores some of the reason why, despite significant investment, Thai students lag behind their peers in this area. It identifies five policy issues that may be holding Thailand back: 1) inequity in infrastructure provision; 2) limited digital learning materials relevant to the national curriculum; 3) teachers' confidence and capacity to use ICT in the classroom; 4) lack of effective monitoring of ICT policies; and 5) no coherent framework for investment in ICT.

It recommends the development of a national strategy to enhance the use of ICT in education as part of a broader long-term vision for education in Thailand. This strategy should focus on how teachers can integrate ICT into their teaching including the development of appropriate learning materials; improving Internet access, particularly in remote areas; and improved data gathering to monitor not just inputs but outcomes of its policy implementation.

Introduction

In the digital age, information and communication technology (ICT) plays a key role in creating and exchanging knowledge and information around the globe. ICT affects the everyday lives of citizens in many areas – at school, in the workplace and in the community. Knowledge about, access to and the ability to use ICT are vital for effective participation in an information society. ICT is transforming the nature of how work is conducted and the meaning of social relationships. Decentralised decision making, information sharing, teamwork and innovation are key in today's enterprises. Countries wanting to adequately prepare young people for the challenges and opportunities of a globalised economy need to make long-term, incremental changes in their education systems to adapt to these new demands. Acquiring and mastering ICT competencies has thus become a major component of education today. As UNESCO (2002) observes: "ICT adds value to the processes of learning, and in the organization and management of learning institutions. The Internet is a driving force for much development and innovation in both developed and developing countries. Countries must be able to benefit from technological developments."

Thailand has made significant investments in ICT education over the past few decades, setting out plans to use ICT as a tool to enhance teaching and learning, particularly at the basic education level; to encourage the acquisition of ICT competencies needed for success in the 21st century; and to put the infrastructure in place to support these efforts (Ministry of Education, 2008; Ministry of ICT, 2009a; Thai Consulate-General, 2015). However, Thailand's schools currently lack stable nationwide access to the Internet and widespread access to digital learning materials, Thai teachers lack confidence and competence in the use of ICT, and the country needs to establish data-gathering mechanisms and a coherent, overarching ICT strategy to support the ongoing development of aligned, evidence-based policies in this area. This chapter begins with an overview of Thailand's reforms relating to the use of ICT in education, and then provides an analysis of the policy issues surrounding this area, presenting recommendations for improvements to support ICT use to enhance the quality and equity of the education system as a whole.

Thai policies on ICT in education

ICT has been a central component of Thailand's economic development strategy for several decades, as evidenced by a series of national ICT policy frameworks. These include Thailand's ICT2010 (Ministry of ICT, 2009b, 2009a) and ICT2020 reports, which give a broad outline of the overall ICT development strategy, as well as a series of ICT Master Plans, which give more specific implementation details and progress updates. The goal of these strategies has been to use ICT to create a "Smart Thailand": a society that is "smart and information literate," where knowledge benefits citizens and "society as a whole" (Ministry of ICT, 2009a). Education has been a key pillar in these efforts.

The first phase of ICT use in Thailand's education system began in 1984, when Thai schools began offering computer courses to students in order to provide them with basic skills for operating and applying ICT (Meleiseia, 2008). The courses were compulsory within the mathematics subject cluster and were revised in 1990 and 1997 to respond to technological developments. When Thailand introduced a new basic education curriculum in 2001, it included standards for what students in all 12 grades should know about ICT. Technological education comprised ICT and content on design and technology.

The second phase of ICT reforms began after the publication of the 2001 Second Information Technology in Education Study (SITES), which showed that the use of ICT in Thailand at the primary and secondary levels was below international averages (Pelgrum and Anderson, 2001; Waitayangkoon, 2007). Thailand expanded its efforts to integrate ICT in education by developing a series of four-year strategy documents and amendments to the basic education curriculum. The Ministry of ICT produced the first of these strategy documents, the *Master Plan for ICT in Education, 2007-2011*. It proposed the following:

- teach students to use ICT so they can compete in a global society
- integrate ICT into the classroom to unlock its pedagogical potential
- further develop ICT infrastructure in the education sector
- take advantage of ICT to more effectively manage the school system (Ministry of ICT, 2009b).

Thailand's 2008 revisions to its basic education curriculum added "capacity for technological application" as one of five key competencies to be taught across all subjects in the basic education system, and included ICT as a topic of study in all grades (OBEC, 2008). Special attention was given to ICT proficiency at the lower secondary level (Grades M1 to M3), the last stage of compulsory education in Thailand (see Chapter 3) (OBEC, 2008). The Ministry of Education has since produced two subsequent Master Plans setting out additional strategies for ICT integration for 2011-13 and 2014-18.

The importance of ICT to Thailand's education reform and broader social and economic development is evident in the breadth of initiatives introduced by the government and the royal family in recent years. HRH Princess Sirindhorn has initiated projects to reduce inequity by providing computer technology to students from disadvantaged backgrounds, as well as students with special needs, in over 72 rural schools (UNESCO, 2005). Between 2011 and 2014, the Thai government proposed seven priority programmes focused on the use of ICT in education, of which the flagship was the One Tablet Per Child (OTPC) policy. These programmes were intended to:

- provide students at all levels with tablet computers for educational purposes

- set up a student-centred national e-learning system to encourage lifelong learning

- develop an information network for education

- establish the "Cyber Home" system by which academic lessons can be transmitted to students at home via a high-speed Internet network

- increase the coverage of educational TV channels

- turn pilot classrooms into electronic classrooms

- enable the "Fund for Technology Development for Education" to fulfil its objectives (OEC, 2013).

Despite these investments in ICT in education, there is evidence that Thai students do not fully possess the level of computer, information processing and communication skills needed today.

ICT proficiency among Thai students

In 2013, Thailand participated in the International Computer and Information Literacy Study (ICILS), which tested the digital skills of 14-year-old students in 23 countries (Box 6.1; Fraillon et al., 2014). Thai students finished second from the bottom on the study, above only Turkey. Among Thai students, 64% scored below the lowest level of ICT proficiency, 23% scored at the lowest level (Level 1), 11% scored at Level 2 (the proficiency level of most students in other participating countries), 2% scored at Level 3 and none reached Level 4, the highest level.

Thai students also reported lower confidence than students in other countries in carrying out certain ICT tasks like locating a file on a computer; using software to eliminate viruses; working with digital photos; creating or editing documents; finding information on the Internet; and uploading text, images, or videos to an online profile.

Thai and Turkish students also had the greatest spread in national scores out of the countries participating, suggesting ongoing issues with equity in access to ICT, a problem also highlighted in the results of the OECD Programme for International Student Assessment (PISA). The 2012 PISA survey revealed a 71.4% difference between the percentage of disadvantaged students and advantaged students in Thailand who reported they were connected to the Internet at home, greater than the 66.5% difference in Malaysia and much higher than the 13.4% average difference across OECD countries (OECD, 2015).

Recent OECD analysis (2015) suggests that a higher rate of ICT use is not necessarily associated with greater ICT proficiency. This seems to be the case in Thailand, where students reported an above-average use of computers. Some 60% indicated they used computers to prepare reports or essays at least once a month, 51% said they had given presentations with computers and 23% stated that they had worked with a student from another school using a computer compared to ICILS averages of 45%, 44% and 13% respectively (Fraillon et al., 2014).

Above-average percentages of Thai students reported having learned to provide references to Internet sources, access information using a computer, determine whether to trust information from the Internet, and choose where to look for information about an unfamiliar topic. Thai students also reported above-average use of computers in seven of eight learning areas, including mother tongue, foreign languages, mathematics, sciences, humanities, creative arts and other.

However, Thai students reported lower than average computer use in the area of information technology and computer studies. They also experienced above-average obstacles to the use of ICT because their schools reportedly had too few computers connected to the Internet, insufficient Internet bandwidth or speed, insufficient computers for instruction, and unsatisfactory ICT skills among teachers (Fraillon et al., 2014). Together, these results suggest that, even if Thai students spend more time on computer tasks than many students elsewhere, variable quality of infrastructure and instruction limit the effect this has on their ICT proficiency.

> **Box 6.1. Assessing the computing and information literacy skills of young people**
>
> The ICILS studied the extent to which young people have developed computer and information literacy. Fourteen-year-old students from a variety of countries were given a computer-based test together with a survey. This was complemented by questionnaires to teachers and school managers.
>
> The study constructed a four-level scale to measure and compare students' performance. Advanced students (Level 4) selected only the most relevant information to use for communicative purposes. They evaluated the usefulness of information based on criteria associated with need, and evaluated its reliability based on its content and probable origin. At Level 3 students demonstrated a capacity to work independently when using computers as information-gathering and information-management tools. Level 2 students were able to use their computers to complete basic and explicit information-gathering and information-management tasks. At Level 1 students demonstrated a functional working knowledge of computers as tools and a basic understanding of the consequences of computers being accessed by multiple users.
>
> *Source*: Fraillon et al. (2014), *Preparing for Life in a Digital Age. The IEA International Computer and Information Literacy Study International Report.*

Policy Issue 1: Thailand lacks the infrastructure to support effective ICT use in schools

In order to use ICT in teaching and learning, students need access to a digital device of some kind, whether it be a computer, tablet PC, mobile phone or interactive whiteboard, and to have a stable, reasonably fast connection to the Internet. An education system that aims to prepare its students for full social and economic participation has to provide good access to the Internet and to all the information, communication opportunities and learning resources it has to offer. Thai students need to learn how to harness the potential of the Internet, making good use of the abundance of information it provides while understanding and managing risks. Thailand has made significant investments in hardware, but teaching and learning are hindered by slow, unstable Internet connections. Thailand's new hardware policies should be informed by its experiences implementing past digital device initiatives.

Access to computers and the Internet

The growing and critical importance of connectivity

During the 1980s the main focus of ICT use in education was on the computers themselves and on their basic applications such as word processing, calculation and database management. In time, the concept of information technology grew to also encompass laser discs, CDs and DVDs. With the emergence of the Internet in the mid-1990s the concept of ICT has expanded to include all technologies and applications intended to provide access to information and media and to support communication, such as Internet browsers and e-mail. Finally, the new generation of mobile phones that can access the Internet has further expanded the concept. The expression "information and communication technology" now comprises all the elements listed above, together with a number of hybrids such as smartphones, tablet PCs, netbooks, projectors, digital cameras and interactive whiteboards (OECD, 2012).

With cheaper hardware and software, as well as an ever-expanding Internet with less and less expensive high-speed access, attention is moving away from devices and towards the information, services and resources that can be used on line. As the OECD (2012) puts it, "although the concept of technology or ICT was a useful construct in the eighties and nineties, since the progressive generalization of access to the Internet, what really matters is the ability to connect either to others or to the Internet, irrespective of the type of device, service or platform used." According to the OECD, these changes require a shift in the focus of policy discussion away from access to particular types of technology, devices or gadgets, and towards the vast range of activities that can be carried out and the services accessed on line. Using the Internet for teaching and learning requires both digital devices and access to the Internet. To achieve this, many countries have made significant investments in computers and improved Internet access for schools.

The learner-to-computer ratio

Internationally, countries strive for a low learner-to-computer ratio (LCR) in schools, as a lower ratio means each pupil has more time to access a computer. Research shows that the more computers are present in a classroom, the more likely it is that a teacher will have students use them frequently (Becker, 1999). Where students share a computer, group work complemented by structured sharing schedules may have significant learning benefits, especially if based on collaborative and co-operative learning models. On the other hand, if too many learners are sharing a single computer, the time required for different tasks may not allow each student to have a meaningful learning experience. In most countries, the LCR is typically greater than 1:1, meaning that more than one student must share a single computer or device. In Europe, there are between three and seven students per computer on average, and nine out of ten students are in schools with broadband connections (European Schoolnet, 2013).

Thailand has made significant investments in hardware for schools in recent years. In 2008, the Ministry of Education recorded an average LCR in secondary education of 14:1 (Ministry of Education, 2011). More recent estimates vary considerably but suggest that this has improved (UIS, 2014a). According to data from PISA, in 2012 Thailand had a higher ratio of computers for educational purposes per student in secondary school than other countries with a similar level of development in the region: 0.48 in Thailand compared to 0.24 in Viet Nam, 0.19 in Malaysia and 0.16 in Indonesia (Figure 6.1; OECD, 2013). Moreover, the ratio was higher in Thailand than in well-developed countries like Korea (0.40), and not far from that of Japan (0.56) (OECD, 2013).

Figure 6.1. Availability of computers at school, selected countries, 2012

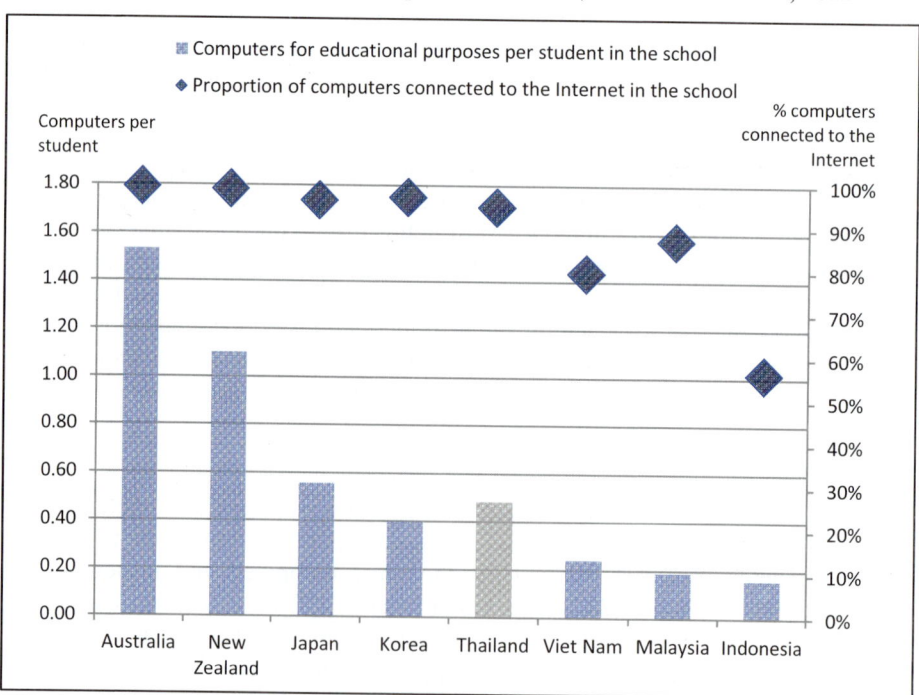

Note: Results based on school principals' reports.

Source: OECD (2015), *Students, Computers and Learning: Making the Connection*, http://dx.doi.org/10.1787/9789264239555-en.

While average LCR figures shed light on the infrastructure available to support the integration of ICT-assisted instruction, they can mask sub-national differences, also known as the internal digital divide. Internationally, LCR values are frequently low in urban centres (indicating greater access) but high in rural and remote areas. For example, research in the People's Republic of China has shown that urban primary education centres have an LCR of 14:1, compared to 29:1 in rural centres (Zeng et al., 2012). By contrast, in Tajikistan computers are more available in rural areas due to the decision to provide all schools with a laboratory with the same number of devices regardless of enrolment. This has the effect of favouring pupils in small rural schools over large urban institutions (Asian Development Bank, 2012). The use of multi-seat computers or networked PCs, where users simultaneously operate from a single central processing unit (CPU) and server while using their own individual monitors and keyboards, is one possible option to minimise the effects of computer shortages.

Thailand's national data on computer access do not permit comparisons between schools of different socio-economic backgrounds or across different regions. PISA 2012 results suggest no significant difference in the LCR between advantaged and disadvantaged schools or between schools in urban and rural areas. However, these data do not reveal the age of the computers in use across the country's schools nor whether they are in good working condition. Evidence from PISA on the overall adequacy of educational resources in schools as reported by principals, which includes but is not limited to ICT resources, reveals significant differences in quality between rural and urban areas in Thailand and a close correlation between schools with poor-quality resources and high levels of socio-economic disadvantage (OECD, 2013).

Internet access

If schools are to make the best use of rich online curriculum resources, online assessment tools, web-based collaboration systems, digital textbooks and a host of Internet-based technologies such as online collaboration tools, Internet-enabled communication services and cloud computing, they need sufficient broadband bandwidth to facilitate their seamless use in schools (Cosgrove et al., 2014). Improved broadband access and wireless connectivity can also reduce inequity across an education system, extending learning opportunities beyond traditional classroom boundaries to meet the needs of under-served populations. This is a driving force behind ICT policies to improve service to rural communities in Australia, Canada, Iceland and New Zealand, (Bakia et al., 2011, in Cosgrove et al., 2014).

The density of devices and users in a school can be among the highest in any work environment (CISCO, 2013). Research recommends that education systems determine the bandwidth schools need to accommodate demand by using a bandwidth-per-student measure, which directly correlates with the quality of a student's online experience across a range of activities (Table 6.1; Fox et al., 2012; CISCO, 2013; Cosgrove et al., 2014). In America, some have set ambitious targets for schools of 2 Mbps per student or even 10 Mbps per student by 2018 (Fox et al., 2012; CISCO, 2013).

Table 6.1. Recommended download speeds

Activity	Recommended download speeds per user
Email and web browsing	500 Kbps
Download a 1 MB digital book in 5.3 seconds	1.5 Mbps
Online learning	250 Kbps
HD-quality video streaming	4 Mbps
Skype group video session, 7+ people	8 Mbps
Download a 6 144 MB movie in 8 minutes	100 Mbps
Multiple choice assessments	64 Kbps/student

Source: Fox et al., (2012), *The Broadband Imperative: Recommendations to Address K-12 Education Infrastructure Needs;* p. 21.

Information about the level of Internet access in Thai schools presents a mixed picture. According to PISA 2012, based on principals' reports, the proportion of school computers connected to the Internet was relatively high in Thailand (95%), particularly in comparison to other countries in the region (Figure 6.1), while the ICILS 2013 study found that 74% of Thai students were attending schools where too few computers were connected to the Internet (OECD, 2013; Fraillon et al., 2014). The latter result may be related to the poor quality of Internet connections across the country (Table 6.2; UIS, 2014a; OEC, 2015). In Thailand, whole schools share a connection of 6-8 Mbps, which is more appropriate for single-family use, and most use satellites for network connections, which are unstable and slow (Table 6.3; OEC, 2015).

Table 6.2. Type and speed of Internet connections in schools, 2012

Share of schools	Type of connection	Average speed
42%	XDSL	8 Mbps
33%	Wi-Fi	6 Mbps
11%	Analogue modem	4 Mbps
6%	Leased lines	8 Mbps
5%	ISDN	6 Mbps
3%	Cable modem	10 Mbps

Source: OEC (2015), *Master Plan for ICT in Education, 2014–2018*.

Table 6.3. Internet connections for schools, 2012

Linkage format	Schools	Educational service areas	Total
Leased line	1 468	85	1 553
ADSL	5 710		5 710
Satellite	22 939		22 939
Total	30 117	185	30 302

Source: OEC (2015), *Master Plan for ICT in Education, 2014-2018*.

The Thai government has taken measures to improve connectivity across the education system, with plans to upgrade Internet access in over 30 000 schools by leasing networks at a cost of approximately THB 1 000 million (Thai baht) per year beginning in fiscal year 2014, and proposed funding for Internet capacity in the Master Plan for ICT in Education, 2014-2018.

Although international targets for connectivity may not be realistic for Thailand in the short term, the country should consider using Mbps per student or per 1 000 students as a metric for bandwidth needs than Mbps per school. Thailand should also expand Internet access in rural areas, and look at similar projects implemented in the European Union to support this work (Box 6.2).

> **Box 6.2. The European Commission's rural broadband proposal**
>
> In 2009, the European Commission committed to supporting the economic recovery of the European Union through a development policy that provided funding to expand broadband infrastructure in rural areas. Broadband connectivity was viewed as key to the use of ICT to spur growth and innovation for the benefit of the economy and society. Specifically, the commission provided funding to:
>
> - create new broadband infrastructure (e.g. fixed, terrestrial wireless, satellite-based or a combination of technologies)
> - upgrade existing broadband infrastructure
> - lay down passive broadband infrastructure in tandem with other infrastructure projects (e.g. civil engineering work).
>
> *Sources*: European Commission (2009a), "Commission earmarks €1bn for investment in broadband – Frequently asked questions", http://europa.eu/rapid/press-release_MEMO-09-35_en.htm; European Commission (2009b), *Community Guidelines for the Application of State Aid Rules in Relation to Rapid Deployment of Broadband Networks*, http://ec.europa.eu/competition/consultations/2009_broadband_guidelines/guidelines_en.pdf.

One Tablet Per Child policy

A lack of equipment is often cited as an obstacle to ICT use in classrooms (Becker, 1999; European Schoolnet, 2013). A number of countries have introduced one laptop per child (OLPC) programmes, although the results of these initiatives have thus far been mixed (Box 6.3). Thailand implemented a small-scale OLPC programme in 2008, comprising approximately 500 XO laptops designed to be low cost and durable machines for school use (Ibarrarán, 2012). A 2009 evaluation of the programme found no strong indication that the academic performance of students using the laptops was appreciably different from that of other students (Mahachai, 2010). However, there were positive differences among participating students, such as enthusiasm about work, and the ability to link computers into their learning and searches for information (Mahachai, 2010).

A more recent One Tablet Per Child policy was launched in Thailand by the government of former Prime Minister Yingluck Shinawatra (2011-14).

A 2012-13 Office of the Basic Education Commission (OBEC) evaluation of the use of tablet computers in a sample of 596 schools in 175 Educational Service Areas, along with other research relating to Thailand's OTPC policy,[1] found that:

- A total of 28 413 schools (99%) had received their tablets, although delivery was late in 22% of the cases and defects were found in 44% of the tablets and in 28% of the software.

- Half of the teachers involved in the programme found the speed of the distribution of the tablets too slow, but 93% of school administrators and 88% of teachers were satisfied with the digital content.

- Teacher attitudes were positive overall: 58% of teachers liked to use the tablet device in their teaching and 62% believed it was of benefit to their students.

- The programme would benefit from the development of contextualised content, greater usability, teacher support and an assessment of learning outcomes. (OBEC, 2013; Viriyapong and Harfield, 2013).

Box 6.3. International one laptop per child policies

One of the most extensive long-term initiatives providing one laptop per student began in the state of Maine, United States, in the 2002/03 school year. More than 17 000 seventh graders and their teachers in over 240 middle schools across Maine received laptop computers. The following year all eighth graders and their teachers also received laptops, and each subsequent year thereafter all students entering the seventh and eighth grades, as well as their teachers, have been supplied by the state with laptop computers. A 2011 review of the programme concluded that it has had a significant impact on curriculum, instruction and learning, improving students' performance in writing, mathematics and science. The elements that have made the Maine programme successful include:

- a focus on teacher and school leader professional development, including seven contracted tech professionals who train teachers, principals, superintendents and technology co-ordinators
- well-developed support and Internet infrastructure
- political commitment and long-term funding.

> **Box 6.3. International one laptop per child policies** *(cont.)*
>
> By contrast, a similar programme in Syracuse, New York, that began two years later ended due to implementation failures, including a lack of clear and measurable goals and a lack of in-service training for teachers, who were not given laptops before their students.
>
> India's Aakash Project and Turkey's FAITH project are OLPC programmes that have advanced slowly, contending with logistical challenges posed by large geographical areas. Peru and Uruguay both began implementing OLPC programmes in 2007. Evaluations of these programmes have found mixed results regarding the effectiveness of laptops in improving educational quality and equity, although questions have been raised about the focus and methodology of these evaluations. What has not been questioned is the finding that technology alone does not solve educational deficiencies.
>
> *Sources*: Silvernail and Gritter (2007), *Maine's Middle School Laptop Program: Creating Better Writers*; Waters (2009), "Maine ingredients", *T H E Journal*; Mahachai (2010), "Laptops a success only in some cases", www.nationmultimedia.com/home/2010/11/22/national/Laptops-a-success-only-in-some-cases-30142835.html; Silvernail et al. (2011), *A Middle School One-to-One Laptop Program: The Maine Experience*; Cristia et al., (2012), "Technology and child development: Evidence from the One Laptop per Child Program". Ibarrarán (2012), "And the jury is back: One Laptop per Child is not enough", http://blogs.iadb.org/desarrolloefectivo_en/2012/03/06/and-the-jury-is-back-one-laptop-per-child-is-not-enough; Trucano (2013), "Big educational laptop and tablet projects: Ten countries to learn from", http://blogs.worldbank.org/edutech/big-educational-laptop-and-tablet-projects-ten-countries.

In June 2014, after approximately 1.2 million tablets had been distributed to students in Grade 1 (P1), Thailand's new government suspended the OTPC programme. Based on information obtained during the review, funds remaining from this programme are to be used for an initiative called Smart Classroom. According to OBEC and Microsoft, this programme aims to integrate four factors into the classroom: 1) teaching with technology; 2) digital content; 3) cloud-based services and Microsoft Office 365; and 4) technological devices. These are intended to create a classroom environment that is more conducive to learning and teaching (Bangkok Post, 2014). The design and implementation of this and other new programmes should be informed by evidence gathered from evaluations of the OTPC initiative and any similar programmes involving the provision of digital devices to Thai schools.

Moving forward, Thailand could continue to invest in television as a potentially powerful educational tool to decrease social and economic inequality. Currently, the "Kru Truu", Educational TV and Tutor Channel projects produce and distribute educational content to Thai television (Laohajaratsang, 2010). While many Thai students do not have access to computers or the Internet at home, 99.6% of Thai households have a television (Bangkok Post, 2013). This near universal access means that televised educational content has the greatest chance of reaching the most students in disadvantaged and rural areas.

Thailand may also wish to explore unorthodox methods of using ICT in education, such as bring your own device (BYOD) policies as applied in the United States or in Scandinavian countries, providing these do not disenfranchise students from disadvantaged backgrounds. As of December 2014, Thailand had 97.7 million mobile subscribers (Leesanguansuk, 2015). It currently has the third highest mobile broadband penetration rate among Association of Southeast Asian Nations (ASEAN) countries, around 50 million users, and will become the second largest mobile broadband subscriber in Southeast Asia after Singapore once the rollout of the high-speed, fourth generation (4G) network is complete.

Recommendations

The review team recommends that Thailand:

- **Address the need for a stable, responsive and widely available ICT infrastructure by setting clear, long-term goals to expand Internet access backed by adequate funding to cover devices, connectivity and maintenance.**

While broadband connections cannot be used without digital devices, computers or tablet PCs are of limited value for learning where there is no access to the Internet. Thailand should continue its digital investments in both, making sure it balances spending between expenditure on devices and Internet access, and expenditure on technical maintenance costs for schools. It should also invest in professional development for educators and digital learning resources, addressed later in this chapter.

Policy makers might consider including BYOD approaches in this investment strategy, but with special support for students from disadvantaged backgrounds or those living in remote rural areas to ensure the policy does not further disadvantage them. In order to reach all regions of the country, Thailand should continue to use television as a medium for providing educational content.

- **Prioritise investments in ICT infrastructure and connectivity in remote areas to ensure equity of access.**

Providing Internet connectivity to schools in remote areas is expensive, as is technical maintenance. Nevertheless, they are necessary to support any initial investment in hardware. Without Internet access in schools and trained teachers who can use computers to their best advantage, very little of the equipment's potential can be harnessed, increasing the risk of a digital divide between urban and rural areas. To support the expansion of ICT infrastructure, Thailand should begin to use bandwidth-per-student to measure progress and look at similar projects undertaken in other regions, including the European Union.

Policy Issue 2: Digital learning materials are not yet fully incorporated into the basic education system

Improving the quality of education relies to a significant extent on ensuring teachers and students have access to relevant and high-quality textbooks and other learning materials, in printed and digital format. For most teachers, there is a close relationship between being able to implement the school curriculum and having access to high quality learning materials. Digital learning resources such as audio or video files, images or software have great potential to promote learning, particularly in comparison to traditional, static textbooks (OECD, 2009). Unlike printed material, digital learning resources can be interactive, receiving and responding to input from the user, making simulations and hypertext possible. For example, a simulation might represent a physical environment that would otherwise be too difficult, expensive or dangerous for students to explore. Although there is some evidence that these types of resources are used in Thailand's basic education system, more could be done to ensure their quality, relevance and widespread availability.

Developing and using digital learning resources

Policies aimed at promoting the use of ICT in schools often focus on infrastructure, equipment and the in-service training of teachers. Realising the full potential of ICT to support teaching and learning also means investing in the development and publication of digital learning resources. In contrast to textbooks, which are generally created within the traditional framework and rules of the public school system, digital learning resources tend to arise from a broad commercial market or social or research context. They are often available for free on the Internet. They may take the form of open educational resources (OERs), which are "teaching, learning or research materials that are in the public domain or released with an intellectual property license that allows for free use, adaptation, and distribution" (UNESCO, 2015). OERs are particularly important in developing countries where students may not be able to afford textbooks, access to classrooms may be limited, and professional learning programmes for teachers may be lacking. In industrialised countries, OERs can also offer significant cost savings.

> **Box 6.4. The Paris OER Declaration**
>
> In 2012, UNESCO issued the Paris OER Declaration, which encourages governments to develop strategies to integrate OERs in education. To support the declaration, UNESCO is working with five member states, including Indonesia in the Asia-Pacific region, to conduct activities in three key areas:
>
> 1. Advocacy – organising events and creating publications to raise awareness of OERs, building the capacity of policy makers and educators to increase their understanding of open licences and issues surrounding the use of OERs, and introducing standards to increase sharing of OERs.
>
> 2. Policy development – developing plans for the production and use of OERs and policies to encourage the open licensing of learning materials produced with public funds.
>
> 3. Teacher development – developing training materials using OERs and about OERs, within the context of UNESCO's ICT Competency Framework for Teachers (Box 6.7).
>
> *Source*: UNESCO (2012a), *Implementing the Paris OER Declaration*, www.unesco.org/new/en/communication-and-information/access-to-knowledge/open-educational-resources/implementing-the-paris-oer-declaration/.

Due to language issues and the need for "localised" learning materials adapted to national curricula, countries should not rely solely on internationally developed OERs but should invest in developing their own digital learning resources. These can be created by the public sector or procured, directly or indirectly (e.g. by having students' families purchase them) from educational publishers. In either case, governments should design a clear and consistent policy setting out the processes they will follow to make the digital learning resources available. In addition to governments, the private sector, bottom-up entities such as non-governmental organisations (NGOs), or users themselves may establish initiatives to develop digital learning resources (OECD, 2009). The changing education landscape makes new scenarios for the production of these resources possible. Involving teachers in their production can be a particularly effective way to reduce costs and improve teachers' digital competency (Box 6.5). As Thai teachers' capacity to work with ICT increases, the country should explore the role they can play in developing digital learning resources.

> **Box 6.5. The Norwegian Digital Learning Arena**
>
> The Norwegian Digital Learning Arena (NDLA) involves teachers in the production of digital learning material. In 2007, the Norwegian government decided to provide students in upper secondary education with free educational materials. The regional educational authorities were tasked with distributing these resources, using funds provided by the national government. A total of 18 out of 19 regional educational authorities teamed up to produce some of their own learning materials instead of purchasing materials produced by publishers.
>
> The regional educational authorities designated a group of teachers to author the new material. Because the teachers produced this material on behalf of their employers and used their schools' own resources, all intellectual property rights to the material belonged to the regional educational authority. The material they produced was combined with content purchased from publishers and media companies. All materials were scrutinised by university experts before publication and then issued in digital format using Creative Commons licenses. This project is still ongoing. It represents not only a cost-efficient way to make digital learning materials available across the country, but also a new way to improve the digital skills of teachers.
>
> *Source*: OECD (2009), *Country Case Study Report on Norway*, www.oecd.org/edu/ceri/42214660.pdf.

Digital learning materials in Thailand

Thailand has invested in the development of digital learning resources. The country's One Tablet Per Child project involved the production of e-books, learning objects, multimedia and songs to be installed on tablets distributed to students. For this project, OBEC produced 336 learning objects in 5 clusters – Thai language, English language, mathematics, science and social studies – which paralleled the textbook content. It is unclear whether these materials were also made available to students who lacked a tablet but had access to a computer.

In recent years, the Institute for the Promotion of Teaching Science and Technology (IPST) has made significant investments in digital learning materials, primarily for science, technology, engineering and mathematics (STEM) subjects. However, this review could not determine the use and quality of these digital learning materials. It was also not possible to determine whether high-quality digital learning materials are widely available on the private market.

The government's Master Plan for ICT in Education 2014-2018 states that digital learning materials have not yet been developed for a number of basic education subjects and grade levels (OEC, 2015). In addition, most high-quality OERs are not available in Thai, limiting their potential use unless teachers translate them or students are capable of working in English. The 2013 ICILS study found that while Thai students have levels of access in school to some software resources (e.g. software for word processing and spreadsheets) and Internet-related resources (e.g. websites, wikis) that are on par with or higher than the average across other countries, only 75% had access to interactive digital learning resources such as learning objects compared to an ICILS average of 84% (Fraillon et al., 2014). All of this suggests the need for a national strategy to produce digital learning materials, including OERs, for the basic education system.

Repositories for digital learning resources

A national hub or repository for teachers to use to find and compare digital learning materials like OERs can stimulate the use of ICT in schools (OECD, 2007). Such a repository need not be in a central physical location. Storage can be decentralised, with materials hosted by an organisation or company that owns the copyright on the material. An outstanding example of a repository for digital learning materials is the European Schoolnet Learning Resource Exchange for Schools. It is a federation of repositories from across Europe, allowing schools and teachers to search for educational content from different countries and providers. All materials are free and most are published under a Creative Commons license. Denmark has a national repository containing both OERs and commercial learning materials. Foundations like the Khan Academy and the CK-12 Foundation offer high-quality materials mainly in the STEM area.[2]

In Thailand, the Asian Institute of Technology initiated the Knowledge, Imagination, Discovery and Sharing – Digital (KIDS-D) project in 2008 as a network of digital libraries for collecting and sharing OERs through the Internet (Bacsich and Salmon, 2014). KIDS-D@SWU is one of the digital libraries under the KIDS-D project that aims to assist educational development by providing high-quality, on-demand learning resources to schools, university students and the general public through the Internet. The project also promotes the sharing of learning resources, knowledge, and thinking between schools, universities, organisations and students.

Of the three different network providers that offer Internet access to schools in Thailand, two also have repositories for learning resources: the National Learning Centre as part of NEdNet and the Digital Content Centre as part of the OBEC-Net (Bureau of Information and Communication Technology, 2015). Thailand's Master Plan for ICT in Education 2014-2018 contains plans to integrate these networks. These plans should also apply to the repositories, so that teachers can visit a well-curated one-stop shop for digital learning materials rather than having to search multiple repositories.

Recommendation

The review team recommends that Thailand:

- **Build a national strategy for developing digital learning materials, and create a national repository where such materials can be accessed.**

Policy makers should address the limited access to digital learning materials in Thailand in part by encouraging and enabling Thai teachers and students to make use of high quality OERs. Thailand should also expand its work on OERs and integrate ongoing projects such as KIDS-D into a national strategy. Thailand could follow UNESCO's advice under the Paris OER Declaration of 2012 (Box 6.4), specifically working to build the capacity of policy makers and educators to understand, develop and use OERs (UNESCO, 2012a). In particular, Thailand should explore the role teachers could play in developing digital learning materials for use in the basic education system.

Thailand should establish a common national repository or a one-stop shop for digital learning materials, where teachers could search for material by grade level and subject, thus stimulating the use of such materials. In creating such repositories, it is recommended to involve or at least consult teachers in how these repositories should be laid out, the relevance of content to curriculum, curation tags, etc. Such repositories are most effective if they are online and allow teachers to rate/comment on available content as well as share content.

Policy Issue 3: Teachers need more confidence and capacity to use ICT effectively in the classroom

Research points to the following pre-conditions for teachers' effective use of ICT: 1) access to computers and the Internet at school; 2) competence in using software and the Internet and applying it to teaching; and 3) motivation, gauged by the attitude that using computers in classrooms results in significant learning benefits (Empirica, 2006). Teachers' confidence in their expertise, as well their opinions and attitudes about ICT, affect not only their use of it but also their students' ICT competency (European Schoolnet, 2013; Fraillon et al., 2014; Box 6.6). Teachers in Thailand need more effective preparation and professional learning to increase their confidence and competency in using ICT to support student learning.

Thai teachers' use of ICT

Thai teachers are not as confident about their ICT use as their counterparts in other countries, and they have mixed attitudes to ICT as a teaching and learning tool. In the ICILS 2013 study, they reported a low level of confidence with regard to basic ICT skills like writing a letter with a word processing programme, e-mailing a file as an attachment, storing digital photos on a computer, filing digital documents in folders and subfolders, and monitoring student progress (Fraillon et al., 2014). While over 90% agreed that ICT helps students access better sources of information, consolidate and process information more efficiently, and develop a greater interest in learning, teachers in Thailand were more likely than in other countries to endorse the view that ICT "only encourages" students to copy material from published Internet sources (68%) and report that it "merely distracts" students from learning (48%).

Box 6.6. Norwegians SMILE

A Norwegian study called SMILE, conducted in 2012 among 17 500 students and 2 500 teachers, looked at the relationship between ICT use and learning outcomes in secondary schools. It focused on how school officials exercise leadership, how teachers teach, and how students learn in technology-saturated classrooms. Those teachers who are successful in their pedagogical ICT use are characterised as having high digital competency, good classroom management skills, the ability to master digital formative assessment, and flexibility in adapting their teaching to an increasingly digitalised society. The study also found that students look up to digitally competent teachers as role models of professional ICT use. More specifically, they need teachers who exercise strong leadership in the classroom, who possess an array of teaching modalities, and who monitor students closely with formative assessments and individualised instruction.

The researchers concluded that the relationship between students' ICT use and their learning outcomes seems to be closely related to digital formative assessment in the SMILE schools. The SMILE study also reveals that the pedagogical use of ICT varies substantially between different groups of students, groups of teachers, professional groups and education programmes. Some of these differences are related to the characteristics of different subjects, the lack of appropriate digital tools in different subjects, as well as a lack of digital competence. For this reason, one of the most important implications of the findings of the SMILE study is that an increase in digital competency among teachers is one of the most important means of increasing students' learning outcomes in schools and subjects that make use of ICT.

Source: Krumsvik et al. (2013), *Sammenhengen Mellom IKT-bruk og Læringsutbytte (SMIL) i Videregående Opplæring*.

The ICILS 2013 study indicates that for some tasks, Thai teachers use ICT at the same rate or more frequently than teachers in other countries. These include providing remedial or enrichment support to individuals or small groups of students, student-led classroom discussions and presentations, and assessing student learning (see Chapter 4 for more information about student assessment). However, other results were significantly below the ICILS 2013 average. Some 68% of Thai teachers said they used ICT in any given class, compared to 94% in Australia and 81% in Korea, and just 22% reported that they "often" use ICT to present information in the classroom, compared to the average of 33% (Table 6.4; Fraillon et al, 2014). These results, combined with Thai teachers' reported negative views about ICT use, suggest a need for the government to do more to ensure all teachers understand the benefits of ICT in teaching and learning and to build teachers' confidence and capacity to use ICT through effective preparation and professional learning, particularly within collaborative school environments.

Table 6.4. Use of ICT for teaching practices in classrooms

National percentages of teachers often using ICT for learning activities in classrooms, 2013

	Presenting information through direct class instruction	Providing remedial or enrichment support to individual students or small groups of students	Enabling student-led whole-class discussions and presentations	Assessing students' learning through tests
Czech Republic	31	4	7	8
Denmark	41	22	23	18
Germany	13	4	5	3
Croatia	28	10	14	5
Lithuania	36	15	15	14
Netherlands	44	14	11	15
Poland	23	19	10	28
Slovenia	35	15	19	7
Slovak Republic	29	10	13	9
Australia	46	19	18	10
Chile	43	20	22	22
Hong Kong, China	38	9	8	12
Korea	42	22	10	12
Norway (Grade 9)	33	12	9	14
Russian Federation	43	21	24	33
Thailand	22	13	14	25
Turkey	22	15	15	20

Source: Fraillon et al. (2014), *Preparing for Life in a Digital Age: The IEA International Computer and Information Literacy Study International Report*.

Table 6.4. Use of ICT for teaching practices in classrooms *(cont.)*

National percentages of teachers often using ICT for learning activities in classrooms, 2013

	Providing feedback to students	Reinforcing learning of skills through repetition of examples	Supporting collaboration among students	Mediating communication between students and experts or external mentors	Enabling students to collaborate with other students
Czech Republic	11	14	8	1	3
Denmark	21	16	16	4	4
Germany	4	4	4	1	2
Croatia	8	14	9	3	3
Lithuania	17	19	12	3	5
Netherlands	10	26	11	1	3
Poland	28	24	24	3	5
Slovenia	13	21	12	3	5
Slovak Republic	11	18	10	3	3
Australia	17	20	14	3	7
Chile	33	29	27	6	12
Hong Kong, China	15	16	8	3	5
Korea	15	20	8	5	8
Norway (Grade 9)	25	11	6	1	5
Russian Federation	16	34	26	5	10
Thailand	19	21	30	10	18
Turkey	17	20	11	7	7

Source: Fraillon et al. (2014), *Preparing for Life in a Digital Age: The IEA International Computer and Information Literacy Study International Report.*

Developing innovative teaching practices

ICT can support innovative teaching practices and the creation of learning environments intended to develop students' competencies for success in the 21st century, such as problem solving and critical thinking (see Chapter 3). Rather than being used as a means to simply transmit information and content to students, ICT can be used as a tool to support students' higher order learning. For example, research recommends that teachers use ICT to develop authentic learning environments that offer students contexts and activities that reflect the way the knowledge will be used in real life (Herrington and Kervin, 2007). Within these learning environments, authentic activities involving ICT could include: planning a trip to a foreign country; using online discussion forums and email; creating a digital story (movie or slides) to raise awareness of local issues; facilitating an exchange of views with peers from other countries; collecting credible data and inferring possible solutions from Internet research. Such approaches can be engaging for both students and teachers.

Innovative teaching practices are more likely to flourish when certain supportive conditions are in place. These conditions include:

- teacher collaboration that focuses on peer support and the sharing of teaching practices
- professional development involving the active and direct engagement of teachers, particularly in practicing and researching new teaching methods
- a school culture with a common vision of innovation, and consistent support that encourages new types of teaching (Wong et al., 2008; ITL Research, 2011).

In Thailand, teachers do collaborate and participate in professional development devoted to ICT, but these elements are not working optimally to increase their confidence and capacity and, ultimately, improve their students' ICT proficiency.

Pre-service preparation in ICT

Thailand has made significant efforts to improve the ICT skills of teachers, both through government-initiated programmes and through public-private partnerships. These efforts focus on pre-service education as well as in-service competency development. In 2002, Thailand's pre-service programmes expanded from four to five years to include an entire year of practicum time. One reason given for this expansion was to prepare teacher candidates for "the real life situation of twenty-first century Thai classrooms, which are equipped with educational television, networked computers, and interactive whiteboards, not to mention the pedagogical skill to interact with self-directed students" (OEC, 2014).

Accreditation requirements mandate that pre-service programmes include ICT as an area of skill and knowledge to be covered. For example, programmes are required to prepare primary teacher candidates to analyse, communicate and draw conclusions about appropriate information for primary school students in an ICT context. Typically, teacher candidates also exercise ICT skills during pre-service programmes through the use of PowerPoint, word processing software and the Internet. However, as highlighted in Chapter 5, pre-service programmes reportedly do not provide sufficient preparation in key areas, including the use of ICT, and teacher preparation needs to be strengthened to support Thailand's education reform.

Professional development in ICT

In the early years of integrating ICT into education in Thai schools, most in-service professional development programmes were designed specifically to build the capacity of teachers assigned to teach computer classes. Today, all teachers are required to participate in ICT training. Schools can organise and deliver this professional development in-house to save on travel expenses, or they can send teachers to attend training offered by Educational Service Areas (ESAs). In practice, only large or medium-sized schools can afford to organise their professional development in-house.

Several ICT in-service training programmes have used the "training-the-trainer model", an educational model in which a group of teachers are trained in ICT skills and then required to train other teachers in their schools. One of the largest programmes of this kind was the IPST's Lead Teacher Programme, which began in 1999 and focused on training secondary ICT teachers to become lead teachers. These ICT lead teachers became valuable resources for the IPST and the Ministry of Education and provided expertise on a range of ICT projects (Waitayangkoon, 2007). They were in charge of reviewing digital materials and creating educational resources and training course content, and they "played a major role in building the capacity of both ICT and non-ICT teachers and in creating a technology-friendly culture in their schools" (Waitayangkoon, 2007). By 2007, 555 lead teachers were providing both ICT and non-ICT training to approximately 1 000 teachers a year at 20 ESA training centres. However, the programme faced a number of challenges, including the need to scale up to provide training opportunities to more teachers, and a lack of co-ordination between the elements of the education system to provide adequate support to enable teachers to change their practices (Waitayangkoon, 2007). Possibly as a result of these challenges, the programme was discontinued, although there is no information available as to when and why. Unfortunately, there was no evaluation of its impact and there is no record of the total number of teachers it trained.

A number of public-private (PP) teacher-training initiatives have also used the training-the-trainer model. These include Microsoft's Partners in Learning programme, which began in 2003 and has currently trained more than 12 000 school leaders and 160 000 teachers in over 12 000 schools.[3] The overall programme objectives include improving teachers' ICT literacy, integrating technology into pedagogy and developing students' competencies for the 21st century.[4] Another private initiative is Intel's Teach Thailand programme, which has a similar profile and content. Since 2002, the Intel programme has trained more than 150 000 teachers,[5] and has received positive feedback from participants (SRI International, 2012). Since 2013, Samsung has been engaged in a Smart Classroom project that has built futuristic classrooms and provides training for 21st century competency development in 15 schools (Nation, 2014).

Overall, PP initiatives make a significant contribution towards preparing Thai educators to use ICT in their teaching. However, they also suffer from limitations, for instance in terms of scale, alignment with the basic education curriculum and reaching teachers in disadvantaged areas of the country. It is also risky for national school systems to become too dependent on private initiatives for their development. It is far better for a government to provide an overall vision and a clear focus and to build momentum for activities to ensure equitable development in line with government policies, which might then be supplemented by various private initiatives.

Research indicates that Thai teachers have relatively high participation rates in professional development devoted to ICT, including school-based collaboration. Over 80% of Thai students in the ICILS 2013 study reported that their teachers have attended courses provided by their school on the use of ICT in teaching; 78% have a teacher who has worked with another teacher trained in an ICT course and who has, in turn, trained other teachers; and 65% have teachers who have participated in professional training programmes delivered through ICT (Fraillon et al., 2014). These figures are well above the average for the study. Among teachers, 91% reported working together with other teachers to improve their use of ICT in classroom teaching (the average in the ICILS study was 71%); 91% report systematically collaborating with colleagues to develop ICT-based lessons using the curriculum (the highest proportion in the study); and in 64% of Thai schools, teachers are part of a community of practice involved in using ICT in teaching, more than double the ICILS average of 29% (Fraillon et al., 2014). These practices are very much in line with those in innovative schools.

Given these relatively high levels of reported ICT training and collaboration, it is unclear why Thai teachers are still less confident at using ICT and why the ICT achievement scores of Thai students are lower than their international peers. However, it is likely that the professional development intended to develop ICT competency has not been effective and/or it has been delivered using an approach that does not prepare teachers adequately, which would be consistent with findings presented in Chapter 5. One observation made by the review team suggests that at least some of the training courses might not have had an optimal design: the IPST courses were largely technological, rather than pedagogical (Waitayangkoon, 2007). Thailand may wish to borrow elements from the UNESCO ICT Competency Framework for Teachers, as well as whole-school approaches, to develop future professional learning on ICT (Box 6.7).

Box 6.7. Professional development to foster ICT competency

UNESCO has developed a comprehensive ICT Competency Framework for Teachers, outlining the policy context needed; specifying the scope, structure and modules for in-service training for teachers; and providing guidance for its implementation. The Framework argues that teachers need to use teaching methods that are appropriate for evolving knowledge societies. Students need to be enabled not only to acquire an in-depth knowledge of their school subjects, but also to understand how they themselves can generate new knowledge, using ICT as a tool. The teacher competencies and associated professional development modules relate to six areas of teachers' work: 1) understanding ICT in education; 2) curriculum and assessment; 3) pedagogy; 4) use of ICT; 5) organisation and administration; and 6) professional learning.

Twenty-First Century Learning Design is a professional development programme for teachers and schools that encourages the creation of innovative pedagogies to prepare students with skills for the contemporary world. The programme is sponsored globally by Microsoft Partners in Learning, and builds on the findings of the Innovative Teaching and Learning (ITL) study. Its purpose is: to inspire teachers and school officials to analyse and "code" learning activities to determine how deeply they integrate 21st century skills; to collaborate in designing new learning activities that provide greater development of those skills; to examine the impact of these learning activities on student work; and to use ICT as part of the overall process. Its goal is to provide teachers with practical guidance on how they may incorporate ICT into their own teaching.

One country that has taken a holistic approach to upgrading the digital skills of its teachers is Ireland, where a government agency, PDST Technology in Education, has developed a range of ICT-related support services for schools. PDST emphasises a whole-school approach involving the principal, an ICT co-ordinator at the school, an e-learning team to provide informal support to teachers, the teachers themselves, and other stakeholders, such as parents.

The four-step PDST approach begins with a review and the prioritisation of aims:

1. The school answers questions including: Where does the school stand at present in relation to ICT?; Where would it like to go?; and, What does it need to do to get there?
2. The development of an action plan.
3. Implementation and monitoring, including professional development for teachers.
4. Evaluation.

For each of the steps, PDST provides services and support – online, through printed materials, and face-to-face. Online courses for teachers have the advantage of being scalable. They also employ the same tools during teacher training that teachers will use in the classroom.

Sources: ITL Research (2011), *Innovative Teaching and Learning Research, 2011 Findings and Implications*; UNESCO, (2011), *UNESCO ICT Competency Framework for Teachers;* PDST (2015), "The e-learning roadmap" (accessed April 2015).

Recommendations

The review team recommends that Thailand:

- **Define the ICT competencies teachers need and provide relevant high-quality teacher preparation and professional development based on these competencies.**

Thailand should assess the current ways teachers are trained to use ICT use to determine how they could stimulate increased familiarity with ICT and increased use. This could be done by emphasising how teachers can integrate ICT into pedagogy in ways that support the learning goals set out in the basic education curriculum. The UNESCO ICT Competency Framework for Teachers provides good advice on how to design such training. ICT-enabled distance training might be a good way to ensure that teachers in rural areas also have the opportunity to participate, providing this does not replace collaborative practices within the school. In addition, teachers' reflective practices, such as action research and lesson study have huge potential, especially if shared through an online community.

This work would be informed by a thorough review of the basic education curriculum, as recommended in Chapter 3, as well as efforts to amend Thailand's teacher standards, as recommended in Chapter 5. It also aligns with the recommendations in Chapter 5 that Thailand strengthen the accreditation process for pre-service programmes to ensure they cover content in essential areas, like the basic education curriculum and the use of ICT, and establish a nationwide strategy for professional development to support the country's education reform.

- **Invest in equipment, Internet access and on-line services to support teachers' use of ICT as a pedagogical tool.**

Provision should be made for pedagogical guidance and support, online and offline, to assist teachers in their daily work. Building on the work of OBEC and the IPST to develop digital learning resources, Thailand should provide national online pedagogic services. These should include access to subject-specific online communities that 1) exchange ideas and experiences; 2) offer digital learning materials; 3) provide handbooks and guidelines for teachers wanting to learn how to use social media sites; and, 4) make suggestions for incorporating student-owned mobile phones into their teaching (UNESCO, 2012b).

Policy Issue 4: Thailand lacks adequate capacity to monitor and assess ICT use in schools

A solid evidence base is essential for informed, effective and timely policy development (Davies, 2000). In contrast, opinion-based policy relies on the selective use of evidence (such as the results of a single survey, irrespective of quality), or on the untested views of individuals or groups. There is wide consensus on the need for effective mechanisms to gather information on the inputs, outputs and outcomes of different policy areas. At present, Thailand has limited evidence about ICT use in its education system to support the development of policies in this area.

The importance of evidence-based policy development

In order to make evidence-based policy decisions about ICT in education, Thailand needs mechanisms in place to collect reliable data. The World Bank and the UNESCO Institute for Statistics (UIS) have developed an Education Data Quality Assessment Framework (Ed-DQAF) to help countries ensure that their data-gathering practices and statistical analysis techniques are methodologically sound, their data sources are accurate and their data are timely and consistent (UIS, 2014b). Key indicators should include the conditions for using ICT (e.g. regional or grade-level differences in the number of students and teachers per computer); the age and quality of the equipment; the availability of digital learning materials; classroom Internet access and speed; teachers' competence in using ICT for teaching and learning; access to ICT competency development for teachers; technological and pedagogical support for teachers and students; and attitudes toward the use of ICT for teaching and learning. Data should take into account not just inputs, but also outputs and outcomes. Output data might include the number of hours per week a student uses ICT in school, broken down by age and subject area; the number of hours per week teachers use ICT to prepare and present their classes; or a list of typical tasks students perform using ICT. Outcome data might be statistics assessing student confidence in using ICT, skills acquired and learning outcomes.

It is also important to understand the results of previous investments and expenditures of resources. Baseline information is essential to measure the effectiveness of programmes. Indicators for target outputs and outcomes must also be clear. One might ask questions such as:

- What are the outcomes of past initiatives to improve teachers' ICT competency or provide digital learning resources?
- If prior investments in hardware, software or competency training were not as successful as expected, why was this the case and what can be done to improve future outcomes?

Questions of this kind require in-depth evaluations built on statistical evidence. Gap analyses can be conducted to determine where additional resources should be spent in order to achieve the greatest impact. In

Thailand, data gathering, evaluation and analysis are not happening on a regular basis to inform the development of policies related to the use of ICT in education.

The limited knowledge base about ICT use in Thailand

In the past, Thailand has gathered, analysed and disseminated information on the status of ICT in its education system. The Ministry of Education's Information and Communication Master Plan for Education, 2011–2013, outlines four groups of key ICT indicators to be used to monitor implementation of the plan over time:

- the number of personnel receiving ICT professional training, and statistics on teachers with access to technology at the school level for learning, e-mail, etc.
- growth of ICT infrastructure and Internet accessibility for schools
- school practices that integrate ICT in teaching
- statistics on ICT use for administrative purposes by schools (OEC, 2014).

The only official statistics regarding ICT use in Thai schools made available for this review appear in a summary of the 2011-2013 Master Plan, and relate mainly to the situation as it was in 2008. They consist of a mixture of input and output data, such as ratios of students and teachers per computer, the percentage of teachers who use their own computer, and average hours per week that teachers or lecturers use computers to support their teaching, broken down by education level (basic education, vocational education, higher education and non-formal education). The figures are not disaggregated by region, which is a problem given the disparities between large urban and small rural schools in Thailand. No chronological data showing development over time seems to be available, nor are there comparable statistics for the period after 2008. The educational data collected annually in Thailand are reportedly unsuitable for comparative purposes because the format and methods for data collection frequently change. There is no system for rechecking and developing data quality, nor is there any means to use the collected data to inform the administration of the education system (OEC, 2015). This lack of readily available data suggests a major challenge for the Thai government.

Thailand has a good record of participating in comparative international studies assessing the use of ICT in education, which can be of real help to policy makers (SEAMEO, 2010). For example, the ICT in Education in Asia study (UIS, 2014a) provides information on areas such as policies to integrate ICT in education, ICT in the national curricula, infrastructure to support the integration of ICT in educational institutions, participation in ICT-assisted instruction, teacher preparedness, and education outcomes. This type of study could be of great use, but all the data on Thailand's practices, except information on ICT in relation to the curriculum, relied on estimates by the government or by UIS rather than solid statistics, and it is difficult to determine their accuracy and reliability.

The ICILS 2013 study also presents an important source of information. Although built on a sample of only 200 to 250 schools in Thailand, it gives a broad range of data on access, utilisation and attitudes regarding ICT use in education. But unless Thailand plans to participate in the next ICILS study scheduled for 2018, there will be no chronological data or comparative information to inform the country's policies and practices. The PISA study (OECD, 2013) also provides useful data on ICT use in Thai schools in comparison to other countries but international data cannot be a substitute for solid national data. A number of countries have developed national data-gathering mechanisms to ensure their ICT in education policies, and broader education reform efforts, are rooted in evidence (Box 6.8). Their practices could inform Thailand's work in this area.

Box 6.8. Promising cases: Systematic monitoring systems

Schools in the Netherlands are served by two public (semi-governmental) organisations. One is called Kennisnet ("knowledge net") and the other Schoolinfo. Taken together, the monitoring of ICT use by Kennisnet and Schoolinfo provide school administrators, parents and policy makers with the information needed to make informed decisions on how to further improve the Dutch school system.

Kennisnet's mission is to ensure that educational institutions avail themselves of the opportunities offered by ICT. The organisation monitors how Dutch schools develop in four areas essential to effective ICT use in education. This model is based on studies showing that investments in infrastructure did not lead Dutch teachers to alter their teaching practices or use ICT tools to impact student learning. The four areas are:

- **vision**: the school's objectives; the role of the teachers, pupils, and administration; the content to be taught; and the ethos of the school
- **expertise**: technical skills, and the ability to combine them with pedagogical techniques in order to present subject matter effectively
- **digital learning materials**: all digital educational content that is used in the school
- **ICT infrastructure**: the availability and quality of computers, networks and Internet connections.

> **Box 6.8. Promising cases: Systematic monitoring systems** *(cont.)*
>
> The four basic elements apply equally to a single school or the whole country. Schoolinfo helps individual schools make the best use of their resources in a transparent and accountable way by providing an online system for gathering and sharing information. The data assembled include the number of students, exam results, the use of ICT, student and parent satisfaction, characteristics of teaching teams, schools' financial situation, partnerships and school plans. Its guiding principle is to use existing data wherever possible in order to eliminate repetitive surveys of schools (thus reducing workload). The system is currently used in 88% of primary schools and 95% of secondary schools in the Netherlands.
>
> In Norway, the Centre for ICT in Education has developed a longitudinal study called *Monitor* that annually charts the digital skills of students in Grade 7 and 9, and in upper secondary level 2. It covers attitudes toward ICT, use of ICT, selection and development of teaching strategies, and learning outcomes. The study highlights links between the use of digital tools and learning outcomes for students. It also provides additional information to teachers, schools, local governments, guardians and authorities regarding the use of ICT and digital teaching resources in schools.
>
> *Source*: ten Brummelhuis and van Amerongen (2010) *Four in Balance Monitor 2010: ICT at Dutch Schools*; Norwegian Centre for ICT in Education, (2010), *Information and Communication Technology (ICT) in Norwegian Education.*

Recommendations

The review team recommends that Thailand:

- **Puts in place a centralised system for periodic (annual or biannual) collection and publication of statistics, fed by school-level data regarding infrastructure, equipment, training and use of ICT.**

Ideally this would involve a central database system, such as the one employed in Norway, so that schools do not have to correspond with various ministries or national agencies separately. The system should be available for relevant ministries and government agencies to use for planning and policy-making purposes. Data should reflect not only resources put into schools, but also outputs and ultimately outcomes.

The statistics should provide an overview of the situation in specific regions of the country. Special attention should be paid to the size of the schools, since there are indications that smaller schools have less Internet access. Special attention should also be paid to geographical differences, taking into account the risks of a digital divide between rural and urban areas. In order for Thailand to measure and monitor progress, the statistics should be comparable over time. The quality of the data should be ensured, for example, by using the World Bank / UIS Education Data Quality Assessment Framework, and it must be accessible to both government agencies and the general public. There should be an agreement between the Ministry of Education and its main and subordinate offices (OBEC, OVEC, OHEC, OEC and the Office of Permanent Secretary) on what data to collect and on the definitions of concepts employed. This would facilitate the use of data and co-operation between agencies.

- **Complement the gathering of statistics with evaluations (qualitative data) and continued participation in international surveys to enable a deeper understanding of the issues at hand and a comparative perspective on how Thailand is progressing.**

The Ministry of Education should organise evaluations of policies and programmes to support the use of ICT in education and use them to inform evidence-based policy making. They should be conducted by individuals – whether within or outside the government – with qualitative research expertise. Although not essential, there is an argument for procuring the services of external researchers such as university faculty or private research organisations to ensure evaluations are impartial. International organisations such as UNESCO can provide relevant ICT in Education indicators and the required capacity building to ensure that they are used to inform policy-making and practice. Efforts should be made to develop broad research strategies, encompassing the evaluation of different policies and programmes, to align efforts and ensure schools are not overburdened by the demands of the research.

At the same time, Thailand should continue its commendable participation in international comparative studies regarding the use of ICT in education. These studies can yield important information about the country's own practices, as well as international practices Thailand could explore and adapt. To make the most out of these studies, it should make every effort to provide reliable and timely data to the study organisers to ensure the results present an accurate picture of the practices that are being implemented in the country.

These recommendations align with the advice in Chapter 1 that Thailand work to increase its capacity for evidence-informed policy development.

Policy Issue 5: Thailand lacks a coherent framework for its significant investments in ICT

Successful policies are coherent, meaning that they are aligned to support the attainment of shared objectives. Insufficient coherence can lead to inefficient use of resources, as well as conflicts among stakeholders over goals. Thailand has made significant investments in hardware, infrastructure, software and "people-ware" in the past, but these have been based on a series of fragmented strategies and initiatives. Thailand needs a coherent national strategy for ICT in education that will improve students' competencies and prepare them for today's society and labour market. This strategy could be articulated within a broader long-term vision for education in Thailand, as described in Chapter 1.

Why coherence is important for ICT policies in education

Policy coherence encompasses a number of aspects, including systemic coherence, chronological coherence, vertical coherence and cross-organisational coherence.

- Systemic coherence means co-ordinating the actions of various parties. If different parties spend time and resources on activities which pull in different directions, this can lessen the impact of their efforts. Systemic coherence may be compromised, for example, if a country allocates significant resources to in-service training for teachers but not to infrastructure or learning materials. In such a case, skilled teachers may be unable to use their knowledge to its full potential.

- Another aspect of coherence is chronology. For example, large investments in hardware and infrastructure, but not in teacher training, may leave the equipment underutilised or standing idle while once teachers do receive training, the equipment may have deteriorated or become obsolete.

- Vertical coherence refers to the alignment of stakeholder initiatives at different levels. For example, if schools wish to allow students to use their smart phones in class, but the Ministry of Education has prohibited this, policies lack vertical coherence.

- Finally, cross-organisational coherence refers to the need for a common vision and strategy across organisations, as in the case of public-private partnerships.

Current technology policies in education

Thailand is committed to modernising its education system, which will involve further integrating ICT into pedagogy, ensuring Thai students acquire the ICT competencies they need, and using ICT to support educational administration. In 2015, the Ministry of Education proposed five general and seven specific policies to further the country's education reform efforts. These included policies related to ICT, including the expansion of the Smart Classroom programme, which would equip schools with Internet access and laptops or desk computers, and the use of ICT for efficient resource-management and data gathering (Ministry of Education, 2015). Such policies need to be aligned with a new coherent strategy for ICT in education.

In developing this strategy, Thailand should learn the lessons of previous initiatives. It should examine in detail, for instance, the impact of the policies and programmes in the Information and Communication Master Plan for Education, 2011–2013 as well as the One Tablet Per Child initiative. These were intended to provide a pathway toward continuous development in the area of ICT in education but their implementation seems to have been unbalanced, with too great a focus on investments in hardware and digital learning materials to be used offline and lower priority given to essential elements, such as Internet access in classrooms and professional learning for teachers. Inefficiencies have been apparent in multiple areas: networks, hardware, software and people-ware (OEC, 2015). Thailand has also lacked a long-term, integrated approach across government agencies. As a result, schools have not been able to make full use of their ICT resources, diminishing the effectiveness of teaching and learning.

Thailand would benefit from ensuring that its strategy emphasises continuity with previous strategies and programmes and, as recommended above, makes use of solid data on infrastructure (networks and hardware), digital learning materials and competencies as well as findings from international research on effective ICT programmes in other countries. Change will take time and often requires longitudinal studies in order to detect differences in student performance due to the intervention of technology. Research suggests it takes at least three years, and up to five or eight years, for stable results to be apparent (Owen et al., 2005; Silvernail and Gritter, 2007).

Recommendation

The review team recommends that Thailand:

- **Develop a coherent national strategy to further integrate ICT into pedagogy, ensure equity of Internet access for Thai students across the country improve students' ICT competencies, and use ICT to support educational administration.**

At a minimum, this strategy should encompass four elements:

- A vision shared by all stakeholders of how ICT will be used in the Thai basic education system over the course of five years to improve student ICT proficiency and transversal skills.

- An inventory of existing digital learning materials, focusing in particular on subject areas and grade levels that are under-supplied, combined with a schedule and operational plan to address gaps (including through the use of OER).

- A map of teacher competencies and competency gaps, focusing in particular on regional differences and the needs of teachers and administrators in small schools, combined with a timetable and plan of action.

- A description of existing ICT infrastructure (Internet access and digital devices per school) together with a plan on how to reach agreed targets in time. This plan needs to take into consideration the age and condition of existing equipment, and the inventories and connectivity in different regions (especially urban vs. rural areas). Targets should be formulated in terms of number of students and teachers per computer, the number of computers connected to the Internet and the bandwidth capacity per student.

The strategy should have clear annual milestones with regard to digital learning materials, competency development and infrastructure so that progress can be measured every one or two years. The responsibilities of different stakeholders on the national, regional and local levels should be made clear and a strong leadership role should be defined. Adequate financial and human resources should be made available, including funds for the maintenance and replacement of older equipment. Targets, resources, and responsibilities should be co-ordinated. If the annual or biannual follow-up indicates that targets have not been met, the reasons for these shortfalls should be the object of thorough discussion, and the targets, resources or responsibilities should be adjusted as required.

This strategy would be informed by a thorough review of the basic education curriculum, as recommended in chapter three of this report, and would be an essential component of a new long-term vision for education in Thailand, as described in Chapter 1.

Conclusions

This chapter has analysed Thailand's use of ICT in education. Over the years, Thailand has made significant investments in hardware, software, people and infrastructure to support the use of ICT in its education system. It has also developed and adopted a basic education curriculum in which ICT is taught as a separate subject and also as a competency across subjects. Despite this, the ICILS 2013 study found that Thai students' proficiency in ICT was low. This chapter has identified a number of reasons for this.

Thailand's schools lack a stable, responsive and countrywide ICT infrastructure, encompassing devices, connectivity and maintenance. Teachers and students require better quality digital learning materials, which are an essential to increasing the use of ICT to improve the quality of education. Teachers need the confidence and capacity to use ICT and digital learning materials effectively; their competencies and attitudes with respect to ICT use have a real impact on student performance. Accordingly, investments in teacher education, both pre-service and in-service, are vital. Mechanisms for gathering, developing and disseminating information are needed to continually strengthen the development of evidence-based ICT policies, as well as Thai schools' ability to use ICT to facilitate students learning.

As a priority, Thailand should create a coherent national strategy to enhance the use of ICT in education. This strategy should be informed by a review of the country's basic education curriculum and it should form part of a broader long-term vision for education in Thailand (see Chapters 1 and 3). The strategy should focus first on the essential role of the teacher by identifying the ICT competencies teachers need and developing relevant and effective professional development to address them. It should emphasise how teachers can integrate ICT into pedagogy in ways that support the learning goals set out in a new basic education curriculum. This work would form part of a holistic plan to build the capacities of teachers and school principals to drive forward Thailand's education reform (see Chapter 5). Expanding and improving Internet access in all regions of the country would also be particularly important, not only to increase ICT use but also improve equity across the education system.

Notes

1. An independent assessment of the OTPC programme by Chulalongkorn University has not been made publicly available (Intellectual Repository: http://cuir.car.chula.ac.th/handle/123456789/43482).

2. These repositories can be found at http://www.eun.org/teaching/resources (Schoolnet), http://materialeplatform.emu.dk/materialer/index.jsp (Materialplatformen), www.khanacademy.org/ (Khan Academy) and www.ck12.org (CK-12 Foundation).

3. E-mail from Mr Srinutanpong, Director, Public Sector Programme, Microsoft Thailand.

4. Partners in Learning, Thailand Infographic. E-mail from Mr Srinutanpong, Director, Public Sector Programme, Microsoft Thailand.

5. E-mail from Ms Langkhapin, Education Manager, Intel Thailand.

Bibliography

Asian Development Bank, (2012), *ICT in Education in Central and West Asia,* http://public.eblib.com/choice/publicfullrecord.aspx?p=3110766.

Bacsich, P. and T. Salmon (2014) "Thailand", in *Researching Virtual Initiatives in Education*, www.virtualschoolsandcolleges.eu/index.php/Thailand#Educational_Internets_in_Thailand .

Bakia, M. R. Murphy, K. Anderson, and G.E. Trinidad (2011), *International Experiences with Technology in Education: Final Report*, US Department of Education, Office of Educational Technology, http://tech.ed.gov/files/2013/10/iete-full-report-1.doc.

Bangkok Post (18 June, 2014), "Tablets swapped for 'smart classrooms'", *Bangkok Post*, www.bangkokpost.com/learning/news/415918/tablets-swapped-for-smart-classrooms.

Bangkok Post (8 July, 2013), "TV ownership nears 100% nationwide, says Nielsen Thailand", *Bangkok Post*, www.bangkokpost.com/tech/local-news/358819/tv-ownership-nears-100-nationwide-says-nielsen-thailand.

Becker, H.J. (1999), *Internet Use by Teachers: Conditions of Professional Use and Teacher-Directed Student Use,* Teaching, Learning, and Computing: 1998 National Survey Report #1, Center for Research on Information Technology and Organizations, The University of California, Irvine and The University of Minnesota, http://files.eric.ed.gov/fulltext/ED429564.pdf.

Bureau of Information and Communication Technology (2015), PowerPoint presentation dated 18 February 2015, Office of the Permanent Secretary.

CISCO (2013), *High-Speed Broadband in Every Classroom: The Promise of a Modernized E-Rate Program*, Computer Information System Company, www.totalcomm.com/total/Literature/VerticalBrochures/ERATEConnectedLearning.pdf

Cosgrove, J. et al. (2014), *The 2013 ICT Census in Schools: Main Report*, Educational Research Centre, Dublin.

Cristia, J. et al. (2012), "Technology and child development: Evidence from the One Laptop per Child Program", *IDB Working Paper Series*, No. 304, Inter-American Development Bank.

Davies, Philip (2000), "The Relevance of Systematic Reviews to Educational Policy and Practice", *Oxford Review of Education*, pp. 365-278.

Empirica (2006), *Benchmarking Access and Use of ICT in European Schools 2006: Final Report from Head Teacher and Classroom Teacher Surveys in 27 European Countries*, European Commission.

European Commission (28 January 2009a), "Commission earmarks €1bn for investment in broadband – Frequently asked questions", *European Commission Press Release*, http://europa.eu/rapid/press-release_MEMO-09-35_en.htm.

European Commission (2009b), *Community Guidelines for the Application of State Aid Rules in Relation to Rapid Deployment of Broadband Networks*, European Commission, http://ec.europa.eu/competition/consultations/2009_broadband_guidelines/guidelines_en.pdf.

European Schoolnet (2013), *Survey of Schools: ICT in Education. Benchmarking Access, Use and Attitudes to Technology in Europe's Schools*, Final Study Report, European Union, https://ec.europa.eu/digital-single-market/sites/digital-agenda/files/KK-31-13-401-EN-N.pdf.

Fox, C., J. Waters, G. Fletcher and D. Levin (2012), *The Broadband Imperative: Recommendations to Address K-12 Education Infrastructure Needs*, State Educational Technology Directors Association (SETDA), Washington, DC, www.setda.org/wp-content/uploads/2013/09/SETDA_BroadbandImperative_May20Final.pdf.

Fraillon, J. et al. (2014), *Preparing for Life in a Digital Age: The IEA International Computer and Information Literacy Study International Report*, International Association for the Evaluation of Educational Achievement (IEA), Springer Open.

Government of India (2012), *National Policy on Information and Communication Technology (ICT) in School Education*, Department of School Education and Literacy Ministry of Human Resource Development, Government of India, New Delhi.

Hattie, J. (2008), *Visible Learning: A Synthesis of Over 800 Meta-Analyses Relating to Achievement*, Routledge.

Herrington, J. and L. Kervin (2007), "Authentic learning supported by technology: 10 suggestions and cases of integration in classrooms", *Educational Media International*, Vol. 44/3, pp. 219-236, http://ro.uow.edu.au/cgi/viewcontent.cgi?article=1027&context=edupapers.

Hoosen, S. (2012), *Survey on Governments' Open Educational Resources (OER) Policies,* Prepared for the World OER Congress, June 2012, Commonwealth of Learning and UNESCO.

Ibarrarán, P. (6 March 2012), "And the jury is back: One Laptop per Child is not enough", Effectiveness Blog, Inter-American Development Bank, http://blogs.iadb.org/desarrolloefectivo_en/2012/03/06/and-the-jury-is-back-one-laptop-per-child-is-not-enough/ (accessed 5 April 2015).

ITL Research, (2011), *Innovative Teaching and Learning Research: 2011 Findings and Implications*, Innovative Teaching and Learning, www.itlresearch.com/images/stories/reports/ITL%20Research%202011%20Findings%20and%20Implications%20-%20Final.pdf.

Jeradechakul, W. (2012), "Foreword", *ASEAN Curriculum Sourcebook*, Association of Southeast Asian Nations, www.asean.org/storage/images/2012/publications/ASEAN%20Curriculum%20Sourcebook_FINAL.pdf.

Krumsvik, R.J. et al. (2013), "Sammenhengen Mellom IKT-bruk og Læringsutbytte (SMIL) i Videregående Ppplæring", Final Report, University of Bergen.

Leesa-nguansuk, S. (23 January 2015),"Thailand expected to move up mobile broadband rank", *Bangkok Post*, www.bangkokpost.com/print/459387/.

Laohajaratsang, T. (2010), "e-Education in Thailand: Equity, Quality and Sensitivity for Learner and Teachers", http://thanompo.edu.cmu.ac.th/load/research/Eeducation.doc.pdf.

Machado, A., G. de Melo and A. Miranda (2014), "The impact of a One Laptop per Child program on learning: Evidence from Uruguay", *Working Papers*, N° 2014-22, Banco de México, www.banxico.org.mx/publicaciones-y-discursos/publicaciones/documentos-de-investigacion/banxico/%7B8AFE28DC-EFE9-E675-6452-A44F480CDA47%7D.pdf.

Mahachai, S.N. (22 November 2010), "Laptops a success only in some cases", *The Nation*, www.nationmultimedia.com/home/2010/11/22/national/Laptops-a-success-only-in-some-cases-30142835.html.

Meleisea, E. (2008), *ICT in Teacher Education: Case Studies from the Asia-Pacific Region*, UNESCO Bangkok.

Miao, F., S. Mishra and R. Mc Greal (eds.), *Open Educational Resources: Policy, Costs and Transformation*, UNESCO, Paris; Commonwealth of Learning, Burnaby.

Microsoft (2007), *Partners in Learning, Progress Report: 2007*, Microsoft.

Ministry of Education (2015), *The Ministry of Education's Policy Fiscal Year 2015*, Ministry of Education of Thailand, Bangkok.

Ministry of Education (2011), "Executive summary", *Information and Communication (ICT) Master Plan for Education, 2011-2013*, Ministry of Education of Thailand, Bangkok.

Ministry of Education (2008), *Towards a Learning Society in Thailand: An introduction to Education in Thailand,* Ministry of Education of Thailand, Bangkok, www.bic.moe.go.th/newth/images/stories/book/ed-eng-series/intro-ed08.pdf.

Ministry of ICT (2009a), *The Second Thailand Information and Communication Technology (ICT) Master Plan 2009-2013*, Ministry of Information Communications and Technology, Bangkok.

Ministry of ICT (2009b), *ICT for Education Master Plan, 2007-2011*, Ministry of Information Communications and Technology, Bangkok.

Nation (9 March 2014), "Working for the community", *The Nation*, www.nationmultimedia.com/business/Working-for-the-community-30228411.html.

Norwegian Centre for ICT in Education (2010), *Information and Communication Technology (ICT) in Norwegian Education*, Norwegian Centre for ICT in Education.

OBEC (2013), "Assessment of One to One Initiative in Thailand, The Scheme of One Tablet per Child: OTPC", presented by Secretary-General, Thailand Education Council.

OBEC (2008), *Basic Education Core Curriculum* B.E. 2551, Ministry of Education of Thailand, Bangkok.

OEC (2015), *Master Plan for ICT in Education, 2014-2018,* Ministry of Education of Thailand, Office of the Permanent Secretary, Bangkok.

OEC (2014), "Country background report – Thailand", internal report provided to the OECD, Office of the Education Council, Bangkok.

OEC (2013), "Mobile learning policy guideline: Thailand experience", presentation at the International Conference on Education 2013, 23-25 June 2013.

OECD (2015), *Students, Computers and Learning: Making the Connection*, PISA, OECD Publishing, Paris, http://dx.doi.org/10.1787/9789264239555-en.

OECD (2013), *PISA 2012 Results: What Makes Schools Successful (Volume IV): Resources, Policies and Practices*, PISA, OECD Publishing, Paris, http://dx.doi.org/10.1787/9789264201156-en.

OECD (2012), *Connected Minds: Technology and Today's Learners*, Educational Research and Innovation, OECD Publishing, Paris, http://dx.doi.org/10.1787/9789264111011-en.

OECD (2009), *Beyond Textbooks: Digital Learning Materials as Systemic Innovation in the Nordic Countries*, Educational Research and Innovation, OECD Publishing, Paris, http://dx.doi.org/10.1787/9789264067813-en.

OECD, (2009), *Country Case Study Report on Norway*, OECD Study of Digital Learning Resources as Systemic Innovation, Centre for Educational Research and Innovation, OECD, www.oecd.org/edu/ceri/42214660.pdf.

OECD (2007), *Giving Knowledge for Free: The Emergence of Open Educational Resources*, OECD Publishing, Paris, http://dx.doi.org/10.1787/9789264032125-en.

Owen, A., S. Farsaii, G. Knezek and R. Christiansen (2005), "Teaching in the one-to-one classroom: It's not about the laptops, it's about empowerment!", *Learning and Leading with Technology*, Vol. 33/4, pp. 12-16.

PDST (2015), "The e-learning roadmap", Professional Development Services for Teachers webpage, http://www.pdsttechnologyineducation.ie/en/Planning/e-Learning-Roadmap/ (accessed April 2015).

Pelgrum, W.J. and R.E. Anderson (2001), *ICT and the Emerging Paradigm for Lifelong Learning: A Worldwide Educational Assessment of Infrastructure, Goals, and Practices in Twenty-six Countries*, IEA and University of Twente OCTO, Amsterdam.

Pichaichannarong, S. (2014), "Assessment of One to One initiative in Thailand: The scheme on One Tablet per Child: OTPC", Attachment Chapter 5, Country Background Report – Thailand, OEC, Bangkok.

SEAMEO, (2010), *Report: Status of ICT Integration in Education in Southeast Asian Countries*, Southeast Asian Ministers of Education Organization (SEAMEO) Secretariat, Bangkok.

Silvernail, D. and A. Gritter (2007), *Maine's Middle School Laptop Program: Creating Better Writers*, Research Brief, Maine Education Policy Research Institute University of Southern Maine Office Gorham, Maine.

Silvernail, D. et al. (2011), *A Middle School One-to-One Laptop Program: The Maine Experience*, Maine Education Policy Research Institute, University of Southern Maine.

Simons, P.R.-J. (n.d.), "Authentic learning and ICT", www .outlab.ie/forums/documents/authenticity_in_learning_118.pdf.

SRI International (2012), *Intel(R) Teach Elements Impact Study*, Intel, www.intel.com/content/dam/www/program/education/us/en/documents/teach-elements-impact-2012-report.pdf.

Stavert, B. (2013), *Bring Your Own Device (BYOD) in Schools: 2013 Literature Review,* Department of Education and Communities, New South Wales Government, Australia.

ten Brummelhuis, A. and M. van Amerongen (2010), *Four in Balance Monitor 2010: ICT at Dutch Schools*, Kennisnet, Zoetermeer, the Netherlands.

Thai Consulate-General (28 January 2015) "News update: Developing Thai education and workforce for ASEAN", Thai Embassy website, www.thaiembassy.org/chennai/en/news/4113/53242-Developing-Thai-Education-and-Workforce-for-ASEAN.html accessed on May 23 (accessed 23 May 2015).

Trucano, M. (31 July 2013), "Big educational laptop and tablet projects: Ten countries to learn from", Edutech blog, http://blogs.worldbank.org/edutech/big-educational-laptop-and-tablet-projects-ten-countries.

UNESCO (2015), "What are Open Educational Resources (OERs)?", UNESCO website, www.unesco.org/new/en/communication-and-information/access-to-knowledge/open-educational-resources/what-are-open-educational-resources-oers/ (accessed 10 April 2015).

UNESCO (2012a), "Implementing the Paris OER Declaration", UNESCO website, www.unesco.org/new/en/communication-and-information/access-to-knowledge/open-educational-resources/implementing-the-paris-oer-declaration/.

UNESCO (2012b), *Turning on Mobile Learning in Asia: Illustrative Initiatives and Policy Implications*, United Nations Educational, Scientific and Cultural Organization, Paris, http://unesdoc.unesco.org/images/0021/002162/216283E.pdf.

UNESCO (2011), *UNESCO ICT Competence Framework for Teachers*, Version 2.0, United Nations Educational, Scientific and Cultural Organization, Paris, http://unesdoc.unesco.org/images/0021/002134/213475e.pdf.

UNESCO (2005), *Infoshare Sources and Resources Bulletin,* ICT for Education in Asia and the Pacific, Volume 6, 2004/05, The ICT Unit, Asia and Pacific Regional Bureau for Education, UNESCO Bangkok, Thailand, http://unesdoc.unesco.org/images/0013/001382/138251e.pdf

UNESCO (2002), Information and Communication Technology in Education: A Curriculum for Schools and Programme of Teacher Development, United Nations Educational, Scientific and Cultural Organization, Paris, http://unesdoc.unesco.org/images/0012/001295/129538e.pdf.

UIS (2014a), "Information and communication technology (ICT) in Asia: A comparative analysis of ICT integration and e-readiness in schools across Asia", *Information Paper,* No. 22, UNESCO Institute for Statistics, Montreal, www.uis.unesco.org/Communication/Documents/ICT-asia-en.pdf.

UIS (2014b), "Assessing education data quality in the Southern African Development Community (SADC)", *Information Paper*, No. 21, UNESCO Institute for Statistics, Montreal, www.uis.unesco.org/Education/Documents/IP-2014-education-data-quality-africa.pdf.

Valtonen, T. et al. (2015), "The impact of authentic learning experiences with ICT on pre-service teachers' intentions to use ICT for teaching and learning", *Computers & Education,* Vol. 81, pp. 49-58.

Viriyapong, R. and A. Harfield (2013), "Facing the challenges of the One-Tablet-Per-Child policy in Thai primary school education", *International Journal of Advanced Computer Science and Applications,* Vol. 4/9, pp. 176-184.

Waitayangkoon, P. (2007), "ICT professional development of teachers in Thailand: The lead-teacher model", in *ICT in Teacher Education: Case Studies from the Asia-Pacific Region*, UNESCO Bangkok, pp. 110-115.

Waters, J., (2009), "Maine ingredients", *T.H.E Journal,* Vol. 36/8, pp.34-39.

Wong, E.M.L., S.S.C. Li, T.-H. Choi and T.N. Lee (2008), "Insights into innovative classroom practices with ICT: Identifying the impetus for change", *Educational Technology & Society,* Vol. 11/1, pp. 248-265.

Zeng, H., R. Huang, Y. Zhao and J. Zhang. (2012), *ICT and ODL in Education for Rural Development: Current Situation and Good Practices in China*, UNESCO International Research and Training Centre for Rural Education (INRULED), Beijing; Beijing Normal University, R&D Center for Knowledge Engineering (BNU-KSEI).

Annex A
Contribution of stakeholders in Thailand

The OECD and UNESCO review team would like to convey our sincere appreciation to the many participants who took time from their busy schedules to share their views, experience and knowledge during the review visits, which took place in June and November 2013 and February 2015. This report is the result of a collaborative effort and we are grateful to the many stakeholders within Thailand who provided a wealth of insights to this review, namely:

- Mr. Virachai Srikajon, Thailand Professional Qualification Institute (TPQI)
- Dr. Gwang-Jo Kim, Director, UNESCO Bangkok
- Mr. Tony Lynch, Ambassador, New Zealand Embassy
- Dr. Sasithara Pichaichannarong, Office of the Education Council (OEC)
- Dr. Suthasri Wongsamarn, Office of the Education Council (OEC)
- Dr. Emmet McElhatton, Senior Policy Analyst, New Zealand Qualification Authority
- Ms. Peggy Wong, Assistant Manager, Qualifications Framework Secretariat, Hong Kong, China
- Mr. Anthony Tung-Shan Chan, Education Bureau, Government of Hong Kong, China
- Ms. Suzanne Cheung, Qualifications Framework Secretariat, Hong Kong, China
- Dr. Anatchai Rattakul, Chief Advisor on Education Affairs to the Deputy Prime Minister, Prime Minister Office

- Dr. Amarjit Singh, Department of School Education and Literacy, Ministry of Human Resource Development (India)
- Prof. Dr. Somwung Pitiyanuwat, Member of the Royal Institute
- Associate Prof. Dr. Samphan Phanphruk, Director, National Institute of Educational Testing Service (NIETS)
- Prof. Emeritus Dr. Montri Chulavatnatol, Chairman of the Governing Board, Institute for the Promotion of Teaching Science and Technology (IPST)
- Dr. Amporn Pongkangsananant, Director, General Administration Bureau, Office of the Education Council (OEC)
- Dr. Samsak Dolprasit, Director, Educational Policy and Planning Bureau, Office of the Education Council (OEC)
- Dr. Sakolwan Plienkum, Deputy Director, National Institute for the Development of Teachers, Faculty, Staff and Educational Personnel (NIDTEP)
- Mrs. Suchitra Pattanaphum, Office of the Teacher Civil Service and Educational Personnel Commission (OTEPC), Ministry of Education
- Mr. Chanchai Chiarakul, Vice Chairman, The Federation of Thai Industries, Rubber-Based Industry Club
- Dr. Prasong Praneetpolograng, Advisor to the Minister of Information and Communication Technology
- Ms. Megawati Santoso, Vice Chair, ASEAN Qualification Reference Framework
- Mr. Tom Burns, Global Director, Content and Services World Ahead Programme Team, Intel Semiconductor Limited
- Mr. Thanin Pa-Em, Deputy Secretary-General, Office of the National Economic and Social Development Board
- Mr. Gwang-Choi Chang, Senior Programme Specialist, Chief of the Education Policy and Reform Unit, UNESCO Bangkok
- Dr. Chanavee Tongroach, Office of the Education Council (OEC)
- Dr. Skolwan Pleinkum, Deputy Director, National Institute for the Development of Teachers, Faculty, Staff and Educational Personnel (NIDTEP)
- Mr. Somyos Siribun, Director, Bangkok Primary Educational Service

- Ms. Praiwan Piraksalee, OBEC Director, Bureau of Academic Affairs and Educational Standard, Office of the Basic Education Commission (OBEC)

- Mr. Pithan Puenthong, OBEC Director, Education Innovation Bureau, Office of the Basic Education Commission (OBEC)

- Dr. Panya Khaewkeyoon, Advisor on Teacher Development for the Permanent Secretary; former Senior Advisor at the Office of the Basic Education Commission (OBEC)

- Mr. Thanin Paem, Deputy Secretary General, National Education Standard Bureau

- Dr. Chanita Rukspollmuang, Dean, Faculty of Education; and Jutarat Vibulphol, Associate Dean, Chulalongkorn University

- Mr. Krissanapong Kirtikara, Advisor to King Mongkut's University of Technology Thonburi, Quality Learning Foundation

- Mr. Precharn Dechsri and Ms. Supattra Pativisan, Representatives of the Institute for the Promotion of Teaching Science and Technology (IPST)

- Mr. Khanchai Wijakkana, President of Teachers-Parents Associations, and OVEC Representative, Office of the Vocational Education Commission

- Mr. Kosin Tetvong, Director of Education Bureau, Bangkok Metropolitan

- Mr. Krai Kettan, OBEC Director, Evaluation Bureau, Office of the Basic Education Commission (OBEC)

- Ms. Jirapan Punkasem, Inspector General, Office of the Permanent Secretary, Ministry of Education

- Professor Dr. Channarong Pornrungroch, Director, Office for National Education Standards and Quality Assessment (ONESQA), National Institute of Educational Testing Service (NIETS)

- Dr. Rawiwan Taneissara, Deputy Director, Institute for the Promotion of Teaching Science and Technology (IPST)

- Dr. Khemar Cotati and Dr. Chanol, and the PISA (Dr. Chaiwut) and TIMSS directors

- Dr. Wilawan Makhum, Director, Teachers' Council of Thailand (TCT)

- Dr. Sakowon Plienkhum, Deputy of the Teacher and Professional Training Institute/In-service Training (NIDTEP)

- Miss Wanida, Director and Owner of Silpadeg Day Care Centre. The Representative of the Bangkok Metropolitan
- Prof. Banchar Chalapiron, Dean, Faculty of Education for Chulalongkorn University
- Mr. Chaisak Changjai, Associate Professor, Director of Chulalongkorn University Demonstration Secondary School
- Chiang Mai, Team Temple School Representative, Rural School Representative, Deputy Director of the Primary Educational Area of the District of Chiang Mai, and other colleagues
- Associate Prof. Dr. Numyoot Songthanapitak, President, Rajamangala University of Technology Lanna of Chiang Mai, and other colleagues
- Mrs. Lumyai Sananrum, Representative of the Bureau of Testing, Office of the Basic Education Commission (OBEC)
- Dr. Prachakom Chantachit, Director of the Standard of TVET, Office of the Vocational Education Commission (OVEC)
- Ms. Thantida Wongprasong, Quality Learning Foundation
- Dr. Benchajaluck Namfa, Senior Specialist in Academic Affairs and Learning Development, Consultant to Secretary General of the Office of the Basic Education Commission (OBEC)

OECD PUBLISHING, 2, rue André-Pascal, 75775 PARIS CEDEX 16
(91 2016 08 1 P) ISBN 978-92-64-25909-6 – 2016